The Referendum Device

A Conference Sponsored by the
American Enterprise Institute for Public Policy Research
and the Hansard Society for Parliamentary Government

The Referendum Device

Edited by Austin Ranney

American Enterprise Institute for Public Policy Research
Washington and London

Library of Congress Cataloging in Publication Data
Main entry under title:

The Referendum device.

(AEI Symposia; 80G)
Includes bibliographical references.
1. Referendum—Congresses. 2. Referendum—
United States—Congresses. 3. Referendum—Europe—
Congresses. I. Ranney, Austin. II. American
Enterprise Institute for Public Policy Research.
III. Hansard Society for Parliamentary Government.
IV. Series: American Enterprise Institute for Public
Policy Research. AEI symposia ; 80G.
JF491.R39   328'.2   80-25657
ISBN 0-8447-2196-4
ISBN 0-8447-2195-6 (pbk.)
AEI Symposia 80G

Printed in the United States of America

List of Participants

KENNETH BAKER is Conservative member of Parliament for St. Marylebone and chairman of the Hansard Society for Parliamentary Government.

WILLIAM J. BAROODY, JR., is the president of the American Enterprise Institute for Public Policy Research.

VERNON BOGDANOR is fellow and tutor in politics of Brasenose College, Oxford, and author of a study of the 1979 devolution referendums in Scotland and Wales.

DAVID BUTLER is a fellow of Nuffield College, Oxford, adjunct scholar of the American Enterprise Institute, senior author of the Nuffield general election studies, and coeditor of *Referendums: A Comparative Study of Practice and Theory.*

RONALD BUTT is a leader writer for the *Sunday Times* of London.

JOHN COURTNEY is professor of political science at the University of Saskatchewan and author of *The Selection of National Party Leaders in Canada.*

THOMAS E. CRONIN is professor of political science at the University of Delaware, coauthor of *The Presidency Reappraised* and *Government by the People*, and director of a study of the operation of the initiative and referendum in the American states.

GEORGE CUNNINGHAM is Labour member of Parliament for Islington South and Finsbury and author of the "40 percent amendment" to the 1979 devolution referendums in Scotland and Wales.

TAM DALYELL is Labour member of Parliament for West Lothian; he took a leading role in the antidevolution campaign in the Scottish referendum of 1979.

ROBIN DAY is a journalist and political interviewer and commentator for the British Broadcasting Corporation and a member of the Hansard Society Council.

HENRY DRUCKER is senior lecturer in politics at the University of Edinburgh and editor of *Multi-Party Britain.*

THOMAS S. FOLEY, a Democrat, is United States Representative for the Fifth District of Washington State, chairman of the House Committee on Agriculture, and chairman of the House Democratic Caucus.

PHILIP GOODHART is Conservative member of Parliament for Beckenham, parliamentary under secretary of state for Northern Ireland, and author of *Referendum* and *Full-Hearted Consent*.

RICHARD HOLME is director of the (British) National Committee for Electoral Reform, member of the Green Alliance, and member of the Hansard Society Council.

CHRISTOPHER J. HUGHES is professor of politics at the University of Leicester and author of *The Parliament of Switzerland*.

NEVIL JOHNSON is professorial fellow of Nuffield College, Oxford, and author of *Government in the Federal Republic of Germany* and *In Search of the Constitution: Reflections on State and Society in Britain*.

JAMES R. JONES, a Democrat, is United States Representative for the First District of Oklahoma, former special assistant to President Lyndon B. Johnson, and a leading sponsor of a constitutional amendment to establish a national referendum by popular initiative in the United States.

MARTIN N. KARMEL is deputy secretary of the Committee of London Clearing Bankers.

BRYAN KEITH-LUCAS is emeritus professor of government, University of Kent, and vice-chairman of the Hansard Society.

ANTHONY KING is professor of government at the University of Essex, adjunct scholar of the American Enterprise Institute, author of *Britain Says Yes: The 1975 Referendum on the Common Market*, and editor of *The New American Political System*.

DAVID E. LEA is assistant general secretary of the Trades Union Congress.

EUGENE C. LEE is professor of political science and director of the Institute of Governmental Studies at the University of California, Berkeley. He has written extensively on California politics and is the author of the chapter on California in *Referendums*.

DAVID MARQUAND is professor of contemporary history and politics at the University of Salford, former Labour member of Parliament for Ashfield, former employee of the Commission of the European Economic Community, and author of *Ramsay MacDonald*.

DAVID MCKIE is deputy editor of *The Guardian* of London.

JACK W. PELTASON is president of the American Council on Education, author of *Federal Courts in the Political Process* and *Understanding the Constitution*, and coauthor of *Government by the People*.

J. ENOCH POWELL is Official Unionist member of Parliament for South Down, former Conservative member for Wolverhampton South-West, former Conservative cabinet member, and a leading opponent of British membership in the European Economic Community.

Austin Ranney is a resident scholar at the American Enterprise Institute, former president of the American Political Science Association, and coeditor of *Referendums: A Comparative Study of Practice and Theory.*

Malcolm Rutherford is political editor for the *Financial Times* of London.

Michael Ryle is clerk of select committees of the House of Commons and a member of the Hansard Society Council.

Richard M. Scammon is director of the Elections Research Center, former director of the United States Bureau of the Census, and editor of the series *America Votes.*

Peter Shore is Labour member of Parliament for Stepney and Poplar, former Labour cabinet member, and a leading Labour spokesman on foreign affairs.

Michael Steed is senior lecturer in government at the University of Manchester, a regular contributor to the Nuffield general election studies, and former president of the Liberal party.

Jürg Steiner is professor of political science at the University of North Carolina and at the University of Geneva and author of *Amicable Agreement Versus Majority Rule.*

Raymond E. Wolfinger is professor of political science at the University of California, Berkeley, author of *The Politics of Progress*, coauthor of *Dynamics of American Politics*, and author of a study of referendum voting in California.

Vincent Wright is a fellow of Nuffield College, Oxford, and author of *The Government and Politics of France* and of the chapter on France in *Referendums.*

Contents

Preface

For whatever reasons, the economic and social problems of Western democratic nations have grown more severe in the 1970s and 1980s, and their governments' efforts to deal with those problems have produced fewer successes. As a result, the traditional institutions of representative government, whether arranged according to the Westminster model or the Washington model, have come under increasing attack as unresponsive and ineffective. Many people in these countries are searching for devices to reform, supplement, or even bypass representative government.

The essays and discussions in this book focus on one of these devices, the referendum—defined throughout the book as a direct popular vote to approve or reject a proposed or existing governmental policy or institution. The referendum device is not a new invention. It has been used in some Swiss cantons since the sixteenth century and in some states of the United States of America since the eighteenth century. To be sure, Switzerland is the only nation that has held a great many nationwide referendums (nearly 60 percent of all national referendums ever held in the democratic countries have been held in Switzerland). Most Western democracies have used the device on at least some occasions; indeed, the United States and the Netherlands are the only such nations that have never held a national referendum.[1]

While the referendum device has existed for some time, a number of developments in the 1970s and early 1980s have greatly increased interest in its record and possibilities. In America, for example, the usage of the device in states where it already exists has increased significantly as a number of political groups—notably tax cutters, environmentalists, and persons seeking more severe penalties for convicted criminals—have grown impatient with what they see as the temporizing and unresponsiveness of the state legislatures. Moreover, for the first time since the early 1900s, serious consideration is being given to a constitutional amendment that would establish a national referendum by popular initiative. One of the participants in this conference, Repre-

---

[1] See David Butler and Austin Ranney, eds., *Referendums: A Comparative Study of Practice and Theory* (Washington, D.C.: American Enterprise Institute, 1978), especially chaps. 1 and 3 and the appendix, pp. 227–237.

sentative James R. Jones of Oklahoma, is a chief sponsor of this measure. A recent Gallup poll reports that 57 percent of the people support the amendment, while only 21 percent are opposed and 22 percent are undecided.

Major national referendums on a variety of controversial questions have recently been held in a number of other democracies. In November 1978, for example, the Austrians voted, by the narrow margin of 50.5 percent to 49.5 percent, to prevent the country's first nuclear power plant from becoming operational. In March 1980, 58 percent of the voters in a Swedish referendum voted to continue the limited use of nuclear power plants. In May 1980, the voters in a Quebec referendum, by 59 percent to 41 percent, disapproved the Lévesque government's proposal to begin negotiations with Ottawa over something called "sovereignty association."

In some respects, however, the most dramatic recent developments have taken place in the United Kingdom. Prior to the 1970s, in all of its long history, Britain had never held a nationwide referendum. After winning office in the general election of February 1974, the Labour government of Harold Wilson faced a serious intraparty split over the issue of continuing British membership in the European Economic Community (EEC). Wilson finally decided that the best way to resolve the issue while holding his party together was to hold a referendum, no matter how radical a departure that might be from previous constitutional practice. Accordingly, on June 5, 1975, British voters were called upon to vote on the proposition, "Do you think that the United Kingdom should stay in the European Community (the Common Market)?" On a 65 percent turnout, 67 percent voted yes and 33 percent voted no.[2]

The EEC controversy receded for a time, but the referendum device did not. In a television interview in September 1977, Margaret Thatcher, then leader of the opposition, unexpectedly suggested that it might be a good idea to invoke referendums in certain strike situations. Then came the devolution controversy and referendums. After some preliminary setbacks in 1977, the Labour government, led by James Callaghan, in 1978 introduced bills calling for devolution of some powers to new assemblies to be established in Scotland and Wales, if approved by the voters in referendums held in those areas (the English were not invited to vote in either). A rebellion in early 1978 by some Labour backbenchers, led by George Cunningham, also a participant in our conference, amended the bills against the government's wishes to

---

[2] The leading studies are David Butler and Uwe Kitzinger, *The 1975 Referendum* (London: Macmillan, 1976); Anthony King, *Britain Says Yes* (Washington, D.C.: American Enterprise Institute, 1977); and Philip Goodhart, *Full-Hearted Consent* (London: Davis-Poynter, 1976).

provide that if in the opinion of the secretary of state less than 40 percent of the Scots or Welsh entitled to vote voted for the act in question, the secretary would be required to lay a repeal order before Parliament.

Thus, turnout as well as preferences became critical. There was no problem in Wales, for the voters divided 80 percent no to 20 percent yes. The result in Scotland was more equivocal:[3]

	Votes	Percent of Votes Cast	Percent of Electorate
Yes	1,230,937	51.6	32.9
No	1,153,502	48.4	30.8
Did Not Vote	—	—	36.4

This result put the Callaghan government in a difficult position. On the one hand, there were clearly more yes than no votes. On the other hand, the 40 percent requirement had clearly not been met. That being the case, should the government press on for the final passage of the Scotland Act, or should it withdraw the act? Callaghan tried to play for time, but on March 28 his government lost a vote of confidence by 311 to 310; a general election was announced for May 3.

Whatever else could be said about the referendum device in Britain after 1975 and 1979, it had clearly played a major role on both occasions. What role it would play in the future was unclear, and what role it should play became an issue of growing concern.

It was against this background that the American Enterprise Institute (AEI) and the Hansard Society agreed to cosponsor a conference on the referendum device, with AEI to publish a volume of its proceedings.

The conference was organized by Kenneth Baker and Philip Goodhart for the Hansard Society and Austin Ranney for AEI. Maxine Vlieland of the Hansard Society efficiently and cheerfully performed the countless chores that made the conference possible, and it was held October 26 to 28, 1979, at Ditchley Park, Oxfordshire. A list of the participants follows this preface.

Seven essays were commissioned for the conference; they appear here as chapters 2 through 8. A general discussion in the conference's opening session, presented as chapter 1, was followed by a series of discussions of the essays. The conference ended with a summing-up by Professor Bryan Keith-Lucas, which appears as chapter 9.

All the discussions were recorded and transcribed; the editor

---

[3] The figures are taken from David Butler and Dennis Kavanagh, *The British General Election of 1979* (London: Macmillan, 1980), p. 115.

selected from them the exchanges that appear in the book. Each participant was given the opportunity to convert his oral remarks into written English.

If undisputed answers indeed exist to the many questions about the role and proper organization of the referendum device in democratic governments, they will not be found in this book. But the pages that follow, I believe, raise most of the hard questions that must be answered, one way or another, by any person or government trying to decide what role and organization referendums should have.

AUSTIN RANNEY

Washington, D.C.

1
Reflections on Referendums

KENNETH BAKER, *chairman:* This discussion will focus on the desirability or undesirability of the referendum device as a supplement to—or possibly a substitute for—representative institutions. To begin, we shall have a statement by Philip Goodhart, an avowed supporter of referendums, followed by a statement by Enoch Powell, who has considerable doubts about referendums.

PHILIP GOODHART: I became an enthusiast for referendums because I was unwise enough to listen to some speeches that I gave in my constituency more than ten years ago about the importance of the Common Market, perhaps the greatest constitutional issue to come before the British electorate since the end of World War II. I was the sitting member. I was more or less in favor of our going into the Common Market. My nice moderate Labour opponent was also more or less in favor of going into the Common Market. My nice moderate Liberal opponent was also more or less in favor of going in. Consequently, there was no way in which a constituent of mine in the 1970 general election (or at any general election before or after 1970) could cast a meaningful vote on this supremely important issue.

This realization converted me to the idea that on certain issues it would be useful to have a referendum available. It is necessary in the constitutional field because, as our American and Continental friends are well aware, Britain does not have the benefit of a written constitution. It is possible to make dramatic changes in the constitutional balance of this country virtually overnight provided there is a parliamentary majority. Since the 1975 Common Market referendum, one has seen a government elected by a minority of votes want significant constitutional changes because of the pressures of a parliamentary majority. One has seen that last government completely change its position on the question of more seats for Northern Ireland, as the balance of power in the House of Commons changed and the base of the Ulster Unionists became all important. One has also seen the attitude of the last Labour government change on the question of devolution as the votes of the

1

nationalists became all important. It is curious in retrospect to remember that a government actually proposed a massive constitutional change in the status of Scotland and Wales without consulting the people of Scotland and Wales as to whether they wanted the change. Because of the referendums we have had, it would be difficult for any future government to make a major constitutional change of that sort without putting the issue to the people directly.

It is perfectly true that the referendum is a limit on full parliamentary sovereignty, but in recent years other patterns, for example, the growth of trade union power, have also imposed substantial curbs on the powers of Parliament. The referendum is an important constitutional tool; we need it in this country without a written constitution. It is a delaying weapon, one that reasserts the right of the majority to have its voice listened to at a time when active, well-organized minorities too often can shift the balance of power irreversibly.

ENOCH POWELL: In reading some of the essays circulated in advance of this conference and reflecting, perhaps superficially, upon what we should be discussing, it seemed to me clear that we will all need to disentangle our own national backgrounds and presuppositions from the abstract question, if there is one, of the validity or desirability of a referendum. That is because the referendum institution may be accepted or rejected according to the constitutional habits and assumptions of the country concerned. I want to comment, at this stage, against the background of the institutions of the United Kingdom as I understand them. I insert that caveat because I did not think that, when Philip Goodhart used the words "we do not have the benefit of a written constitution," he was being ironical. I would be using those words wholly ironically, because my view is that, despite the European Economic Community, which I regard as a temporary aberration, we are unique amongst the countries of the world in that we are a parliamentary monarchy and our Parliament therefore exercises the unlimited sovereignty inherent in a prescriptive monarchy.

In such a parliamentary monarchy, the powers of the crown or of the people are put in commission with a particular institution. Parliament does not occupy that position merely as a numerical expression of opinions in the country itself. It is an expression of opinion that is entrusted, locality by locality, to individuals. This is of the essence, of the nature, of the British Parliament, that it is rooted in locality. That is the context of our constitution to which I have related the experience of the last few years. All the rest of what I have to say deals with our specific experience with referendums in the last five years, first with the 1975 referendum on the EEC.

2

This vote on the EEC had a discreditable genesis from the point of view of the parliamentarian and the believer in parliamentary—that is, parliamentary party—democracy. The Labour party in 1974 arrived at certain electoral propositions with regard to the EEC and crowned them with the offer that, when it had completed the promised renegotiations (which, taken literally, would have been equivalent to a complete renunciation of the Treaty of Rome), the result would be submitted to the electorate either by a general election or by a referendum—an incredible piece of levity, to treat the two as optional alternatives.

There are two salient factors of the 1975 referendum that should be taken into account. One was embodied in a sentence in the official document accompanying the proposition presented to the electorate. The sentence ran as follows: "If the result of the referendum is affirmative, our continuing membership of the Common Market will depend upon the continuing assent of Parliament." That states the correct constitutional position—that the House of Commons at any moment can do anything, including repealing the 1972 act or refusing to accept a directive of the EEC. It states correctly the constitutional position that the powers of the Crown and people are in commission with the House of Commons. There was an inherent contradiction in the referendum itself in that those voting were told,"Your votes will make no difference, because the day after, and every day after that, Parliament can decide, and is expected to decide, whether it wants to go on with the show at all." Every vote that the House of Commons takes on an EEC proposition is a vote on continuing membership. That is why, to the distress of those who hold other views, every debate has turned into a debate on membership, even when the vote has been on the minutest matter of EEC detail.

how would that have been different?

There was this inherent contradiction in the very posing of the referendum; it was posed in terms that denied its significance and reasserted parliamentary sovereignty. It was treated by the electorate as an opinion poll on the current performance of the Labour government. The electorate will usually behave this way. If a question is put to them, they will judge it in terms of party politics, because that is how they get their way through the parliamentary institutions. At that time, a large number of people wanted to give a slap in the face to the Labour administration. In addition, they had the further idea that the fashionable thing at the moment was to be pro-EEC; all the best people were certainly voting pro. It was a typical piece of English humbug, probably irreproducible in any nation that does not have the blessings of that ineffable quality of the English. It was a discreditable episode from beginning to end, and not least discreditable because it deceived

3

the outside world. The unhappy Germans and French, who, like all foreigners, think they understand the British better than the British understand themselves—that is almost the definition of a foreigner— were led to believe that the British had come to a binding, permanent commitment to being a member of the Common Market. They will be correspondingly surprised when they discover, perhaps not long in the future, that there is no such commitment. Then we shall have the usual nonsense about "perfidious Albion."

I now come to the other referendums we had, on the Scottish and Welsh devolution proposals. This was, if anything, even more sauce. Somehow the Labour party got itself hooked on the idea that proposals for devolution in those two countries would be a vote winner. They were also thought to be a preservative against the further growth of nationalist members, who are a confounded nuisance anyhow because they are not on one side or the other; the House of Commons is not equipped for dealing with more than two sides.

The Labour government introduced the bill; all the forces—proper and very necessary to parliamentary democracy—of patronage and the rest were put into operation. Then there occurred the most disgraceful scenes that I have witnessed in thirty years in the House of Commons: honorable members stating on the second reading of the bill that they were opposed to the bill, that they regarded it as damaging and inconsistent with the parliamentary union, but that they were going to vote for it, on condition that there would be a referendum afterward, because they were convinced that the electorate thought as they did and would throw it out. It was a shameless renunciation of the function entrusted to members of Parliament when they are elected. They are elected in each locality "to grant and to consent on behalf of the community." The House of Commons is not a house of the common people; it is a house of the communities who send the members there. Yet, these members stood up and said, "We are all out for the Whips; we are all out for the government; we are voting straight—but only because, in due course, we shall campaign for what we believe will be a successful referendum to throw the whole thing into the dustbin afterwards." That was how it worked, by a whisker—but all the best things are by a whisker. The electorates of Wales and of Scotland, recognizing the practical consequences of the devolution and rejecting those practical consequences, made it clear they would not have it.

My last observation is this. The fact that those referendums were conducted only in Scotland and Wales respectively was the refutation of the claim of those conducting the referendums that devolution did not call in question the United Kingdom. The assumption underlying the submission of the question only to the populations of Scotland and

Wales was that the matter concerned only those populations. In other words, it was claimed not to affect the populations of England or of Northern Ireland in any way, although it manifestly did. There was yet another contradiction at the heart of the referendums of 1979, the contradiction between a referendum designed to rescue a government from the consequences of an incautious and unwise commitment and a referendum to ask one section of a country whether, by a majority, it wished to remain a part of that country.

With regard to the first of those alternatives, the Labour party did not have the services, usually available to it, of the House of Lords. Normally, the House of Lords enables a Labour government to get out of inconvenient commitments, because the party can get them voted down in the House of Lords, then blame the House of Lords for the action, and say it will reform or abolish the House of Lords in the next Parliament. On the other hand, in terms of the English background, the sole justification of a plebiscite—that is what it was called in the good old Woodrow Wilson days—is to ascertain whether there exists in a part of a country a majority, and if so what size of majority, in favor of remaining or ceasing to be part of the state to which it belongs.

There had been, of course, a sort of referendum in 1973—we called it "the border poll," a marvelous Anglicism—that asked the people of Ulster whether they wanted to remain part of the United Kingdom. It produced an answer. Ninety-eight percent of those who voted said that they wanted to remain part of the United Kingdom. Why? Because the terrorists have a sufficient grip upon the areas in which persons likely to vote the other way live that they were able to prevent people in those areas from voting, that being their only way of reducing and destroying the significance of the resulting figures.

Those are my reflections on recent British experience with this new-fangled device. In every case, they have been miserable, disgraceful, and damaging to the maintenance of parliamentary democracy. They have been, in Mr. Goodhart's words, a blow to parliamentary sovereignty. That is the only respect, I think, in which I find myself in agreement with my colleague.

ROBIN DAY: Does Mr. Powell think that it was wrong to hold the border poll, that it was of no assistance at all?

ENOCH POWELL: It was not valuable because of the nugatory result produced.

DAVID BUTLER: If I remember rightly, 58 percent of the total electorate cast yes votes, which actually proved that the majority of the people in

Northern Ireland wanted to preserve the situation that Enoch wanted them to preserve.

ENOCH POWELL: We knew that anyhow, because of the results of parliamentary elections, which had produced large majorities in all elections in favor of the union.

VERNON BOGDANOR: A referendum can be used to defuse a political issue by taking it out of the hands of extremists. This is what the Scottish referendum did in 1979. It defused the devolution issue in the only way possible.

I am puzzled why the referendum should necessarily be a barrier to good parliamentary government. It seems to me that if the referendum is confined to the approval or rejection of a bill passed by Parliament, the bill's supporters will be more concerned to seek defensible legislation rather than cobble together a bad bill and push it through willy-nilly. One of the reasons why the Scotland Act and the Wales Act were not more strongly supported in the referendums was that they were terrible pieces of legislation; if there is another round, the proponents of devolution will have to do a bit better than they did last time. So it seems that referendums can be an aid to good parliamentary government and do not necessarily undermine it.

JÜRG STEINER: We have a different view of referendums in Switzerland because we do not think that we are a parliamentary democracy. We call ourselves a direct democracy; therefore constitutionally it is clear that the ultimate say is with the people. The ultimate power, not only to elect representatives but to make decisions, is with the people. Constitutionally, the question of compatibility with parliamentary democracy is not relevant at all. What *is* relevant is the question of what happens if the people make foolish decisions or immoral decisions or maybe unconstitutional decisions. Is there a danger in Switzerland of dictatorship by popular majorities? There is always a risk.

Now I come to my main point. The Supreme Court in Switzerland is never asked whether a popular referendum is permissible. The final power is with the people. They are higher than any branch of government. The Supreme Court would never declare any referendum unconstitutional. Let me give two examples. The female vote was not introduced in Switzerland until 1971 (I am ashamed to say there are still two cantons not having female votes). Is this unconstitutional? It is not, as long as the people say it is not. It is not possible for a Supreme Court to say that the people are violating basic human rights.

The next example is the situation with the foreign workers. Many foreign workers in Switzerland have legal work permits, yet a constitutional initiative was launched to kick those people out within two or three years. In many other countries, that would be unconstitutional. The Swiss people were mature enough to reject this proposal by a majority of nearly 60 percent.

In changing from representative democracy to direct democracy, there is always the risk that this sovereignty is immoral, unethical, even unconstitutional. The only counter argument that we Swiss have is that if the people use referendums long enough, if they are mature, they will abuse their power relatively rarely.

MICHAEL STEED: Empirically, it always has seemed that the problem with the Swiss use of the referendum is that the turnout has steadily dropped from a reasonably high level in the early part of this century to an average of below 50 percent. In other words, the Swiss have used the referendum so frequently that the sovereign people now abstain in large numbers every time an issue is put to them. This seems to be the problem with the frequent use of referendums.

Also, I want to defend the moderate use of referendums by referring to my experience as a Liberal parliamentary candidate in 1970. I fought the 1970 election in the constituency of Truro, where there was a large number of small village meetings. The Common Market was an issue; the situation was not unlike that in Philip Goodhart's constituency of Beckenham in that each of the three candidates took a similar position. I was clearly the most pro-European; the Labour candidate clearly the most equivocal. None of us stood clearly against the Common Market. I faced question after question of "OK, you may be right, you may have some good arguments, but shouldn't we have the right to vote on the matter?" I used the argument, which perhaps Philip Goodhart could not use, that in a better electoral system one would have that choice. The voters countered with the argument that, even with a perfect electoral system, they should have that choice in a clear and direct manner. As that election campaign progressed, I became less and less convinced of my answers to those questions. Consequently, at the 1971 Liberal Assembly, the Truro Liberal Association put up a resolution, which I moved, enthusiastically supporting entry into the Common Market *and* use of the referendum. We did not advocate it for the reasons that Tony Wedgewood Benn, Douglas Jay, and others were pushing it. We supported it because we believed that, given the deep divisions among the British people which were very evident, and which were not appreciated by the Conservative government, the matter would not be settled easily. We would not, therefore, become a permanent member of the EEC unless it were settled in a much clearer manner than by a simple majority in the House of Commons.

Even now the issue may not be as settled as I would like it, but it became more settled after 1975. In fact, those few of us who argued that a referendum was desirable from the pro-Common Market point of view have been proved more right than those who hit upon the referendum as a means of objecting to the Common Market. It was one of those rare matters dividing people so deeply that some sort of appeal is needed that is accepted as more legitimate than a simple vote in the House of Commons. To get the matter settled, to resolve the issue in favor of going in, one had to find a mechanism for legitimacy. Consequently, I would defend in a pragmatic way the occasional use of the referendum on major constitutional issues where one can guarantee a reasonably high level of interest among the people and where, because of the nature of the party system or the electoral system or a combination thereof, the choice between parties cannot easily settle the matter. I would advance perhaps a more moderate acceptance of the value of referendum than either the extreme opposition to it put by Enoch Powell or the more extreme acceptance of it put by some others.

ROBIN DAY: I am in some difficulty, because I was, on the whole, in favor of referendums as a general idea until I heard Philip Goodhart and then I was against them until I heard Enoch Powell. He has made me think again.

Philip Goodhart said he came round to the idea of referendum when he found that nobody in his constituency had the opportunity of voting on whether we go into the Common Market, because all three candidates were middle-of-the-road, well-meaning chaps who wanted to join Europe, and there was no opportunity available to vote on this matter without a referendum. This, of course, is not strictly true, because anyone who felt that way could have stood for Parliament and offered himself as an anti-European candidate.

MICHAEL STEED: That is difficult within the rules of the British political system.

ROBIN DAY: Constitutionally, there was a clear alternative that has always existed under our system. In certain by-elections, anti-Common Market candidates have stood and have been elected. I am not saying it works generally, but it is constitutionally inaccurate to say that there was no alternative to a referendum.

Second, if Philip Goodhart feels we should have referendums because no one in a constituency has the opportunity to vote on a particular issue when all the candidates in that constituency take the same view or do not say anything about it, what are we going to do about capital punishment, what are we going to do about whether immigrants should be repatriated, what are we going to do about whether the closed shop should be abolished? Nobody has any doubt that if there were a referendum on capital punishment there would be an 85 percent majority in favor of it; there would probably be an 85 percent majority in favor of repatriation of immigrants; there might well be a majority in favor of abolishing the closed shop and doing all sorts of terrible things to trade unions. Whether those matters should be put to referendums is an interesting question. Many people think that there are far more important things than the so-called constitutional issues on which intellectuals and establishment people think the people should be allowed to express their direct opinion. I was not impressed with that aspect of Mr. Goodhart's argument.

Then I heard Mr. Powell say that referendums undermine the central principle of our parliamentary democracy, which he called a parliamentary monarchy, and they undermine Parliament. Of course, our constitution exists in six unwritten words: *The Queen in Parliament is supreme.* Those of us who believe in that kind of constitution and do not want a written constitution must admit that there is nothing incompatible with that and a referendum; if Parliament in its supreme wisdom decides that a referendum is an aid to its processes, then it is perfectly constitutional. How can it be said to undermine parliamentary government? If Parliament says it would like to know whether the people of Northern Ireland want to be part of a united Ireland, then it seems constitutionally pure and impeccable within the domain of parliamentary sovereignty for Parliment to hold a consultative referendum.

On the question of the border poll, I am amazed to hear Mr. Powell say that the border poll in Ulster was useless. Of course, we knew that the bulk of the people in Northern Ireland wanted to remain part of the United Kingdom, and, of course, we knew that that was proved by elections to the Westminster Parliament. What we did not know and what the border proved is that a substantial proportion of the Catholic population wanted to remain in the United Kingdom; that is a rather good fact to have at one's disposal.

HENRY DRUCKER: Mr. Powell was entirely right when he said that referendums entrap parliamentary democracy. He put it quite the wrong way round in that we have referendums because parliamentary democracy is failing to do certain things that we want it to do. Members of Parliament have to face the fact, specifically in the case of the Scotland and Wales bills, that we had referendums because the government realized that the only way they could get these bills through Parliament was to promise Labour MPs a referendum; clearly, the referendum was used to save Parliament's face. The referendum was a solution to a difficult parliamentary situation, not the cause of it.

It is important to remember that, because the referendum is one device among many being talked about to fill a number of the gaps that have opened up because of the current problems in Parliament. We do not want to get too bogged down in discussions about how the device should work. We in Britain have had three referendums in the last five years and we have set a precedent of a 40 percent rule. If we are going to keep having referendums, we are going to have to keep this experience in mind.

KENNETH BAKER: Perhaps I should explain to our foreign visitors that the 40 percent rule was introduced in the Scottish and Welsh referendums. It required approval by 40 percent of all those *entitled* to vote— not just a majority of those who voted.

THOMAS FOLEY: It is obvious that in every type of constitutional system a referendum can be useful particularly for politicians who face difficult and intractable problems of public importance. Its usefulness will depend upon the particular policy and constitutional arrangements of the country involved. Professor Steiner made the point that referendums are perfectly consistent with the direct sovereignty of the Swiss people and pointed out that they are inconsistent with parliamentary democracy. They are unconstitutional at a national level in American politics. Congress cannot make a decision by a referendum; it is clear that the courts will say that Congress could not put to a referendum a binding question of national policy. Second, it is inherently inconsistent in the federal system; that does not say it is not convenient, it is merely inconsistent. The full arrangement of the American political system at the federal level is a delicate balance between population and geography; it is inherently unrepresentative in many of its aspects. We give the states of Rhode Island and Oklahoma the same power in the United States Senate as the states of California and New York. A national referendum would be totally based on population. The county of Los Angeles would have about three times the voice of Oklahoma and twice the voice of the state of Washington; that would be not only politically difficult but unconstitutional. I come from a state where referendums and initiatives are common; they have the great vice of weakening the will of legislators to tackle difficult problems. It is so easy to let the public decide whether there should be abortion, whether there should be immigration, whether there should be a tax, as we legislators say that we will leave that to the sacred and sovereign judgment of the people. When we do so, we are escaping our responsibility. From that standpoint, the referendum is a dangerous institution. It may be useful, it may be convenient in exceptional circumstances, but it tends to have the vice of intruding upon the responsibility of elected representatives.

RONALD BUTT: I sympathize with the motives that lead to the demands for referendums. Representative government in England over recent years has consistently disregarded the opinion of the majority on a number of particular issues. One of the most obvious, and incontrovertible, instances is immigration.

The tendency of governments, at any rate in Britain, to ignore public opinion is damaging to democracy. The only time they do not ignore it is when they try to win elections by expanding the economy at the opportune time, whatever the eventual cost to stability. People increasingly feel that they have the form of democracy but not the reality. In the democracy of Athens, all the people could meet and have a voice in settling particular questions. In a representative democracy with a mass electorate, however, people are bound to cast their votes according to their opinions about the way this or that party will behave on the one or two questions that are uppermost in the individual voter's mind. Generally, the decisive question for most people is bound to be concerned with the government's likely performance in dealing with the complex of economic issues—prosperity or poverty, employment, inflation, pensions, and so on.

It must be so. The more governments take over the things that control a man's ability to earn his and his family's living, the more these things will determine the individual's voting behavior; a man's livelihood must (for most people) come first. Obviously, there are many who do cast their votes according to their opinions or interests on some other questions, such as immigration or education. They are not the majority.

Most people probably subordinate their opinions on such other matters to their views of the government's economic program and competence. This does not mean that voters who do this lack strong feelings on these "secondary" subjects. On the contrary, they feel strongly about them and they feel frustrated by the way in which their opinions are ignored by governments. Governments' actions on such questions increasingly are determined by their obedient response to pressure groups with clearly defined social objectives that know how to use the political process to achieve certain sorts of social change that they want and that the majority of people plainly do not want.

To respond to popular instincts in these matters is, of course,

11

customarily sneered at as *populist*—but the increasingly *elitist* approach of governments to many questions vitally affecting the daily lives of the citizens is liable to create a disillusion with democracy that, in certain circumstances, could be highly dangerous to democratic institutions. I am naturally drawn by instinct toward the idea of the referendum to ascertain the people's real will on particular matters and to place some obligation on the government to heed it.

Nevertheless, the referendum device has one enormous danger; used as it is likely to be used in Britain, it places an undue power in the hands of the parliamentary majority of the moment. That majority can exploit it and misuse it. The EEC is a classical case of this. The point about the EEC referendum was that the decision to hold it was entirely in the hands of the parliamentary majority. Mr. Heath's Conservative government, which took us into the EEC, would never have considered a referendum because it knew that it would get a different answer from the answer wanted, which was the answer actually given when the referendum finally did take place. If Mr. Heath's government had put the proposition for British membership of the EEC in a referendum, it would have been turned down flat—principally because people do not like leaps in the dark, they are naturally conservative, they do not like new ideas, and they would not have been willing to face the dangers of this leap.

When it came to the 1975 referendum, in which the people did confirm the existing membership on the so-called renegotiated terms, the sole reason the vote went that way was not the one named by Enoch Powell. It was not a slap in the eye to one party or the other, not a judgment on one party's general performance compared with the other's. The result in favor of continued membership came simply because people felt that, once we were already in, it would be dangerous to come out. There was a feeling that somehow membership might, after all, be handy; there had been an enormous amount of propaganda saying that, if we came out, we should be made to look like idiots in the eyes of the world and would get the worst of both worlds.

The Wilson government knew that if, from its declared position of scepticism about membership, it nevertheless recommended continued membership, the answer would be yes to membership. It chose to hold a referendum to get the answer it wanted, and to escape from its own internal party difficulties. In the end, the referendum was chosen because it could achieve one particular result. Whichever side one was on, that is undeniable. Similarly, if Mr. Heath had held a referendum, he would have had a different result. He would never have considered it.

Unless a complete referendum system like the Swiss is used, in overturning seven hundred years of representative government, a dangerous weapon is placed in the hands of the parliamentary majority to manipulate things its way. In certain circumstances, that could be anti-democratic. I need not make any points about the dangers that can lie in the way a particular question in a referendum is phrased. I remember, when I was an undergraduate, my history tutor told me that no dictator ever had to fiddle a referendum, whether it was Napoleon or Hitler or anybody else; when people are asked to answer a question, one half of which is positive and the other half negative, and when to give a nega-tive answer looks like peering into the abyss of uncertainty, the people will choose the certainty. So one rarely has to fiddle an 80 percent majority in those circumstances. It is this combination of the parliamen-tary majority and an appeal to the people in somewhat spurious circum-stances that is the most alarming aspect of the use of the referendum.

RICHARD HOLME: I felt good about referendums until I heard the word "device." The one thing I do not think we should do with devices is to put them in the hands of politicians, because politicians like devices. Our society on the whole is manipulated by politicians using whatever device they have at hand. A device that is useful to politicians is not something that we should embrace. I think that Mr. Goodhart used the phrase "the referendum is a delaying weapon." That is a classically conservative position: It is good to delay things.

There is a second point for some of our foreign visitors unused to the rococo fantasies that Enoch Powell has about constitutions. It concerns this idea of a parliamentary monarchy in which the role of Parliament is to assent or dissent to the Queen or the executive. There are those who think that we are supposed to have a popular democ-racy in this country and that Parliament should reflect as accurately as it can the will of the people. "The people," of course, is not merely a juridical or abstract conception; the idea of popular sovereignty should be the foundation of all our institutions. A word which has not come up so far is "legitimacy"; much of the conversation this week-end should be about legitimacy. It is possible to argue that legitimacy lies in a written constitution, which we do not happen to have in Britain, or it is possible to argue that it lies in the people. If one believes that the people, in whatever way one interprets the word, are sovereign, then Enoch Powell's rather idiosyncratic explanation of the way the British constitution works must be regarded as one point of view, be-cause not all British people think that way.

ANTHONY KING: Before Mr. Butt's view is generally accepted—that referendums are inevitably conservative—refer to pages 11 through 13 of Butler and Ranney's *Referendums* and in particular to the fact that on August 13, 1905, in the first referendum listed, the people of Norway voted by 99.9 percent to separate themselves from Sweden—a country of which they had been a part for two or three centuries. The notion that referendums are barriers to change is simply in sharp contradiction to facts, of which there are large numbers available.

NEVIL JOHNSON: Occasions like this should be used to sharpen one's own thinking by listening to what other people say. What has struck me in this discussion is the fact that underlying it is a serious worry about the present state of representative government and its institutions. Set against this background, some people are inclined to view the referendum device as a means of reinvigorating representative institutions, while others fear that it will further undermine them. It seems that both Philip Goodhart and Enoch Powell, although their conclusions differ, express some of the doubts and questions that affect the operation of representative institutions, and in particular representative institutions in Great Britain. They are concerned with the strength and weaknesses of the case for allowing the people to check, in certain ways, the decisions that representative institutions make on their behalf.

One can pursue the logic of that and make a fairly persuasive argument for qualifying the operation of representative institutions by appealing to the people in certain circumstances to ensure that a particular decision really has majority support. These are, no doubt, issues that will be discussed later. With some of the other contributions, particularly those of Professor Steiner and Congressman Foley, there is the other side of the problem. If one sees the problem of government and the structure of political life as being essentially concerned with the terms on which power is exercised in a society and with the kind of limits that affect what those in office can do, and if, against that background, one turns to the use of popular consultation referendums, one must ask, What are the risks inherent in referendums for the kind of constitution that actually limits the exercise of power?

Written constitutions, and particularly a serious one like the American, lay down a number of principles that apply to individuals living in society, to relationships governing institutions, and so on. If one subjects these principles to expressions of popular will from time to time, a serious question arises as to whether there is any guarantee of limited government at all. Obviously, there may be certain special conditions, as in Switzerland, that moderate in substantial ways what might otherwise be the rather harsh effects of this direct appeal to the sovereignty of the people. If we recommend popular consultation in one form or another as a regular device, we have to think carefully about society's political habits and attitudes—how mature are they?—as well as about its social structure and composition—do they put barriers in the way of dominating blocs of opinion?

These matters have to be weighed before we commit ourselves to popular consultation. Otherwise, we are likely to get into a situation in which the notion of popular consultation becomes a principle that works against the possibility of having limited government and institutions with restricted powers.

JAMES JONES: My good friend Tom Foley and I have a fundamental disagreement on this question of direct voting by the people. In the House of Representatives, I am the chief sponsor of legislation to amend our Constitution to allow direct voting on some kinds of legislation. My amendment takes the middle course to provide for the initiative petition process and, if the required number of signatures is obtained, to allow that issue to be voted on at the next general election. I came to that conclusion because of my experiences in four years on President Johnson's staff during the Vietnam War. I came to feel that the people should have some safety valve through which they can make their voice heard on national laws, if they think the elected representatives are not responding to what they want.

I agree with Tom Foley that it is unconstitutional to have either a national referendum or a petition process in the United States, but I disagree that it is inconsistent with our American experience. To extend this sort of privilege and right is a natural evolution of the Constitution. Most of the amendments to our Constitution, particularly recently, have extended voting rights—to eighteen-year-olds and women and the right of people to vote directly for United States senators. The initiative is a natural evolution. I also disagree with Tom Foley that this sort of direct power to the people will weaken the will of legislators to tackle tough issues. If we use the referendum process, legislators will leave those tough issues to the people. The initiative petition process will strengthen the will of legislators not to avoid those issues, because they will not want that power taken out of their hands in a general election.

As far as turnout is concerned, it has actually been much higher in those twenty-three states that have referendum issues on the ballot than in those states that have no direct voting on issues.

DAVID E. LEA: This whole argument about referendums is tied up with the move toward the Gallup poll approach to politics. Technology— through Gallup polls—can sound public opinion every five minutes; it seems that this is being matched by a fickleness of public opinion. People can test opinion at the drop of a hat and, as someone said, it must undermine the credibility of politics as a profession. It reminds me of the story of the Mississippi senator who spoke for fifteen or twenty minutes to the voters and said, "Well, folks, them's my views and if you don't like them I'll change them." It seems that this problem of whether the politician is supposed to go to the people with his own wisdom and his own experience or respond to what the people tell him is fairly fundamental.

With regard to the fickleness of the whole process, the EEC referendum stands out as a result that would have been different if the vote had been held at any other time. Far from making our EEC commitment permanent, the opportunism of doing it that way has had the opposite effect.

To take another example, the February 1974 general election itself was almost a referendum, in that the government went to the country when it thought it could win on the one issue, "Who runs the country, the government or the unions?" The government did not get the result that it wanted, because there is a difference between consulting the people on one issue and getting a view of what is viable as an overall policy.

This leads to my second point, that in running government there are multiple tradeoffs, and the referendum can produce contradictory results. I will put up a generalization to be knocked down, namely, that referendums can have a diseducating effect. Consulting people about the complexities of society can give the appearance that one does not need any experience in these matters, that one does not need to understand, for example, the relationship between taxes and levels of public service; only a Gallup poll is needed. As the world becomes more complicated, that seems to be exactly the wrong direction.

Finally, referendums can divide rather than enlighten the people by producing so-called solutions that are not solutions at all, given the reality of the political and industrial situations. To say that there are so many sheep and so many goats on a major national issue does not really match up to the crosscurrents of the political party system. Does anyone think that problems are resolved by saying that one can have this direct approach to the people? In Britain our problems will certainly not be solved by making this Gallup poll approach to politics easier than it unfortunately already is.

TAM DALYELL: David Lea is surely right when talking about the diseducating effect. It is sure that we have not had our last referendum in this country; some of us will be paying great attention this weekend to find ground rules for referendums that surely will be necessary in the future.

Thomas Foley said that a referendum weakens the will of a legislature in the face of difficult problems. The American experience, however, is on the state level, not on the national level. We are often faced with a position in which we ask legislators to do things that they would not want to do if they had a free legislative will. It may seem a bit of a cynical proposition from me as an antidevolutionist (of course, the Scottish referendum was about a second bite of the cherry and a desperate situation that we faced, groping around to put a spoke in the wheel of a juggernaut that was coming to a conclusion that we didn't want). Something had to be done; a referendum seemed a handy device because we did not see any other device that was easily available. On the other hand, equally cynically perhaps, some of us thought that a virtue of the referendum was its ensuring a more detailed discussion on the devolution proposal; the more the people knew about the proposals, the less they would like them. How many other referendums on a national level or on constitutional matters are about what they purport to be about? One of the deep-seated objections to referendums is that the question put forward is often far from the real issue. In the case of devolution, the issue was whether there should be a breakup of the British state.

Professor Steiner says it is not like that in Switzerland; the devolution referendum is different from anything in the Swiss experience, because no one in Switzerland has put forward a proposition that a canton should separate from the Swiss federation. There are referendums about all sorts of other things but never on the breakup of the Swiss state. There are two entirely different kinds of issues: fundamental constitutional issues, delicate and emotional, and general issues. No one ever thought that there should be a referendum on whether the state of Oklahoma should secede from the federal union.

The question in Scotland in 1979 was whether a rival government should be set up. The referendum device came to be used for an entirely different purpose from the fairly modest purposes intended by those who originally put it forward. In fact, the real issue was perceived at the end of the day.

The point is that there are referendums and referendums. There are referendums that ask a genuine question, as in Switzerland or in the American states. There are referendums that are used as instruments of policy to get through the legislature measures that would not otherwise pass. I am shoulder to shoulder with Enoch Powell in saying that indeed it was disgraceful that many people in the House of Commons somehow came to terms with their consciences by believing that the people in a referendum would have the courage or sense, according to taste, to do what the MPs, for political reasons, could not. That kind of referendum becomes a discredited instrument of policy. We have to

17

differentiate at this early stage in this conference between the genuine referendum that ascertains the views of people and that which is put forward as political oil to ease through on a temporary basis what is not acceptable to the elected representatives of the people.

ROBIN DAY: Mr. Powell has condemned the Common Market referendum in scathing terms. Why was it, then, that he advised people to vote Labour on the grounds that a Labour government would give people that opportunity of a referendum?

ENOCH POWELL: Not quite. The Labour manifesto promised a renegotiation. I worked through the terms of this renegotiation and concluded that they represented the repudiation of the principles of the 1972 act and the Treaty of Brussels. It was on that ground, not because it would be a yes or no referendum, that I asked those of my countrymen who agreed with me, irrespective of other things, to vote Labour.

KENNETH BAKER: As an elected representative, I have no illusion that I would not be elected if I did not stand in the Conservative interests of St. Marylebone. By that fact, I do not surrender my judgment to either my local party organization or my national party organization on a whole range of issues. If one accepts Dr. Steiner's case for direct democracy, which takes away the individual judgment from the elected representatives, then, as Tom Foley says, we legislators are shrugging off our responsibilities. The only sort of referendum that I would support is a consultative one; beyond that lies a consultative democracy in which elected representatives are barely necessary. The original Wedgewood Benn proposal in 1967 envisaged a terminal in each home, with questions that could be answered by families. That is the logical conclusion, the absolutely logical conclusion, and it is the danger of single-issue politics. That is the road that undermines the individual judgment of elected representatives and it is damaging to parliamentary democracy.

2

Types of Referendum

Nevil Johnson

The referendum device may be used for a variety of subjects and purposes. The political and constitutional implications of the practice vary considerably according to the purpose it is intended to serve and the specific procedures associated with it. This essay briefly outlines the principal forms of the referendum and considers for what kinds of topics and circumstances those different versions of the referendum may best be used. This discussion leads quite naturally to some observations on the constitutional consequences of referendum, particularly in the British context. It must be remembered that the most important feature of the referendum is precisely its quality as a popular consultation: A matter is referred to the people. When taken seriously, this embodies an important principle that can conflict with the theory and practice of representative government as we are familiar with it in most mature parliamentary democracies. We are considering an institutional device that for good or ill may represent a substantial innovation in many political systems.

In one of its most straightforward forms, the referendum is essentially a kind of "people's veto," a controlling device enabling various measures to be accepted or rejected in a popular vote. Usually this form of referendum is provided for in a country's constitution, which specifies that certain matters must be referred to the people for decision. As a rule, this type of referendum procedure applies to constitutional amendments or revisions, as for example, in Ireland, Switzerland, and many American states. Experience suggests that this form of referendum tends to have a negative rather than a positive effect: It acts as a restraint or veto on changes proposed by governments and parliaments rather than vice versa. This will be referred to as the "controlling referendum."

When the referendum is extended more widely and applied to ordinary legislative enactments (or to certain categories of these), problems arise in determining how and when such a reference to the people should occur. The normal and logical solution to this problem is to provide for an initiated permissive referendum, that is, one that must occur if a specified number of electors so request. This link between

19

referendum and popular initiative is relatively common. The initiative is, however, a device that can point in two directions. It can be seen as a means of stimulating participation and of prompting citizens to take the initiative in putting forward proposals (for example, in some of the American states). It can also retain its quality as a restraint on governments and a source of veto (how it often operates under the Swiss constitution, which has extensive provision for referendums on ordinary laws at the behest of 30,000 voters). It also worked like this recently in North Rhine Westphalia, where a successful initiative on school reform proposals brought in by the provincial government compelled their withdrawal, and in Italy, where an initiative a few years ago brought about a referendum that in turn forced divorce law reform on a hesitant government. This type of referendum will be called the "facultative referendum" to indicate that it can be brought about by popular initiative. It is important to underline the connection between initiative and referendum, since reflection on the latter can quickly lead to the conclusion that initiative is but the other side of the referendum coin. Acceptance of referendum may well at some stage entail provision for initiatives, too.

With the "plebiscitary referendum," a popular vote is seen primarily as a means of legitimizing the actions of a government or political leadership. Procedurally, this version of referendum need not differ substantially from the controlling referendum, although there usually are significant differences in the procedural conditions. Historically, the plebiscitary referendum has been associated with regimes anxious to establish a claim to popular support and thus to what is often loosely called democratic legitimacy. There is, for example, a plebiscitary component in the referendum as provided for under the constitution of the Fifth Republic of France (article 11), although the extent of this should not be exaggerated, as it sometimes has been in Anglo-American commentaries on the political system of the Fifth Republic. The referendum as used in the United Kingdom on the European Economic Community (EEC) issue also had a plebiscitary element insofar as it was seen by many as involving to a certain degree a vote of confidence for or against a government. The more overt transformation of the referendum into a plebiscite for or against a government occurs in societies in which authoritarian governments seek to secure or maintain carte blanche by a demonstration of popular support in their favor. The ultimate absurdity in this direction is the totalitarian plebiscite; the people express their support because they fear to do otherwise. The plebiscitary version of the referendum is instructive chiefly because it points to the dangers of popular manipulation in what seem on the surface to be highly democratic procedures. This form of referendum, moreover, necessarily links an expression of opinion on an issue with support for or opposition to a particular political leadership; such a coupling of two different perspectives tends either to be destabilizing or to be associated with degradation of the referendum to a manipulative device.

Finally, there is the "consultative referendum," a popular vote that can be facilitated by various procedures and that is held to be purely advisory; the legislative and executive authorities need in principle pay no attention to the outcome. Certainly, there are reasonably convincing examples of the consultative referendum, notably in Norway and Sweden. (In the latter country, a popular vote went decisively against driving on the right in 1956; within a decade, the Riksdag decided to set aside the popular verdict and committed Sweden to the changeover from left-hand to right-hand driving.) In theory, the British use of referendum has been, and is intended to be, consultative, subject perhaps to the exception of polls on the Northern Ireland border (successive pledges appear to imply that no change could be made without a popular majority in its favor). The consultative referendum is a slippery device. It may remain genuinely advisory if rarely used. If invoked often or in relation to issues which polarize opinion (for example, adhesion to the EEC in the case of Norway in 1972), its consultative status becomes illusory. To defy its verdict would be to flout the most important basis of legitimacy in contemporary democratic states, that of popular consent.

Rules versus Political Discretion

Conditions governing the use of major types of referendum are likely to lie on a scale running from more or less tightly defined rules to untrammelled political discretion. Undoubtedly, in practice, there are real and important differences between referendum according to rules and referendum at the discretion of some person or institution. The former might be termed "prescribed referendum," the latter "discretionary referendum."

In considering the referendum as an institutional practice grounded in the constitution of a country, we are concerned with the rules that permit or require a referendum. If the rules are firm and clear, the referendum becomes in many cases an automatic process, required when certain conditions are met. A clear and simple case of this is the provision in the Irish constitution that amendments to it shall be submitted to popular vote. Roughly the same rule applies to constitutional amendments in Switzerland. These are relatively straightforward rules; the rules can be more or less complex and ambiguous. This is true of the French rules, which vest an initiative in the president but leave rather uncertain how far his discretion qualifies the use of alternative procedures in respect of constitutional amendment (that is, a three-fifths vote by the two legislative chambers in joint session). Nevertheless, these rules do restrict the referendum to matters affecting the organization of the public powers and, in this respect as in others, fall well short of permitting the purely discretionary referendum.

Where the referendum is linked with provisions for a popular initiative to bring it into play, the rules are necessarily fairly complex. In the North Rhine Westphalian case, the signatures of 20 percent of the total electorate (equivalent to 2.5 million voters) had to be secured in order to confront the provincial parliament with the choice of either a referendum on its school reform proposals *or* voluntary withdrawal of them (it chose the latter course). At the other extreme is the referendum held at the discretion of some person or authority. This is not, in fact, found often in association with a written constitution, no doubt because there is a certain tension between a formal and binding constitution on the one hand and, on the other, a provision that appears to permit a purely discretionary procedure. Where, however, there is scope for a discretionary referendum under the provisions of a written constitution, it is usually regarded as a consultative procedure, as in Norway or Sweden. It should be noted that in both these cases the referendum is notable for the rarity of its use and the nonapplicability to constitutional amendment itself, for which different procedures are prescribed.

The purely discretionary referendum is confined to the principal state that has parliamentary government and no written constitution, that is, Great Britain, and to more or less authoritarian regimes in which a referendum can be held if the political authority so decides.

The difficulty with the discretionary referendum subject to no qualifications at all (or only to such as may be laid down in respect of a particular referendum) is twofold. First, it is hard to see what kind of genuine constitutional legitimation it can have. People cannot see it as based on reasonably fair rules, predictable in their application, since by definition no such rules are specified in advance. Second, the procedure for this form is peculiarly exposed to the risks of exploitation for short-term political ends. Under authoritarian regimes, the referendum is used to enhance the position of those in power and to facilitate the achievement of their political aims; in democratic conditions, politicians will resort to the referendum when they wish to avoid taking responsibility, to circumvent problems in party relations that they cannot solve, or to curry favor with the electorate.

The Referendum under the British Unwritten Constitution

It is relatively easy to formulate rules for the controlling, facultative, or consultative forms of referendum and to fit these into a variety of formal constitutional arrangements. Far more difficult is the decision of principle on the desirability of the referendum as a procedure, and the assessment of the likely political consequences of any particular version of the device.

Beforehand, it is worth elaborating on the problems affecting the use of referendums in the British constitutional context. These arise partly because the British constitution is informal and unwritten and, to a substantial extent, consists of shifting conventions. There is also the difficulty that the underlying principle of the constitution is held to be the sovereignty of the crown in Parliament. This is eminently a discretionary principle, implying that Parliament may use its authority for whatever purposes it sees fit. Clearly, it may use—and has used—its authority to establish a referendum; it is questionable whether Parliament could provide a constitutionally satisfactory basis for referendum as a *regular practice*. Here we are confronted by the logical puzzle that frustrates so much constitutional argument in Britain. To have a constitution is to have rules and procedures for changing them. How can a genuine constitution exist at all on the foundation of the unlimited discretionary will of the crown in Parliament? The question has been posed simply to underline the precarious nature of any proposal to introduce the referendum as a normal procedure into the traditional British constitutional framework. It is difficult to devise rules for it; perhaps only the purely discretionary referendum is logically consistent with the doctrine of parliamentary sovereignty. In terms of political realities, that means referendum at the discretion of the government of the day and of the majority behind it in the House of Commons. It is questionable whether this amounts to constitutional justification for the procedure; it is virtually certain that the referendum on such terms must always involve in some measure the standing of the government that initiated it.

Reasons for Using the Referendum

It is appropriate to turn to some of the purposes for which referendum in one guise or another might be used. These matters are conveniently approached through a brief consideration of some reasons why the referendum has been regarded recently by various shades of opinion in Britain as a desirable innovation.

There are three arguments on behalf of the referendum that seem to carry some weight in the British discussion. First, important constitutional changes should not be made over the heads of the people. This argument was used in favor of the EEC referendum (and, incidentally, *against* Edward Heath's reliance on wholly traditional procedures of parliamentary enactment in 1972) and has been deployed on behalf of the referendum provisions in the Scotland and Wales acts. It was also the argument used in 1911 when proposals to vest in the House of Lords the right to initiate a referendum on certain constitutional questions were under consideration by the Conservative party.

The second main argument is in essence a call for more effective popular control of public authorities, usually expressed in the plea for submitting important issues to a popular vote on the grounds that (1) the people have a right to be consulted and (2) government and Parliament often propose matters for which there is no popular majority and in respect of which they may be flouting public opinion. While this argument can apply to constitutional issues, it is chiefly relevant to a wide range of other policy questions. It is usually presented as a plea for more democratic control of governmental bodies on the grounds that it is too easy for minorities to manipulate political decisions in a manner injurious to the majority.

The third argument (although rarely put in unequivocal terms) is that governments can no longer rely simply on the authority of a majority in Parliament (which in Britain may not represent a majority in the electorate). Additionally, they need, from time to time, the reinforcement of an appeal to the people on a specific issue if they are to have the authority to proceed. It should be noted that this argument tends to rest on the assumption that a government will always secure the reinforcing majority that it seeks. As indicated, this condition may often not be fulfilled; if it is not, a government's authority is more likely to be diminished rather than increased by the use of referendum. A classic example is the French referendum of 1969 on regional and senate reform.

A more detailed look at the difficulties presented in practical political life by each of these arguments can be done with special reference to Britain, although many points have a much more general application. If the case for referendum in Britain is based on the constitutional protection argument, the major difficulty is defining what counts as a constitutional matter. We might say that both entry into the European Economic Community and devolution "affected" the sovereignty of Parliament (despite something in the nature of disavowals by Parliament) and were, therefore, plainly constitutional issues. As far as the rights of individuals are concerned, this type of institutional change may have far less direct significance than other pieces of legislation that look less constitutional at first sight. Examples which can be cited are the 1974 legislation enhancing the legitimacy of the closed shop, which plainly affected the right to free association; the exclusion of private practice from the National Health Service by the previous government, a measure that affects the right to choose medical treatment according to the individual's preferences as well as a doctor's right to offer his services for a charge; and much recent local government legislation that might be held to reduce the right to local self-government through elected representatives. These are but three examples of what can be called constitutional ambiguity; none directly affects matters within a narrow definition of constitutional provisions, but each does affect civil and political rights of individuals in significant ways.

Two conclusions are indicated. One, any definition of a constitutional question in traditional terms in Britain would be too narrow to accommodate many issues on which many people seriously believe their rights are adversely affected. Apart from presenting awkward problems under the first argument, it would certainly not accommodate the second argument for referendum. Indeed, in this connection, there is reason to believe that the majority of voters accepted the legitimacy of the EEC decision as taken by Parliament and did *not* want to have to vote on it. With regard to devolution, there is some evidence for the view that it is not (and perhaps never has been) a dominant issue for a majority of voters in either Scotland or Wales. In contrast, there are other issues—notably those affecting the closed shop and the privileges of trade unions, and perhaps measures relating to racial and sex discrimination, the penalties for crimes of violence, and parental rights regarding the provision of education—on which a majority of voters do have strong opinions and might welcome an opportunity to express them. In other words, there may be no strong demand for referendum on traditional constitutional matters, but there may be on matters that undoubtedly have implications for the rights of citizens. It is also in these directions that the definition of what is constitutional becomes highly contentious and in which a consistent definition of rights may lead, at least for a time, to sharp political conflict and social unrest. Moreover, there may be other means than referendum, such as an enforceable bill of rights, by which protection could be offered to individuals in such matters.

The other conclusion is far more limited in scope. Even in the traditional constitutional sphere concerned with relations between institutions, to define what should count is probably impracticable in Britain. This point has emerged several times in relation to House of Lords reform and proposals to vest a power in the Second Chamber to call for a referendum on constitutional issues. The Landsdowne proposals of 1911 were a brave but inadequate attempt to do this. Appreciation of this problem undoubtedly influenced the recent Conservative party committee on the future of the House of Lords to decide against making similar suggestions.[1] Ultimately, it is impossible to escape from the difficulty presented by an informal constitution. Nobody knows quite

---

[1] The author was a member of this committee.

what is in it; agreement on what definitely is in it tends to be limited to a few matters affecting institutions, most of which (for example, the position of the monarchy) are not going to be changed anyway.

The Case for Popular Consultations

The second main argument for the referendum also runs into seemingly insuperable problems in defining the terms on which it can properly be applied. It ought to be recognized that there is considerable force in the case for referendum as a means of popular democratic control. This is to some extent a matter of principle: Why should the people be denied a direct voice in determining the laws to which they will be subject? The case for popular consultations may also be reinforced by the growing complexity and remoteness of modern government, as a result of which many people feel alienated from their political institutions and suspicious of the decisions taken through them on their behalf. The serious aspects of this second argument also link with one facet of the third argument, namely, that governments may need the explicit support of a popular majority if they are to secure authority for measures to which powerful minority interests are opposed and for which parliamentary approval alone is an insufficient foundation. The referendum may be needed in order to ensure that the preferences of a genuine majority prevail over those of a minority; this is, of course, a case based on democratic postulates.

The points in favor of the use of referendum for the purposes outlined are persuasive. With the translation of the proposal into practical rules and procedures determining when and under what conditions a referendum may be held, serious difficulties appear. Once again, it is impossible to define coherently the category of issues on which it would be acceptable to provide for referendum. All kinds of objections are raised against referring to popular vote a remarkably wide range of issues. Those of a conventionally liberal and progressive outlook fear the prejudice of ill-informed majorities, much as J.S. Mill did over a century ago. Conservative populists would be happy to see the referendum used for some issues on which they believe enlightened opinion has set itself against popular sentiment and feeling, but they too draw back from accepting the opinion of the people on matters affecting, for example, defense, economic policy, or social benefits. In the end, we are left with little or no agreement on the kind of questions that can be safely left to popular decision of opinion.

Moreover, we encounter other problems. Assuming we could agree on a list of issues appropriate for referral to the people, we should have to decide whether such referral were to be mandatory or discretionary.

If discretionary, the referendum provision has, in effect, been turned into a tool of political expediency to be used by government and Parliament as they see fit. If mandatory, we still must define the terms on which it becomes mandatory. Once an effort is made to do this, it is hard to avoid introducing provisions for popular initiative. In other words, the referendum becomes mandatory when it is invoked by an appropriate number of electors. Whether many advocates of the referendum want to face up to the logic of their position in this way is more than doubtful. There is also the risk of involving the standing of a government. It is hard to see how a referendum on a contentious issue (even if contained in a list of matters suitable for referral to the people) could, in a competitive party system such as the British, result in anything other than a polarization of opinion with one side for the government and another against. If the point of view favored by the government were rejected at a referendum, it is hard to see how the government could long survive. It would have asked for a vote of confidence from the people and have been refused it. The risks for a government initiating a referendum would be all the greater if it were on an issue such as trade union reform, which would be likely to ensure the mobilization against it of those opposed to the measures submitted to a popular vote.

Finally, there are the implications for the role of Parliament. It is not necessary in this connection to plead in aid the sovereignty doctrine, which is anyway a serious obstacle to fruitful constitutional development. Even if it were assumed that Parliament were subject to certain limits, it remains important in a parliamentary democracy that Parliament and governments should accept responsibility for what they propose and undertake. The danger with the referendum on the basis under discussion here is that it encourages those in public office (and that includes all members of the legislature in this context) to abdicate their responsibilities in favor of a popular vote. In small and/or homogeneous societies, this may be tolerable. It is doubtful whether this is a prudent course to follow in political systems of a more complex and competitive kind in which there is no tradition of popular consultations on specific issues.

The third and last argument for the referendum has for the most part been covered by the second one. Additionally, it is understandable that politicians, in what appear to be increasingly difficult political circumstances, should be attracted by the idea of seeking to focus popular opinion on particular issues in order to overcome some of the obstacles created by inertia, the fragmentation of interests in society, and the apparent veto power of sectional interests. It is doubtful whether the referendum offers a safe way out of these difficulties. Rarely can one issue be separated from all others. Public opinion is elusive, complex, and often internally contradictory; the attempt to simplify issues opens the way to demagogues. It is by no means certain that even a popular majority will always overcome the objections of minorities who believe strongly that their interests are at stake. In other words, the referendum looks like a device for simplifying and resolving some of the difficult problems of government by consent. In special conditions, it may succeed; there is not much evidence that it would either in contemporary Britain or in many other countries with similar political and social conditions.

Constitutional and Political Implications

We are now in a position to summarize the results of this exercise in identifying types of referendum and in outlining the constitutional and political implications of different forms of the device.

The referendum on constitutional matters. There is quite a lot to be said in principle for the controlling referendum on constitutional questions, that is, giving the electors the right to make the final decision on the terms by which they are governed. In some countries (for example, the United States), this would represent a simpler and quicker procedure for constitutional amendment; this fact of itself could produce problems. Complex procedures of an indirect kind usually have the effect of protecting special interests and of slowing the rate of change: A popular vote overcomes minority claims and in some circumstances may accelerate the rate of change and thereby encourage instability.

In the peculiar conditions of the United Kingdom, however, the referendum on constitutional questions appears unworkable for two main reasons. Such questions cannot be satisfactorily defined (quite apart from deciding who or what institution would be entitled to initiate a referendum). Second, any likely definition would be far too narrow to encompass some of the issues on which there is some kind of case (grounded in democratic theory and based on the legitimate anxieties of politicians as to the strength of their authority) for referral to the people.

Referendum on ordinary policy questions. When the scope of the concept of a controlling referendum is widened beyond constitutional issues to other matters that cannot be specified in advance as a category, it is difficult to resist the slide toward the arguments for what has been called here facultative referendum. In other words, if the people have a right to express a view on some or all policy issues, the release mechanism ought to be some measure of popular demand rather than the decision of a group of representatives. This is the only method consistent

28

with the logic of the referendum device; the issues to be referred should be determined by a procedure that offers some protection against the risk that a government or party will offer or withhold a referendum to suit its political convenience. There is no reason, however, why the qualifying conditions for the release mechanism of popular initiative, to be effective, should not be set fairly high. In this way, it can be guaranteed that the facultative referendum will be invoked only when a reasonably strong body of opinion demands it.

The consultative referendum. The notion of a consultative referendum is rather artificial. In a democratic age, *vox populi* tends to have a binding effect anyway. The evidence suggests that where the referendum is used rarely, its consultative status may be partially retained. Frequent use is bound to emphasize the dependence of the legislative institutions on the results of the popular vote and thus to bring about a shift from consultative to binding effects.

Plebiscitary referendum. The plebiscitary referendum is necessarily a procedure regarded with suspicion by advocates of representative government and even by many sympathetic to the extension of direct democracy and participation via the referendum. There are some circumstances, however, in which the plebiscitary referendum may be regarded as justifiable, as in the establishment of the Fifth Republic in France and the solution of the Algerian problem. This is highly specific to a particular situation, tradition, and type of politician; we cannot generalize from such an example. Most of the relevant historical experience tells against the plebiscitary referendum, underlining its manipulative character and its association with methods of government directed against genuine citizen involvement in political life. It should be noted, however, that none of the other types of referendum wholly excludes the risk of a plebiscitary element coming into the procedure. This is simply because all questions referred to the people must be capable of a yes/no answer. From this it follows that if one or the other answer is linked with the views of some group of officeholders or aspirants to office, popular attitudes are likely to take shape for or against the holders of such views. Inevitably, therefore, the referendum runs the risk of becoming a vote of confidence in someone; to this extent, a plebiscitary element is present.

Referendum and the British unwritten constitution. In the narrower context of British constitutional traditions, it is particularly difficult to graft the referendum onto them as a regular and constitutionally recognized procedure. The device plainly conflicts with parliamentary sovereignty and with long-held views about the responsibility of members of Parliament for their own decisions in relation to the government of the country. The crucial problem lies in the resistance offered by the unwritten constitutional tradition to any serious constitutional innovation at all. If the effort is made to develop coherent proposals for introducing some form of the referendum, this inevitably affects in all kinds of ways other features of a highly ambiguous constitutional pattern. The only way through this thicket would be to contemplate a substantial formalization of the constitutional tradition itself. This is not a course for which most protagonists of the referendum have shown much enthusiasm.

A Challenge to the Representative Principle

In conclusion it is worth raising an issue that is presented by the discussion of the referendum device and that goes beyond the immediate problems of classification. This is the question whether much of the talk about referendum does not express serious misgivings about the representative principle as it now operates and thus amounts to a plea for a much more serious effort to institute a greater degree of popular participation in political life. The discussion of the referendum, notably in Britain, does amount to a challenge to traditional ideas about representation and its uses, despite protestations to the contrary by some advocates of the referendum. On the other hand, it must be recognized that the case for more popular participation is beset by many difficulties and ambiguities: Who wants participation, when and for what purposes, and what implications does this have for responsibility in government?

There are many reasons why in large, densely organized societies, dependent to a great extent on advanced technology and on their external links with the world economic system, representative government should no longer appear to work as it did in the era in which the theory and practice of it were elaborated. However, it is not pressures of this kind which I will put in the foreground, but rather the impact of the rise of disciplined political parties. In essence, the effect of this has been to confer a high degree of ambiguity on the notion of a representative. What and whom does he or she represent, how is the capacity to represent affected by membership of a party, and how are the claims of party discipline and party advantage reconciled with the idea that representatives should look to a public interest that necessarily cannot always be identical with party interest? Skepticism as to the possibility of answering these questions satisfactorily has stimulated a fairly widespread disillusionment with political parties. Certainly, this can be observed both in Britain and the United States; there are less clear signs of it in some countries of continental Europe. The declining commitment to political parties as acceptable ways of organizing opinion and interest for political action inevitably amounts to a challenge to the representative principle. The alternative in contemporary conditions is taken to be enhanced popular involvement; the representatives are to be tied more closely to expressions of popular preferences and, where practicable, to more extensive popular consultation and participation.

If this challenge is to be met, it would appear that some defects of representative government as currently practiced in many Western countries ought to be admitted openly. Political parties need to be more self-critical about their methods, organization, and sectarianism. In particular, they need to consider how their membership can be widened and in many cases diversified. Parties need to be more restrained in the claims they make, more tolerant of dissent and argument, and less inclined to behave as if securing government office gives them the right to appropriate the state for their own benefit. If meeting the challenge to representative principles requires, in the first place, action by parties, it also affects the structures of government. The weakening of representative practices appears to be correlated positively with the size and complexity of contemporary units of government and the density of administrative organization employed. Such conditions cannot be wished away, nor wholly revoked. Nevertheless, there are few compelling reasons why the structure of government should be as centralized as it often is and the units of administration or service provision as large and ponderous as many are. It is reasonable to hold that, when public organizations are on a scale that allows easy access and appear to the citizen to be manageable, the chances of the representative principle breaking down or being rejected are somewhat reduced. In such conditions, public confidence is generally exposed to fewer strains and there is less demand for direct citizen involvement. (Conveniently, too, direct participation is easier to organize in these circumstances.)

While recognizing that there may be serious shortcomings in the methods by which the representative principle is applied in many contemporary states, it is also important to appreciate the weaknesses in the participationist claims. The great strength of the representative principle lies in the idea of the representative as someone who speaks and acts on behalf of others generally and across the whole spectrum of their interests. The Achilles heel of the participationist argument is that most people do not appear to want to represent others at large in this manner and equally, when engaging in public affairs, do so for narrow and specific reasons. All this is no cause for reproach or condemnation; it merely expresses the obvious fact that human beings are restricted by their situation, interests, and knowledge. Even if an extension of opportunities for direct citizen participation in public affairs can be secured, it is likely to encourage a fragmentation of interests and points of view in the management of public services as a result of the overemphasis of particular individual and sectional concerns.

More fundamentally and seriously, however, the extension of direct participation carries with it the risk of eroding the notion of responsibility vested in officeholders. The proliferation of consultative arrangements and the referendum procedure may in some circumstances work decisively in this direction. The striking thing about consultation and the right to vote on this or that is that the person consulted or voting bears no responsibility for the decision and what follows. He has no duties laid on him, cannot be held accountable, and may not be affected in any way by the consequences of his behavior. The position is in principle quite different for officeholders; they have duties, they can be required to justify their decisions, they may be hauled before the courts, or they may be dismissed from office. None of this applies in situations reminiscent in some degree of direct democracy. If, therefore, one believes that direct democracy expresses an illusion in the modern world, one is bound to view with great reserve measures that work against the maintenance of the representative principle and of the responsibility in officeholders that it can so effectively sustain. Even in Switzerland, the one country in which extensive use of the referendum has been successfully combined with representative methods of government, there are grounds for concluding that the referendum has not infrequently allowed officeholders to hide behind the people.

Discussion

JACK PELTASON, *chairman:* In preparation for this discussion, I pulled off the library shelves here at Ditchley a book on the history of American colleges and universities. A commencement speaker in 1670 said, "If these, our fathers, had not founded the university, the ruling class would have been subjected to mechanics, cobblers, and tailors, the laws would have been made by mobs, nor would we have had rights, honors, or medals worthy of preservation; but plebiscites, fields of great pageants, and revolutionary movements would have prevailed." There is a little wisdom with which to begin.

NEVIL JOHNSON: Mr. Chairman, I think you've chosen an appropriate text for our discussion. My essay is an amended and slightly extended version of something I produced on my own initiative for a committee which the Conservative party set up some time ago to look at the desirability and practicality of referendums in Great Britain. No commitment on this matter actually came into the party's subsequent election manifesto; there is no news of the likelihood of any action being taken by the Conservative government on this particular constitutional possibility. But as you can see, what I tried to do in my paper was, above all, to bring out what I think might be the underlying logic of the device in different forms and applications. When I talk about consequences, for the purposes of this discussion I am thinking much more about the consequences of a constitutional and political nature: How the way in which a country is governed is affected by having the referendum or not having it.

JACK PELTASON: Your essay makes a complex and persuasive argument. You proceed from the premise that there is a demand for more popular participation in government that will not go away. This demand is applauded by some and feared by others. Although you seem to argue that there ought to be some kind of "popular release mechanism," would it be impossible to provide even for a restricted and limited use of the

33

referendum without a revolutionary change in the parliamentary system?

NEVIL JOHNSON: This is a difficult question; the answers differ acording to the level of understanding of and concern about the political order at which the question is posed. For argument's sake, let us assume an arrangement in Great Britain whereby, by petition with a certain number of signatures, a particular bill which had been through Parliament would then be put to popular vote, and, if rejected, would not be promulgated as an act.

Most ordinary voters would not be bothered much by the conflict between such a scheme and one of the basic principles about sovereignty on which our constitution is supposed to work. Yet, at the level of more sophisticated and professional political discourse, the strains caused by this change would be considerable. It would make no sense to keep talking of an omnipotent Parliament, with each Parliament able to do what it liked with the enactments of its predecessor. With this kind of referendum provision in relation to ordinary legislation, there would have to be a shift in beliefs about how our major institutions work and what they are entitled to do.

VINCENT WRIGHT: Is there not a series of inherent conditions involved in the use of the referendum that is much more likely to compound the problems of representative democracy than to solve them? After all, if one looks at some of the pressures pushing for the use of the referendum, they stem from the defects that are perceived in the legislative process. Since the weakness of the legislature in some measure results not so much from insensitivity to public opinion as oversensitivity to public opinion, one wonders whether a situation may develop in which the instrument designed to remedy the situation has the effect of weakening the legislature.

I am intrigued in listening to our American friends; when pressed, they ultimately believe that their fate resides not so much in the people as in the courts. Would one of the major constitutional implications of the frequent use of referendums in Britain be the creation of a written constitution and the formation of a group of judges empowered to protect that constitution? One therefore may end up paradoxically with a government by judges rather than government by the people.

JÜRG STEINER: The argument has been made that if there is a strong referendum the parliament is destroyed. The Swiss case indicates otherwise. In Switzerland, despite the referendum, the parties are strong and important. The parties in Switzerland, however, act differently; this is strongly linked to the referendum. In Switzerland, the four major parties, which hold more than 80 percent of the seats in parliament, are all represented in the Federal Council. The referendum has not destroyed the parties, but it has changed the interaction among the parties.

Let me give two examples. When we had the Treaty of Association with the EEC, there was quite a lot of opposition at the mass level, so it was necessary for all major parties to unite and to fight the battle to win public opinion. If we wanted to become a member of the United Nations, which we are not yet, there would also be a lot of resistance among the people, and all major parties would have to fight together. Often the parties act together and try to bring through an issue together. Often the parties and the politicians are afraid to have too many referendums, and they try to anticipate the referendum so as to prevent one of the parties from bringing it to the people. A famous tactic in Switzerland for political debate is inclusion of all relevant political groups. This is why the socialists were taken into the cabinet a long time ago and other groups as well. With this kind of party situation and government in which all the major relevant groups are included, one needs some kind of counterbalance and opposition outside the parties and the legislature. Elections for the legislature become less meaningful, and the referendums provide the counterbalance.

ROBIN DAY: I will indulge in a moment in a piece of constitutional heresy. First, Dr. Johnson's essay refers to the problem affecting referendums in the British constitutional context. He says the difficulty is that the underlying principle of the constitution is held to be the sovereignty of the Crown in Parliament. It is questionable, he says, whether Parliament could provide a satisfactory constitutional basis for referendums as a regular practice. I would like to suggest how this could be done and how the principle of the referendum and the principle of the sovereignty of Parliament could be made compatible. That idea may shock some of my British friends.

We start with the point that Parliament is sovereign. That very sovereignty, which is limitless, must include the power to define what Parliament is and the power to state what the manner and form and the procedure are for exercising that sovereignty. In other words, Parliament must define what Parliament means for one purpose or another. If that sounds odd, it has already been done by the Parliament Act of 1911, which says that for money bills Parliament needs the Queen and the House of Commons, and, for all other subjects, it needs the Queen, Lords, and Commons. Of course, Parliament can repeal the Parliament act that defines its procedure, but, in doing so, it has to follow the procedure laid down in the act.

We come here to the question of a referendum. Suppose we had, in Britain, a bill of rights passed like an ordinary statute, safeguarding, for instance, trial by jury, habeas corpus, the duration of Parliament, the British Broadcasting Corporation, the Finsbury Park Foundation. Parliament could enact a referendum law that said that no bill affecting or infringing or amending the bill of fundamental rights shall be presented for the royal assent unless it shall have been approved by two-thirds of the people voting in a referendum. Further, it could say that no bills to amend the referendum requirements shall be presented for the royal assent without the consent of two-thirds of the people voting in a referendum. This obviously would not conflict with the sovereignty of Parliament because at the bill stage, pre-royal assent, parliamentary sovereignty has not been exercised; it is only a bill, only a legislative proposal. The sovereignty of Parliament was used to redefine what Parliament is and to say that for certain purposes—for example, constitutional rights—Parliament is not the Queen and Commons; it is not the Queen, Lords, and Commons; it is Queen, Lords, and Commons *plus* a majority of the people voting in a referendum. If Parliament with its sovereignty wished to do that, it could do so. It is possible to combine the referendum process with a bill of rights so as to achieve that protective value of the written constitution, without having one with all its disadvantages, and without conflicting with the sovereignty of Parliament. That is the heresy I would like to put forward. That is the answer to Professor Johnson's question as to how one can have a genuine constitution on the foundations of the unlimited discretionary will of the Crown in Parliament.

MICHAEL RYLE: I see two difficulties. The first concerns the authority for making a referendum a constitutional provision. If a constitutional provision should allow altering only certain laws by referendum, that itself is a constitutional revision and so should be subject to a referendum. One cannot get behind the ultimate authority of Parliament. The second difficulty is that the courts will not look behind the royal assent and will not inquire into the process by which the act went up for royal assent. If the Commons passed a bill and the Lords passed it and presented it for the royal assent and the royal assent were given, the courts would not challenge its validity. That indicates that in the end you cannot go behind the sovereignty of Parliament.

ROBIN DAY: In my brief intervention I was not drafting an entire statute to meet all the objections that a learned clerk of the House of Commons would feel able to raise. Of course, the matter is perfectly simple. Mr. Ryle says the courts will not look behind the acts of

Parliament, that they will not interfere with the royal assent. If Parliament in its sovereignty said the courts will entertain an injunction to restrain the presentation of a bill for the royal assent, then the courts would be able to do so, because Parliament is sovereign.

MICHAEL RYLE: You are trying to make a man jump on his own shadow. It will not work; the shadow moves as you jump. The only way one can get out of this is by appealing to an authority external to one's own, in other words, an original constituent assembly such as that which established the constitutions of the states of the United States.

VERNON BOGDANOR: Michael Ryle is trying to say that one cannot entrench a referendum act. That is unnecessary for it to be effective. Robin Day has the authority of Professor Dicey behind him for his point that the referendum is not contrary to parliamentary sovereignty. He is suggesting a referendum act that would say that any bill on some particular subject would require direct approval by the electorate, and perhaps it would require some special majority—two-thirds or something similar. The referendum act might declare that any legislation that sought to transfer the powers of Parliament either downward through devolution or upward to the EEC would require a referendum before it could become law. That cannot be entrenched formally, but it can be entrenched politically in that it would be ruinous politically for any government to deprive the people of their rights by refusing to hold a referendum.

Nevil Johnson made two powerful points about the use of the referendum in a country, such as Britain, without a written constitution. The first is to define a category labeled "constitutional." Parliament has already done that in a sense because it has set a persuasive precedent that Parliament should not be able to transfer its powers downward or upward without a referendum. We would not be able to enact another devolution act in Scotland or Wales or to leave the EEC without another referendum. Thus, we already have one principle and there seems to be no reason why we could not develop others.

The second point was who decides whether any particular bill falls under the appropriate category. At the moment, this would be done by the Speaker or the Chairman of the Committee of the Whole House; this gives these officers of the Commons enormous power. Indeed, in the first Scotland and Wales bill, the Chairman of the Committee of the Whole House ruled that a mandatory referendum was not contrary to the British constitution. It was also his view that it could be introduced as a new clause in an already published bill.

Nevil Johnson's argument that the referendum is an appeal from knowledge to ignorance can be met if use of the referendum is confined to bills already passed by Parliament. The people become, as it were, a third chamber, their power like that of the unreformed House of Lords. They cannot initiate policies, but they can veto legislation.

There are three things the referendum can do that no other instrument can. First, it can give everyone voting an equal say on a specific question; in no other way can people decide whether they favor or oppose a particular legislative proposal with their votes counting equally. Second, it can enable people to decide an issue, not on the basis of what is compatible with particular party interests or party gains or party goals, but on the basis of what is in the public interest. Third, it identifies the interest of the people with the government, because it makes them think that laws are not there merely because Parliament has passed them, but that the people themselves are responsible for what is done.

CHRISTOPHER HUGHES: In speaking of parliamentary sovereignty, the House of Commons no longer behaves like the deliberative body it was in the nineteenth century. The House today is a collection of two sets of whipped dogs who follow their masters. The reality of British government is different from what the textbooks say. It is rule by the party bosses modified by two factors. One factor is mob violence, in the form of strikes, sit-ins, demonstrations, and processions, by middle-class mobs as well as working-class mobs. The other modifying factor is fear of the next election. An election settles nothing, but the fear of an election forces changes in policy. It is fear of the election that puts governments on their course toward inflation. The reason why I am advocating the referendum, not merely the once-for-all referendum but the total, integral referendum, is to restore the House of Commons, restore the Privy Council as a sort of federal council, to return England to the principles of 1688. I wish to strengthen government against parties and organized minorities.

I am not talking about the referendum as a device. I am talking about it as an institution. The ad hoc Common Market referendum was unconstitutional, but I favor a general referendum available for all measures, both the popular initiative and the challenge. I take this position on the basis of the Swiss experience, because in Switzerland, while the referendum itself, like elections here, often decides nothing, the *fear* of the referendum profoundly modifies Swiss government in the way that fear of the general election alters British government.

What impact does the referendum have on the legislature? I have studied both the Swiss and the British legislatures. I started out by thinking that the Swiss parliament is hopelessly weak compared to the British Parliament. After studying both, I concluded that the Swiss legislature is in some ways a stronger and more satisfactory parliament for the backbencher to serve in. It is a terrifically boring parliament—our Parliament is a joy to watch. Life in the Swiss parliament has the satisfaction of a certain sort of solid power, which a backbencher in our Parliament does not have. The difference the referendum makes in Switzerland is that it has made public opinion crucial; one must form public opinion, must indoctrinate the public. One must square the big corporations, square the trade unions, square the business people, square all the great forces of society; of course, it makes government regard public opinion as something to be formed.

EUGENE LEE: One of the reasons the initiative and the referendum are on the march both in the American states, which do not have them, and in the Congress is the inability of government to deal with public sector unions. Proposition 13 was a direct result of the inability of the California legislature to bargain with public employees, who are major contributors to the political campaigns to elect the city council and the state legislature. Does this have any relevance to the British Parliament?

NEVIL JOHNSON: It does have relevance. Mrs. Thatcher was perhaps incautious enough on one or two occasions when she was leader of the opposition to speculate in public about the possible use of referendums as a means of controlling the unions, imposing the will of an elected government on the unions. Whether one likes that idea or not, there is a real problem; some organized groups pay little attention to parliamentary majorities. It seems that this is a special aspect of the more general problem, which is most serious and came out in Christopher Hughes's remarks. Political leaders in quite a number of countries, and certainly in Britain, have become, on the whole, much more uncertain as to what they may say and do on any subject, no matter what majorities they have and notwithstanding the institutional authority they claim. They are much more uncertain as to whether the authority derived simply from having a majority in Parliament is enough for them to govern; therefore, some of them are moving toward referendums as a means of creating authority to enable them to do certain things.

DAVID MARQUAND: What does David Lea feel would be the Treasury response to the sort of referendum which Mr. Johnson was discussing? It is not quite analogous to the American Proposition-13-type referendum, but it has certain features in common. If it were to be carried out in the form that Mrs. Thatcher seemed to be implying, it would be an attempt, as Mr. Johnson said, to gain extra authority for the government in dealing with some kind of dispute in which it was not possible to persuade the trade unions to do what the government wanted in any other way. What does David Lea, representing the Trades Union Congress, think would be the trade union response to a situation in which such a referendum had been held and in which, for the sake of argument, the government's position had been endorsed by a substantial majority of the electorate?

DAVID LEA: The proposition is based on a fallacy. If all 30 million voters were asked whether they accepted the settlement of a particular industrial dispute and they said yes, one would be no further forward than without such a referendum. Let us postulate, for example, a national referendum on whether the coal miners should accept a 15 percent increase. Probably 95 percent of the people would say yes, but so what? That is the fallacy of this whole proposition. The answer is that one must deal with the people directly affected by the particular industrial situation.

ROBIN DAY: Would it not give the government greater moral support in taking emergency measures to head off a strike, such as the use of troops?

DAVID LEA: It does not get one anywhere, unless one is prepared to see how it relates to the issue of who is entitled to vote in the context of bargaining with a particular group of workers.

It is not the case that in the United States everything is moving in the direction of referendums and away from the direction of dealing on the basis of a social contract or a national accord. In October 1979, President Carter agreed with the AFL-CIO on a national accord. The Americans are learning a great deal from the British experience about this. There are problems, and those people who want to be cynical about it ought to look at the problems of the 1980s. The fact is that the economies in both countries in the 1980s will only operate effectively if we recognize that large national corporations and trade union organizations have to work together in running the economy. Things cannot be split all the time into contradictory propositions. It is this synthesizing proposition—a concordat, a national accord—that is a major trend in American society. It has also been the trend in British society; governments that have worked in the last few years in Britain have worked on that principle of joint commitment, not on the principle of trying to appeal to the people as a whole as to what to do about a particular industrial situation. The use of national referendums is based on a fallacy.

40

RONALD BUTT: When Mrs. Thatcher commented on referendums, I thought the comments were rather dangerous. What she said was, in effect, that if she got into political difficulties in an industrial situation— one in which the authority of government was challenged by the trade union movement in much the same manner as it was challenged, or was said to be challenged, under Mr. Heath—she might in those circumstances appeal to the people by a referendum.

That is dangerous because, first of all, it raises the question of what happens while she is appealing. If, for example, a government either creates a crisis or has a crisis forced upon it, and gets into conflict with the trade union movement as a whole, if the economic life of the country has come to a full stop and is strike-ridden, if there is chaos all around and the government's authority is challenged, this should be the last moment for the government to appeal to the people and to ask the question: Do you give us authority to govern or not? What happens during the campaign? In such a crisis, could the referendum campaign be carried on fairly and properly?

Let us suppose that the government could achieve that, and a fortnight or three weeks later it got 53 percent in favor and 47 percent against. What would that do for its policy and authority? It would accomplish little or nothing. Such a crisis is precisely the moment when a government needs the support of Parliament, not referendums, to give it the authority to govern. To ask the people in a referendum to give it that authority is to admit a doubt as to whether it has such authority. The use of the referendum in an emergency or short-term crisis could well appear to be a confession of weakness.

THOMAS FOLEY: We still tend to mix up the initiative and referendum. The British are not interested in initiatives. They are only talking about matters being put by Parliament for the people's vote to provide additional legitimacy that Parliament might find useful. In the United States, there is no particular movement toward such a referendum. The movement is totally toward initiative; it stems from a desire on the part of the groups pushing it to break through the seemingly obdurate insensitivity of the national and state legislatures to deal with questions in the manner in which they want them dealt with. When talking about the initiative and the referendum, we are looking at different kinds of movements and different kinds of questions.

No one, not even Mr. Jones, is proposing that Congress be given any authority to refer questions to the public; there is no interest in that. There is an interest on the part of members of Congress and citizens who cannot get their views accepted by Congress to force the public to take over the questions directly and limit the power of Congress. I take the point of Professor Johnson that some parliaments in Europe and in Britain feel that they do not have sufficient authority or legitimacy to make certain decisions without taking broader plebiscites. The classic example of that may be Sweden, where the question of nuclear power is binding the parties and the decision processes of Parliament. That blockage has to be removed, and it is going to be by a referendum. That is the only purpose that a referendum would serve.

NEVIL JOHNSON: I do not accept a sharp dividing line between the initiative and referendum. If one thinks through the notion of referendum, one is likely to come to the initiative also in some form or another. In the British case, we could not leave referendums as a purely discretionary device. One might manage, as the Irish do, for example, with a restricted use: One simply says, well, we have a written constitution, and if it is to be amended, then that amendment must go to the people. One might be able to have that as a possible baseline. If one tries to consider the referendum broadly as an institution to be used effectively and widely in society, intended to serve the purpose of promoting certain political values, then one is pushed from referendum to initiative.

JOHN COURTNEY: Nevil Johnson is absolutely correct in saying that it is difficult to produce some sort of general explanation or general theory of referendums. The problem, as he has pinpointed it, has to do with the nature of parliamentary government. It is true that the logic of referendum is simply not the logic of parliamentary government in the purist sense of the term, but this does not help unless we come to grips with the fundamental issue. That is, if the issue is one of calling for correcting the legislative process, what then will be the relationship between the representatives and the voters in a referendum? What are the categories of questions that should be submitted? These are absolutely essential points to be understood. If we propose to refer to the people questions that we are most keen to have discussed—taxation, capital punishment, and various moral issues—that is one thing. The typical electorate, whether British, Canadian, or American, is not particularly interested in the run-of-the-mill daily affairs that, of necessity, concern governments. It is difficult to propose some sort of blanket category of the kind of questions that should be referred. When referendums are used on an ad hoc basis to get the government out of trouble, or to refer a question because it happens to have had a certain interest expressed by a particularly prominent group, the ad hoc experience is unsatisfactory.

GEORGE CUNNINGHAM: I have a good deal of sympathy with Professor Hughes's criticism of how Parliament in Britain works at the moment and particularly with his criticism of the dominance of the parties. He exaggerated enormously; it is easy to go to any other parliament and to think that an individual member in that other parliament is either more influential or has a more satisfying role than he does in the British Parliament. It is as difficult for me as a British MP to get inside another parliament as it is for Professor Hughes as an academic to get inside any parliament. The British backbencher has, if he wishes to use it, and many do, at least as much possibility of influence on power as in any other parliament. The exception, of course, is the American Congress, where there are no backbenchers.

There has been much talk in this session about the fundamental principles of the British constitution. First, we do not have a constitution, so the term should be banned as far as it relates to Britain. The "fundamental principles of the constitution" have been invented for the purposes of writing books. There are no fundamental principles, there are certainly no fundamental principles that have lasted a thousand years or anything like it. There are habits, and, with great respect to the academics, what they do is to describe habits and then say these are fundamental principles of the British constitution, and one ruins the constitution if these are changed. They said, for example, that if a government were defeated on a budget bill, it absolutely must resign. When it happened, the government did not resign and nothing happened legally. The argument that there is some conflict between the use of referendum and what are accepted as monumental principles of our constitution is wrong.

Second, "entrenching" is not the problem that some have said it is. After all, the British Parliament could legislate in respect to Australia. It would not be wrong in British law to do this, but it does not, in fact, happen. We do not need to find ways of making it impossible to do something.

ROBIN DAY: That happens only with the consent of the Commonwealth of Australia.

GEORGE CUNNINGHAM: If we passed the 1931 Statute of Westminster, we can repeal it. We can legislate for Australia without any breach of convention, if the dominion of Australia asks us to do so, and we have done so long after 1931. If we wanted to do it, it would be valid British domestic law to repeal the Statute of Westminster.

There have been two sorts of issues that we have taken to referendums. On the EEC, there were some people who thought that they could get their way by means of a referendum but not otherwise. On the EEC, there was a justification in having a referendum because one could not estimate what the public wanted from the way it voted in the previous election; the difference of view on the EEC issue was not congruent with the differences between the political parties. That seems to be one of the obvious justifications for a referendum: not knowing what the public wants. One may throw over what the public wants, but at least one ought to have some idea of what people want. If there is no way of telling what they want from the way they voted in the last election, because the parties were not opposed on the particular issue, then a referendum is a natural thing to turn to.

The second case, the one on devolution, was one where it was felt by some of us that a gross error was being made as to the state of opinion in parts of the country. So we were really saying, "All right, since that's a large part of your argument, let us test whether your assertion in that respect is correct." There is nothing wrong with continuing on such an ad hoc basis. If there is some particular justification in a particular case for having a referendum, then let us go ahead and do it. The public would not regard either the EEC or the devolution referendums as having been improper in that respect. We do not need a general referendum act at the present time. If we continue finding more cases where we think we need to have a referendum, then we must have some rules about how to conduct it. Clearly, it would not be right to have a certain condition, such as the 40 percent requirement, that is used on some occasions but not on others. Those rules would be general principles about the way one conducts referendums rather than prescribing the occasions upon which one conducts them.

PHILIP GOODHART: It would not be physically possible to have any sort of national referendum on any sort of specific industrial dispute. Even in Switzerland where they have had, after all, more experience in staging referendums than any other country in the world, it takes some three months to mount a referendum campaign. It would not be possible to mount a national referendum here with the best will in the world in less than three months, given that the legislation would have to go through Parliament. What was discussed after Margaret Thatcher's reference to the use of the referendum in the industrial scene was the question of whether trade unions are not such a major part of the constitutional purpose of this country that any major legislation affecting their powers should be put to a referendum before it became operative. If such a bill were passed by the referendum, it would be rather more difficult to repeal that legislation at a later date. That particular idea could well return to the forefront.

DAVID LEA: What is sauce for the goose is sauce for the gander. Does one think through that logic and apply it, for example, to the city of London? Does one ask a general question of the British people as to whether they think the city of London ought to be more publicly accountable? One gets the same sort of problem.

3

The American Experience, 1778-1978

Eugene C. Lee

In November 1979, several million California citizens went to the polls in a special election to vote on two highly controversial and complicated issues. One was a proposed constitutional amendment, placed on the ballot by the state legislature, designed to stop school busing ordered by the courts to achieve racial desegregation. The second, placed directly on the ballot by citizen petition, proposed a ceiling on state taxing and spending authority, limiting future increases in the budget to an adjustment for growth in the population and the cost of living.

These are among the most recent examples of an ancient, continuing, and apparently growing American institution, the referendum. Indeed, as Austin Ranney notes, the modern referendum, as opposed to face-to-face town or cantonal meetings, was probably first used in 1788, when citizens of Massachusetts considered ratification of a proposed state constitution.[1] By the mid-nineteenth century, it was commonplace to require that state constitutional amendments be approved by the voters. This was extended in many states to the ratification and amendment of city and county charters, the incorporation of cities, and the passage of state and local bond issues. By 1900, Americans were no strangers to the concept of approving changes in their fundamental laws by the use of the referendum. That they should also have the power of *initiating* such changes was, to many, a logical extension of their power; the right of the initiative was adopted quickly in many American states. Neither the initiative nor the referendum, however, has ever been employed at the national level.

We do not know how often these institutions of direct democracy have been employed in the United States. It has been suggested that 12,000 to 15,000 state propositions have been voted upon in this century alone. In the not untypical year of 1968, for example, 320

[1] Austin Ranney, "The United States of America," in David Butler and Austin Ranney, eds., *Referendums: A Comparative Study of Practice and Theory* (Washington, D.C.: American Enterprise Institute for Public Policy Research, 1978), p. 68.

propositions were on state ballots, an average of 7 per state among forty-four of the fifty states, with a minimum of 1 measure and a maximum of 50. In November 1978, there were 380 state ballot propositions.[2] In 1968, approximately 16,000 local propositions were voted upon in various localities across the nation as well.[3]

Several different kinds of referendums—broadly defined—must be distinguished. The "constitutional referendum" noted above—the mandatory referral to the people for ratification of state constitutional amendments passed by the state legislature—exists in all but one state, Delaware. In thirty-nine states, other types of issues are also referred to the voters:

• In twenty-one of these states, certain measures—typically bond issues or debt authorization measures—must be submitted by the legislature to the voters in a "constitutionally mandated referendum."

• In twenty-four states, voters—generally a fixed percentage of the electorate—may use a protest or "petition referendum" to force an issue passed by the legislature onto the ballot, where it must receive majority approval before taking effect.

• In nineteen states, the legislature may voluntarily submit measures to the people for their approval, in a "legislative referendum."

Finally, twenty-two states employ the initiative, the ability of the people by petition to place a measure directly on the ballot.

• Fifteen of these states provide for the "constitutional initiative," the direct placement of a constitutional amendment before the electorate. (In addition, Illinois provides for a limited initiative dealing with only one section of the constitution.)

• Twenty-one states utilize the "statutory initiative," by which a popular petition can force a statute onto the ballot. Five of these states, however, employ the "indirect initiative," whereby such measures must first be considered by the legislature which has the option of approving the measure. In the remaining states, the "direct initiative" bypasses the legislature altogether. (In three of these states, the indirect initiative is also available.)

In all initiative states, the legislature may itself propose a substitute measure—constitutional amendment or statute—and place two competing propositions before the voters.

---

[2] Richard J. Cattani, "Voters Face Growing List of Decisions," *Christian Science Monitor*, November 1, 1978, p. 1.

[3] Jerome M. Clubb and Michael W. Traugott, "National Patterns of Referenda Voting: The 1968 Election," in Harlan Hahn, ed., *People and Politics in Urban Society* (Beverly Hills, Calif.: Sage Publications, 1972), pp. 137, 140, 143.

The two examples of *direct legislation,* the initiative and the petition referendum, are largely a phenomenon of the western states, reflecting the particular impact of the Progressive reforms of the early 1900s on this section of the nation. Currently, only five of the twenty-six states east of the Mississippi River provide for the initiative—either constitutional or statutory—in sharp contrast to seventeen of the twenty-four western states. None of these five eastern states has adopted the direct initiative for statutory changes, whereas fifteen of the western states have done so. Only ten states, all in the West, have *both* the constitutional and direct statutory initiative. Of the twenty-four petition referendum states, only six are in the east. Charles Price suggests a possible explanation for this regional pattern:

> It may well be that the initiative was able to catch on in at least some western states because the political institutions and channels for doing things were not as firmly rooted in tradition as they were in the eastern, southern and mid-western states. After all, the Progressive Movement swept the western states only a few decades after most had attained statehood.[4]

Whatever the reason, these measures—most of which were adopted in the first two decades of the twentieth century—were believed by their Progressive authors to be an instrument to neutralize the power of special interest groups, to curtail corruption on the part of political machines, to provide a vehicle for civic education on major policy issues, to create pressures on state representatives and governors to act on specific measures, and, when they failed to act, to bypass these representative institutions altogether, in short "to make every man his own legislature." Against this vision, what has been the record, not only of the initiative and the petition referendums, but of referendums generally?

The Use of Referendums

For one thing, the use of these different kinds of referendums differs markedly. Accurate national information is available only for initiatives —either constitutional amendments or statutory proposals. Through 1978, 1,197 had appeared on the ballot since the institution was first adopted in South Dakota in 1898.[5] Reflecting the disproportionate

---

[4] Charles M. Price, "The Initiative: A Comparative State Analysis and Reassessment of a Western Phenomenon," *Western Political Quarterly,* vol. 28 (June 1975), p. 248.

[5] Virginia Graham, *A Compilation of Statewide Initiative Proposals Appearing on Ballots Through 1978* (Washington, D.C.: Congressional Research Service, Library of Congress, 1979).

western usage, seven states—Oregon, California, North Dakota, Colorado, Arizona, Washington, and Oklahoma—account for more than three-quarters of these measures, Oregon and California alone for nearly one-third.

Far more frequent than initiated measures, however, are constitutional amendments placed on the ballot by state legislatures. No national figure exists, but in eight states, between 1898 and 1976, some 1,506 proposals were of this character, compared to 409 constitutional amendments that came before the electorate by citizen petition.[6] In California, from 1912 through 1978, for example, 489 constitutional amendments were proposed by the legislature, 91 by initiative petition.[7]

The widespread use of the referendum in American states arises directly from the lengthy and detailed character of their constitutions. Generally containing a mass of technical verbiage on such subjects as taxation, utility regulation, and the like, the typical state constitution is the length of a small paperback book. Such a document requires continual and extensive amendment to maintain its viability in a changing social and economic environment; a great deal of state legislative activity—compared to that in the national Congress, for example—is devoted to the consideration of constitutional amendments.

Bond issues or debt authorization, the subject of constitutionally mandated referendums in many states, also appear on the ballot in large numbers. In Maine, for example, thirty-three bond measures were on the ballot in the 1970–1978 period. In California, voters considered some fifty-five bond referendums from 1912 through 1978.

The remaining institutions of the referendum are far less widely employed. Only a few state legislatures appear to make frequent use of the optional legislative referendum. One of these is Oregon, where the legislature voluntarily placed seven measures on the ballot from 1970 through 1978. In neighboring Washington, 27 statutes were similarly referred from 1944 through 1973, and the device has seen recent increased usage.[8] In Maine, well over 100 statutes have been referred by the legislature to the voters for their consideration since this provision was originally enacted.

Finally, the once popular petition or protest referendum has fallen into relative disuse. Charles Price concluded that it is increasingly difficult to obtain "the specified number of signatures in the abbreviated time period allotted before the act in question goes into effect [for

---

[6] Ranney, "The United States," p. 81.

[7] Eugene C. Lee, "California," in Butler and Ranney, *Referendums*, p. 90.

[8] Hugh A. Bone and Robert C. Benedict, "Perspectives on Direct Legislation: Washington State's Experience, 1914–73," *Western Political Quarterly*, vol. 28 (June 1975), p. 337.

example, ninety days in California]."[9] Hugh Bone and Robert Benedict suggest from their Washington state study that the declining use of the petition referendum, despite its highly successful record in overturning statutes, indicates greater popular agreement with what the legislature has actually passed.[10]

Measures placed on the ballot by the legislature have, as might be expected, a far greater chance of success—an approval rate of about 60 percent—than those arriving by the petition route. Among states that employ both alternatives, measures placed on the ballot by the legislature are approved by the voters at a rate almost double that for measures proposed by initiative petitions. "Evidently," suggests Ranney, "the voters in most states are far more likely to think well of a proposed new law or constitutional amendment if it has previously been considered and approved by their elected representatives than if it is solely the creature of an unofficial pressure group, whether it be regarded as a 'special interest' or 'public interest' group."[11] This may be especially the case in the majority of American states where a two-thirds or three-fifths legislative majority is required to pass proposed constitutional amendments, which then come to the ballot with acknowledged extraordinary support. Even so, the fact that 40 percent of referendums from the legislature are turned down by the voters is noteworthy.

What uses are made of the referendum in American states? Clearly, given the nature of state constitutions, their frequent amendment may involve every conceivable issue, screened in most instances—as noted above—by legislative review. Again, however, the written record and analysis of these constitutional referendums are sparse; commentary on bond issues and the other types of referendums is equally deficient. Only the initiative has drawn the sustained attention of scholars; it is to that institution that one must turn for information and analysis.

Fortunately, Austin Ranney has recently classified all American state initiatives for the period 1898–1976 by subject, revealing the fact that from women's suffrage to the regulation of nuclear power plants, from prohibition on the sale of liquor to a prohibition on the use of busing to achieve racial balance in schools, from the death penalty to abortion, the crucial issues of the moment have come to the ballot via the initiative process.[12] Most frequent of all measures—one-quarter of the total—have been those dealing with the nature of government—

[9] Price, "Initiative," p. 245.
[10] Bone and Benedict, "Perspectives," p. 338.
[11] Ranney, "United States," p. 82.
[12] Ibid., pp. 78–81.

for example, the judicial system and limitations on gubernatorial terms. Revenue and taxation, most vividly exemplified by California's Proposition 13 in 1978, constitute the second most frequent subjects, one-fifth of all questions put to a vote. Issues of public morality—a state lottery, decriminalization of marijuana—and the regulation of business and labor—conditions of union membership, electric utility pricing—have been prominent on the ballot. Most recently, environmental policies have been presented, such as coastal land conservation and the Colorado ban on the use of public funds for the 1976 Winter Olympics, which led to the transfer of the games to Austria.

The California Experience

Who employs the initiative? As implied, the groups do not differ significantly from those lobbying before the legislature. The California experience, where the initiative has been most actively used in recent years, is illustrative.

Many measures have been drawn by proponents with substantial economic means: realtors supporting an anti-open-housing measure, movie theaters opposing pay-television, a state lottery sponsored almost exclusively by the American Sweepstakes Corporation, the railroad industry in support of an antifeatherbedding proposal, land investment companies supporting a property tax shift, agricultural growers opposed to farm-labor unionization, and public employee groups seeking higher salaries. Grassroots organizations have also been active, as in the case of coastal zoning, marijuana decriminalization, nuclear safety, wild rivers preservation, and political reform measures.

Why do these groups promote direct legislation? The reason most often assigned is that the legislature refuses to pass a measure that is dear to the group requesting its passage. Second, groups wish to have measures adopted in the form they desire rather than to have them amended to death in the legislature. The special status attached to an initiative constitutes a third motivating factor. Successful initiatives, once adopted, can generally be amended only by a vote of the people, unless the measure expressly allows legislative revision. The public educational impact of a ballot campaign provides a fourth basis. Some groups, like those proposing a liberalization of marijuana laws in 1972, do not anticipate victory at the polls. Instead, they hope that enlightened public opinion, stimulated by the campaign, will lead to subsequent legislative action, which did result in this instance.

In short, direct legislation, or the threat to circulate initiative petitions, has become an integral part of the strategy of law making. In 1976, for example, statutes to regulate nuclear power plants passed the California legislature only because of the threat of a much more stringent initiative measure on the subsequent June ballot. Important political figures withheld their judgment of the initiative until the legislature had acted and only then suggested to voters that the ballot measure was not needed. In 1968 and 1978, the threat of a radical property tax limitation initiative forced the legislature to propose major adjustments in the tax structure. In 1968, the legislature was successful. In 1978, however, the voters chose the initiative measure, Proposition 13.

What emerges from this review is that, while a few groups outside the main political stream occasionally try to employ the initiative process, the main actors are those who regularly do battle in legislative corridors or in campaigns for elective office. For these groups, the initiative is mainly another weapon, or hurdle, in the contest for political power and influence.

Bone and Benedict draw an additional view from the Washington state experience:

> Time and time again the sponsors [of initiative measures] have been ahead of the legislature. The initiative has been used to liberalize liquor laws, adopt daylight saving time, expand welfare benefits, authorize joint tenancies in property, protect game, advance and protect recreational opportunities, bring about reappointment, and to institute a number of government reforms including the state civil service, open meetings, and regulation of lobbying and campaign practices. The success at the polls of these measures and many others, often by large margins, can be interpreted to mean that the legislature was unresponsive to a wide-spread desire for these certain types of political changes.[13]

Is the Washington state record typical? Ranney concludes that from 1945 to 1976 the national (that is, basically western states) record of the initiative process on six issues that involved clear liberal-conservative choices was as follows:

> ... liberal positions on economic questions (right to work and taxation laws) generally won, conservative positions on social issues (death penalty, abortion, and racial discrimination) won, while the environmentalists broke even with the advocates of economic growth on nuclear power issues. This pattern is consistent with the widely held view that American voters are predominantly liberal on economic questions and conservative on social issues.[14]

---

13 Bone and Benedict, "Perspectives," p. 347.
14 Ranney, "United States," p. 84.

Campaigning

How are these issues brought before the voters? An initiative campaign uniquely involves the circulation of petitions. In some instances, this may be accomplished by volunteer organizations such as the Sierra Club or Common Cause. In many cases, however, especially in a state like California, where more than 500,000 signatures are required to qualify a proposition for the ballot, professional organizations may be employed. In 1978, the cost for such a campaign was 50 cents per signature, with perhaps a minimum fee of $225,000.

In 1980, a technological innovation was introduced in California that may revolutionize the initiative process—the solicitation of signatures by direct mail. Professional campaign firms provide computerized mailing lists, targeted to particular neighborhoods and socioeconomic groups, to sponsors of ballot measures. A typical mailing contains a letter from the sponsor, a short but legally sufficient petition to be returned, and a request for a campaign contribution.

Although differing only in degree from previous efforts involving solicitation door-to-door and at shopping centers, qualification by direct mail appears to be radically different in its impact. The overnight blanketing of the state with individual petitions greatly facilitates the qualification process for groups able to meet the heavy costs of the direct mail campaign. It is highly likely that the 1980s will see a greatly expanded use of this device and subsequent efforts to regulate it by law.

Once an initiative measure has qualified for the ballot, the campaign methods are substantially the same as those employed in contests for public office. Even more for initiatives than for candidates, this has meant the professionalization of campaigning, the dominance of public relations firms with media consultants, public opinion pollsters and direct mail specialists. To be sure, grass-roots organizations are alive and well. Even these groups often succeed because they are able to "out-professionalize" their opponents.

The character of initiative campaigns—frequent reliance on sloganeering and emotional appeals, on propaganda and sixty-second television advertisements—is not unique. Indeed, it seems to parallel the new style of campaigning—the decline of party and the rise of candidate-centered technology—so typical of contemporary American politics. It would appear that the politics of the initiative was a precursor of these developments. Although the "new politics" owes much to the more recent advent of television, it was in California that the current form of political campaigning began to take shape. The campaign management and political public relations firms first cut their teeth on initiative campaigns.

All of this requires money; direct mail campaigns may require even more. In California, proponents and opponents of the sixteen propositions on the ballot from 1972 through 1976 spent a grand total of $22,518,000 on campaigning. The amounts varied tremendously, from under $60,000 spent on both sides of the school busing initiative in 1972 to $3.8 million spent on the nuclear power measure in 1976. There was generally a big difference between the amounts spent by proponents and opponents. In some cases, advocates of a measure were the heavy spenders; in other instances, opponents were forced into massive expenditures to defeat a proposal not of their choosing.

It is even more significant that the expenditure of money on an initiative does not necessarily correspond with its success. From 1972 through 1976, six of the eight measures on which advocates spent more than their opponents were defeated; for all sixteen measures, the side spending the most money was successful in only eight races. In general, opponents of initiatives who spent the most tended to be successful in defeating the measure; on the other hand, high-spending advocates most often saw their cause go down to defeat.

What may one conclude about initiative campaigns and their financing? Drawing from the California experience, between 1964 and 1976, no major economic group was able to enact an initiative measure: realtors and land developers, state employees, agribusiness, farm labor, and greyhound racing interests—all failed in their attempts to bypass the legislative process. Instead, victories were achieved by groups with minimum economic clout but the ability to capitalize upon high public interest in such contrasting issues as coastal conservation and the death penalty, and the ability to mobilize effective political campaigns without massive funding.[15]

The Voter

Voters are the target of all of this effort, of course. To understand electoral behavior in referendums, at least three questions must be asked: To what extent do voters participate? Do they understand the measures on the ballot? What are the factors that shape their decision?

Voting on referendums almost always coincides with a general or primary election and is affected by the differential turnouts for presi-

---

[15] The passage of Proposition 13 in 1978 could be classified as a departure from the above generalization. The proposal was sponsored in large part by apartment building owners, who were slated to receive a substantial financial reward from the passage of the measure, a prospect which has clearly been realized. However, the initiative met with such widespread popular support that it is somewhat misleading to characterize it as a single-interest proposal.

dential and mid-term gubernatorial contests and for congressional and state legislative races occurring at the same time. Whatever the election, however, voting in the United States is at a low point. In California, Massachusetts, and Washington—three referendum states—less than 65 percent of the adult population voted in the last two presidential elections, and less than 50 percent in the intervening nonpresidential years. Numerous studies have demonstrated that the electorate is different in character from the total adult population. Typically, minorities, the poor, and the uneducated vote in smaller numbers, relative to their size. Among these groups, Wolfinger and Rosenstone note that education has the largest impact upon turnout.[16]

The problem is more complicated, however, for not all who go to the polls vote on referendums. Reviewing the national record in 1968, Clubb and Traugott found that the proportion of the estimated eligible population voting on the 320 referendums in that year ranged from a high of 74 percent in Utah to a low of 9 percent in South Carolina, with an average across the country of 40 percent. A postelection survey of voters in 1968 revealed that 75 percent of the respondents had voted, but that of these only 53 percent had voted on referendums.[17] In extending the comparison of voters with the adult population, the referendum voters were "more predominantly white, affluent, better-educated, and of higher subjective social class" than the voters as a whole.[18]

David Magleby's review of more recent evidence parallels this conclusion. Among those who vote, those from upper socioeconomic categories are disproportionately represented among those who decide referendums. Most specifically, education has a strong impact on the likelihood of voting on propositions. Citing a national poll of voters in 1974, Magleby noted that while 89 percent of respondents with college degrees reported voting on all or most of the propositions in that year, only 40 percent of those with an eighth-grade education or less so indicated.[19]

Various kinds of referendums, as expected, command different rates of participation. Examining recent elections in California, for example, Magleby found that the average dropoff (the number of voters

---

[16] Raymond W. Wolfinger and Steven J. Rosenstone, *Who Votes?* (New Haven, Conn.: Yale University Press, 1980), pp. 17–30.

[17] Clubb and Traugott, "Patterns," p. 142.

[18] Ibid., p. 165.

[19] David B. Magleby, "Voting on Statewide Propositions" (Paper presented at the annual meeting of the Western Political Science Association, Portland, Oregon, March 22–24, 1979), pp. 26, 38.

not voting for a candidate or ballot measure) for constitutional referendums was 17 percent, for bond issues 12 percent, but for the generally more controversial initiative proposals 7 percent. This last compares favorably with the dropoff for congressional representatives of 7 percent or state legislators of 8 percent, but is higher than the 2 to 3 percent dropoff in presidential and gubernatorial races.[20] As for types of issues, in Washington, with respect to initiatives and petition referendums, "turnout on morals issues is likely to be greater than for any other type of proposition," with an average dropoff of 11 percent, while questions of government and structure and reform bring out the lowest participation, an average dropoff of over 25 percent.[21]

Regardless of the participation rate, referendum voters often make up their minds on the eve of the election. One month before the November 1976 election, for example, 46 percent of the California public had seen or heard nothing about the controversial labor-agricultural ballot measure sponsored by farm union leader Cesar Chavez. Mervin Field, a distinguished California pollster, suggests that the voter then gets his cues concerning these types of issues by looking "to what other people say, to what respected institutions and leaders say, and to the advertising and other information about the measures that is made available."[22] An official ballot pamphlet, objective information by the League of Women Voters, newspaper and media coverage, and the ubiquitous television commercials provide some of the cues.

This finding is consistent with the 1968 national survey reported by Clubb and Traugott. Over half of the referendum voters indicated they read newspaper articles about the election regularly, in contrast to 35 percent of persons voting for offices only (and 21 percent of nonvoters). Similar contrasts were exhibited with respect to radio, magazines, and television.[23]

As this information is digested, congruence between attitudes on the general issue and views on the specific measure appears to develop. This may be somewhat confused and uncertain, as was the case with the highly technical nuclear power plant initiative in California in 1976. Scientists and engineers argued on both sides; on election eve, only 58 percent of those polled said they knew enough to vote.[24] In contrast, in early October 1972, 80 percent of the public polled had not heard of the forthcoming death penalty initiative but, when told about the measure, only 13 percent were undecided as to how to vote. Their

---

[20] Ibid., p. 8.
[21] Bone and Benedict, "Perspectives," pp. 334, 340.
[22] Mervin Field, *The California Poll*, October 24, 1972.
[23] Clubb and Traugott, "Patterns," p. 147.
[24] Field, *California Poll*, June 4, 1976.

views coincided almost exactly with those already cognizant of the ballot issue.[25]

The campaign over the property tax limitation measure, the famous Proposition 13, provides another perspective. Immediately before the election, only 9 percent of those polled were undecided or unaware of the measure; supporters and opponents alike possessed clear and logically consistent views backing their voting intention.

With respect to the voting decision, no less than in presidential or gubernatorial races, initiatives are influenced by currents of conservatism and liberalism, by socioeconomic status, by age and race, by urban or rural residence, and—related to all of these—by party affiliation. Issues such as school busing, the death penalty, environmental controls, and tax measures involve themes that have long divided the public in familiar ways. In contrast, the salaries of state employees or greyhound dog racing cut across normal political lines. All of these must be put in the context of the absence of the party label on ballot measures and a general lack of party activity, of an often relatively low level of voter awareness, and of frequent last-minute decision making, subject to quick change under the pressure of a massive campaign and emotional appeals.

What does this evidence concerning the voter suggest? Clubb and Traugott concluded that "referenda voters appear as a small, well-informed, well-politicized, and in some respects, elite segment of the total electorate," especially with respect to the less prominent measures.[26] Magleby found "the electorate which votes on propositions is *not* representative of those who turn out, at least for propositions submitted by the legislature."[27]

The California evidence is at least partially supportive. Voting on initiatives is reasonably high among those going to the polls—far less on constitutional referendums from the legislature—but low as a proportion of adults eligible to vote. As is true of statewide candidates—undoubtedly in all states—few, if any, measures ever receive the approval of a majority of adults. With respect to referendums, millions of Americans in effect delegate their vote to their fellow citizens.

These facts concerning both voter turnout generally and referendum participation specifically have led William J. D. Boyd of the National Municipal League to speculate whether "since the arrival of one man, one vote, state legislatures do not represent the entire population (not just those who vote) more accurately than the voters at any

[25] Field, *California Poll*, October 24, 1972.
[26] Clubb and Traugott, "Perspectives," pp. 155, 165.
[27] Magleby, "Voting," p. 49.

single election." From this specific perspective, he asked whether the initiative and referendum are in fact "less democratic" than representative institutions.[28]

Whatever the level of participation and the character of the electorate, we know from the California evidence that referendum voters frequently make up their minds at the last minute. Although they are occasionally uncertain as to the meaning of a measure, they generally vote in accordance with their underlying beliefs and attitudes. Partisan and regional influences are sometimes, but not consistently, evident. With respect to initiative measures, electors tend to vote no two-thirds of the time—regardless of the liberal or conservative nature of the measure—while even with referendums that have passed the legislature, only 60 percent are approved.

The Future of Referendums

Clearly, the referendum is an imperfect instrument of democratic government and one easy to criticize. Yet, the fact remains that, not only is there no move to restrict the referendum in those states where it is widely employed, but it is proposed to extend its use to new states and localities. Indeed, a recent Gallup poll indicated that 57 percent of the American public favored adoption of a *national* statutory initiative.[29] A proposal to amend the United States Constitution to this effect has been placed before Congress but has little chance of success. That it has been taken seriously at all, however, is indicative of the strength of that powerful strain in American political thought that stresses the virtues of direct democracy.

This belief arises, of course, out of the imperfections of representative institutions in this country. The initiative and referendum must be tested not against a theoretical model of democratic institutions but the real world of declining electoral participation, weakened political parties, partisan legislative districting, and television-dominated election campaigns funded by massive contributions from special interests that also dominate legislative lobbying, all set in the context of an economic, social, and political environment of frightening complexity.

American state and local governments are at the center of this activity. Their combined budgets—heavily supported by federal grants and revenue sharing—have skyrocketed in recent years, far outdistancing direct domestic federal expenditures. State and local government employment is nearly four times that of the national government. Taxes at

---

[28] Quoted in Lee, "California," p. 109.
[29] Ranney, "United States," p. 75.

the state and local levels have increased at a more rapid rate than nationally. The pressures of rapid growth and now the added pressures of inflation, energy shortfalls, and tax revolts confront mayors and governors as never before.

It is within this environment of imperfect institutions and extraordinary public problems that the referendum exists. Whether it will strengthen or weaken those institutions or aid or hinder solutions to those problems is uncertain. That it will remain a prominent part of the American political scene is assured.

Discussion

THOMAS CRONIN, *chairman:* Our challenge at this session reminds me of the American who visited India on a three-day trip. When he returned home, he was asked by friends and relatives to write a book about his trip. He protested that he had been in India only three days, that India is a large country with a complex culture, and so on. They persisted, however; he finally relented and wrote a short book on his trip. He tried to find a title that would show his modest and limited knowledge of India. He finally chose the title, "India: Yesterday, Today, and Tomorrow."

We are in a similar situation at this session. The United States is also a large, complex nation, and the American experience is equally complex. It should be understood at the outset that referendums in America are conducted according to the laws of the individual states; we doubtless will frequently suggest that this or that depends upon which state you are discussing.

We are fortunate to have as the author of our paper on the American experience and as our first speaker in this session Professor Eugene Lee. He is one of the foremost experts on politics in California, which is one of the largest, and, in recent times, perhaps the most notorious user of referendums.

EUGENE LEE: The referendum device is clearly an imperfect instrument of democracy. But interestingly, the trend is to expand, not to restrict, its use. In the United States, those states that have never previously considered the initiative are considering it, and it is being discussed by Congress for possible use at the national level. Comparable developments are taking place in many other democratic countries.

The belief in the referendum, of course, arises from the imperfections of representative institutions. It must be evaluated not against some theoretical model of democracy, but in the real world of declining electoral participation, weakened political parties, television-dominated election campaigns funded by massive contributions, legislatures dominated by pressure groups—all set in the context of an economic, social,

60

and political environment of frightening complexity. It is within this environment of imperfect institutions and extraordinary public traumas that the referendum exists. Whether it will strengthen or weaken those institutions or aid or hinder a solution of those problems is uncertain; it will certainly remain a prominent part of at least the American political scene.

THOMAS CRONIN: There are four or five topics that we are likely to touch. How well informed are voters when they are voting on these referendums in America? What does the availability of the referendum procedure do to the representative process? What are the consequences for the will of legislature; what are the costs in terms of representative processes? Professor Lee raises the question of money and manipulation in television-dominated campaigns. To what extent are there fairness and justice in a campaign? What happens regarding the abuse of civil liberties and minority rights?

TAM DALYELL: Professor Lee talked about the threat of an initiative, and I want to ask whether the existence of a threatening initiative makes legislatures behave differently from how they might behave if that threat did not exist?

EUGENE LEE: That is clearly the case. We have limited data, with only impressions from specific races and specific campaigns. There is no question from my own observations, however, that the threat of the initiative does prompt legislatures and governors to do things differently than they would otherwise do. In some instances they avoid issues, but in others they take action to forestall an initiative.

ROBIN DAY: Are most of these referendums binding or consultative? Are they all part of the law-making process?

EUGENE LEE: They are very much so.

MICHAEL RYLE: If they are binding referendums in most cases, they are part of the law-making process?

EUGENE LEE: That is correct.

MICHAEL RYLE: Suppose a fairly complicated financial or constitutional amendment is put to the poll; is there no process of amendment? If so, is this not the only law-making process where a measure cannot be amended as it is considered?

61

EUGENE LEE: No, it cannot be amended while the voters are considering it. That is a major criticism of the process.

MICHAEL RYLE: A lot depends, therefore, on what is asked on the ballot. In a legislative initiative like the legalization of marijuana, if the question is simply—"Are you in favor of the legalization of marijuana?" —does that become law, or must an actual draft piece of legislation be presented for voter study?

EUGENE LEE: The answer is both. The ballot itself typically would have a capsule statement, probably drafted by the state attorney general. The state law would also probably require the full language of the amendment to be made available to the voter. In California, this is in the form of a ballot pamphlet mailed to every voter in the state, which contains arguments, pro and con, and the full legal language; it might run to several pages.

THOMAS CRONIN: It should be pointed out that after a measure has been initiated and passed by the voters, the state supreme court can review it and find it unconstitutional. That occasionally has been done, which complicates matters even further.

EUGENE LEE: My students ask how an amendment to a state constitution can be declared unconstitutional, as has been the case on a number of occasions. The answer is that they are declared unconstitutional under the United States Constitution, which is superior to all state constitutions.

MARTIN KARMEL: As a representative of a pressure group myself, I have dealt with a complex piece of legislation comparable to the usury law in California—the Consumer Credit Act enacted five years ago. A powerful amendment was offered, and the bill was redrafted several times. There is not one single issue in all the many issues involved in that act that could be put, with any ease, to the electorate in a referendum. Even after it had been through Parliament, the complexity of that act is such that it still has not been brought into effect. Yet, in California, a measure of equal complexity could be put to the voters for a simple yes or no vote.

EUGENE LEE: This must be placed in the context of state constitutions in the United States. They typically run to tens of thousands of words and, unlike the United States Constitution, they are full of statutory or technical details on a variety of issues. I was reading to my class two weeks ago the rights of Californians to fish in the public waters of California. The section in the constitution goes on for a full paragraph describing how private owners' property rights cannot infringe the right of the citizen of California to fish in a public stream.

HENRY DRUCKER: I gather that it is possible in California for there to be an initiative referendum and a legislative referendum on the same subject, and therefore it is possible for them both to pass, even though they are contradictory. What happens in such a case?

EUGENE LEE: Whichever of the propositions gets the higher vote takes precedence over the other.

HENRY DRUCKER: On another matter, is there any way of comparing the electorate's knowledge of referendum measures with knowledge of candidates for office?

EUGENE LEE: That is an excellent question, and I think I should ask my colleagues to share in the response. Do we know anything empirically about voter knowledge of candidates and their policy positions compared with voter knowledge of referendum measures?

RAYMOND WOLFINGER: It is hard to imagine how to formulate valid points of comparison, particularly because there are enormous variations in the information that citizens have from one issue or candidate to the next. The Michigan study of the 1978 congressional election found that less than one-fifth of all American adults even claimed to know how their congressman had voted on any issue. A sizable minority of voters in 1972 thought that George McGovern was not a dove but a hawk on Vietnam. Voters are not well informed about the candidates' issue positions.

EUGENE LEE: It seems that one poll showed that more people are acquainted with the referendum measures than are acquainted with the issue stands of candidates on the ballot.

RAYMOND WOLFINGER: The officials who administer California elections, such as the county clerks, say quite proudly, "We have the best informed voters in the world." The reason, they say, is the voter handbook mailed to everybody in California in advance of the election. It has fifty or sixty pages of absolutely impenetrable prose; everybody gets it, so everybody has the opportunity to be informed about the issues. However, I do not read the handbooks and I do not know anybody who does read them except to see who is for and who is against the proposition, so that a vote can be adjusted accordingly. It is fair to say that on a real blockbuster proposition such as the one in 1964 that repealed the laws against discrimination in housing, everybody probably knew that the proposition would end all fair housing laws. Beyond that, there was not much information about the problem or the implications of the proposition.

RICHARD SCAMMON: Recently in Dade County, Florida, a referendum was held on tax cutting; someone made a mistake so that the legislation provided for a 90 percent cut instead of a 9 percent cut, and it was impossible to change the language before the measure went to a vote. In the election, 35 or 40 percent of the people voted for the 90 percent cut. Whether they really approved of it is another question. On the other hand, with all due respect to the legislators in both our countries, this kind of error is not unknown particularly in the United States; it might have happened once or twice in the House of Commons as well.

Second, Proposition 13 was not really an attack on taxes as such. It was an attack on two things. It was an attack on the property tax as such and an attack on a group of men and women referred to collectively as "those clowns in Sacramento," who had sat on a $5-billion surplus in the state of California and, because of their disagreements about how the money should be used, had never done a thing with it. The voters said, "All right, if you cannot make a decision, we'll make it for you"; in effect, this is what they did. They applied the surplus to the reduction of property taxes.

The third point relates to the nature of the referendum at the state level. This is variable. About six years ago, in the state of Maryland, there was an amendment to the state constitution to provide public funding for private schools. There are a few Lutheran and one or two Jewish schools, but many private schools are Catholic. This issue was hotly contested in television advertisements and newspaper advertisements; most people knew about it. The voting turnout on this particular constitutional amendment was high. People knew clearly what they were doing. But I must confess that, in my own case, if I am given twenty propositions to vote upon as an elector in the state of Maryland, my only recourse is to telephone people who know more about it than I do and find out exactly how I am supposed to vote. When there is an issue, such as the public funding of private schools, in which people are concerned and when there is an issue that affects them or is presumed by them to affect them, turnout is good, by American standards at least.

RAYMOND WOLFINGER: Proposition 13 included a number of secondary provisions that illustrate some interesting things about referendums. One such provision said that the assessed value of property was to be cut to what it was in 1975–1976, except that any piece of property sold after that date would be assessed at the sale price. In a building with twenty condominiums, each assessed in 1975–1976 for $50,000, if one were sold in 1979 for $125,000, then nineteen people would be paying taxes on $50,000 and the twentieth person would be paying taxes on $125,-000. That is an example of the kind of kicker often inserted in the language of propositions in California. The people knew what they were voting on, but few knew that the package they were voting on included things like this $125,000 versus $50,000 situation.

PETER SHORE: We are obviously discussing two very different animals, the initiative referendum and the constitutional referendum. They have different implications for political practice or political theory, and indeed for their impact on representative government. Is the constitutional referendum something that is written into the constitutions of the fifty states? Is it the only way in which an amendment to the constitution can be made or are there processes other than the direct reference to the people? Are we really talking about a referendum process that alters the written constitution or are we simply talking about a referendum process that applies to any legislative act of the same government?

JACK PELTASON: All states except Delaware require that an amendment to the constitution be ratified by the voters. Prior to ratification, an amendment must be proposed. Amendments can be proposed in three ways: (1) in some states, especially in the West, by an initiative petition; (2) the most common method, by the legislature; or (3) by a constitutional convention especially called to propose constitutional change.

PETER SHORE: That is not entirely my point. In the forty-nine states that do practice constitutional referendums, is there, as a preliminary to the referendum process, a special legislative procedure, for example, an extraordinary majority?

JACK PELTASON: Proposals of constitutional amendments require action by an extraordinary majority—two-thirds or three-quarters, in each chamber. A few states permit proposal of amendments by a simple majority vote in the legislature, but it takes action in two successive sessions of the legislature.

PETER SHORE: Concerning the distinction between what is written into the constitution of the state and is therefore subject to a constitutional process, a special class of referendum, and the kind of issues that have been cited as referendum examples, property taxes and so on—I understand that those are embodied in the constitution. That must mean that there is no real distinction between legislation and the constitution itself.

THOMAS FOLEY: Some state constitutions, such as California's, do become statutory pipelines, but there is nevertheless a great difference between whether a measure is in the constitution or in the statute book. If it is in the constitution, the legislature cannot amend it; if it is in the statute books, they can. Frankly, the California constitution is a mess, but the notion of a constitution as an organic body of general governmental relationships is not common among the states. Most states have statutory-type constitutions addressing all kinds of specific issues and modeling themselves after the California constitution.

There is some evidence that the voters can be quite remarkably well informed about initiatives and referenda. There are voter's handbooks that spell out the issues in great detail, but there are often enormous differences between the technical information in the handbook and the political arguments in public advertising. The most ingenious public advertising in my state was the huge billboard and radio campaign stressing the simple proposition, "Initiative 26 is a bad initiative!" That was the sum total of all the arguments about it. The initiative failed.

TAM DALYELL: There is a question as to who writes the handbook. Ray Wolfinger referred to fifty or sixty pages of impenetrable prose. Whose prose is it?

THOMAS CRONIN: It depends on the state. In about four states, the secretary of state's office prepares it. In a few other states, different sides are allowed to state their views, as happened in Britain with the Common Market referendum.

TAM DALYELL: Why was there no voter's guide on devolution? There was absolutely no agreement as to what should go into the guide. Let us take the example of nuclear power. Who exactly frames the questions and who gives the voter's guide the information? It is an important question because some might like to frame a question along the lines, "Are you in favor of nuclear power in the knowledge that if you are not in favor of it your grandchildren will not have any electricity?" or some such loaded question. Others may want to put equally loaded questions on the other side. Who, in fact, *is* responsible for producing the voter's guide?

AUSTIN RANNEY: As in other matters, there is considerable variation from state to state as to how this is done. In some states, the petitioners can phrase the proposition as they wish. In some, the contending sides can write the materials in the handbook. (Many of the Americans here have enjoyed observing the faces of our British colleagues. There is nothing like a discussion of California to bring out these expressions, which move from interest to incredulity to consternation and finally to sheer horror. I do not say that any of those reactions are unjustified.)

However, there is one other variant of the referendum that some people who share Thomas Foley's skepticism about the initiative process find more acceptable. It is called the indirect initiative. As it works in the seven states that have it, any citizen group can petition for a certain piece of legislation. The measure is submitted to the legislature and the legislature has a certain period of time to act on it. It may incorporate the measure in a piece of legislation and thereby make a referendum unnecessary. The legislature may suggest a revised version to the petitioners, who may accept or reject it. If they accept it, it becomes law with no referendum. If they reject it and the legislature does nothing further about the original petition, after a reasonable period of time— perhaps six or nine months—the original measure goes on the ballot, usually with a notation that the legislature has failed to act on it; the voters make the final decision. Under the indirect initiative, there is an opportunity for the legislature to act, but the voters have the final word. In the states with the indirect initiative, the numbers of propositions that have been on the ballot are substantially smaller than in those states with the direct initiative, where the legislature has no power to keep a petition measure off the ballot. It might be useful to keep in mind the possibility of that form of the referendum.

KENNETH BAKER: Are there any states with recent referendums that resulted in undue pressure being placed upon minority groups or the rights of minority groups being eroded in any way? This is a danger that people do see in referendums, certainly on this side of the Atlantic.

THOMAS FOLEY: There are several examples of propositions dealing with minority rights. Many of them have been initiated by groups favoring or opposing discrimination against homosexuals. California recently had an antihomosexual initiative that was designed to allow the state to prevent the employment of homosexuals in schools. It was a little too strong, even for California; it was opposed by such a surprising person as Ronald Reagan.

KENNETH BAKER: If it had been passed, then it would not have been possible for the state of California to employ homosexuals? Would that have been the effect?

JACK PELTASON: In the schools, that is true. In the United States, however, an active judiciary hovers in the background. It stands ready to protect us against the excesses of direct democracy. Federal and state judges have had no difficulty in finding ways to set aside initiatives that alter state constitutions in such a way as to threaten the rights of minorities or cause complications in the operation of the government.

ROBIN DAY: What about Dick Scammon's 90 percent tax cut? Did no court intervene there to say it was nonsense?

RICHARD SCAMMON: What would have happened if it had passed? Would Jack Peltason's judicial guardian angels have come to the rescue?

JACK PELTASON: After the California constitution was amended by an initiative in 1964 to nullify open-housing laws, the Supreme Court of the United States said, "We are sorry, but the people of California cannot do that because it violates the Constitution of the United States."

JAMES JONES: In Thomas Foley's state of Washington there was a recent initiative for an antipornography law, an initiative that passed and then was struck down by the courts as violating the First Amendment's guarantee of freedom of speech. By and large, given the thousand or so initiatives we have had in America, less than a handful have actually abused the rights of identifiable minorities; the record is much better than the critics and skeptics back in the 1912 Progressive era thought would be the case. Indeed, most of the political scientists who study initiatives state by state generally are impressed by the ability of the voters to judge public interests as well as popular interests.

THOMAS FOLEY: On the other hand, most initiatives are designed to protect the special and accepted rights of minorities. Most initiatives, for example, are designed to prohibit discrimination in housing because of race, or discrimination in employment because of race. They did not win prior to the time when Congress enacted the federal Civil Rights Act; they failed all over the United States in the most liberal constituencies. Something like a hundred of these initiatives failed; Congress then imposed a national antidiscrimination standard.

JAMES JONES: As a footnote to that, such movements as workmen's compensation laws and direct election of senators have begun through the initiative process.

KENNETH BAKER: Proposition 4, which will be put to the California voters in a few days, ties increases in public expenditure to increases in population and in the cost of living. That is quite clear, but it may well be that the administrators and politicians in the state of California cannot actually live up to that, for all sorts of reasons. They may simply get it wrong; they may not be able to do it in a year or two years. If they cannot, what are the sanctions against them?

EUGENE LEE: In contrast to Proposition 13, Proposition 4 is a carefully drafted proposition but it still holds many ambiguities. The sponsors can go to court. In other words, if a legislature or a city council tries to contravene this amendment, the state controller can be enjoined from authorizing the excessive state expenditure.

ENOCH POWELL: I am interested in the conundrum of how one amends, if at all, the results of a referendum. It is one of the fundamental problems of the whole procedure by referendum, which is by no means limited to questions of the type found in California. It applies as much to yes or no questions of a moral character.

This leads me to introduce a word that has not yet been mentioned, the word "debate." The essential difference is between information that is voluminously available, if they want it, to the electorate and the *meaning* of information as conveyed by events. There should be great emphasis on the significance of debate as a means of assistance. This has an immediate implication for referendums because debates can only take place in some sort of closed or organized environment— debates where people can have their minds changed. This, of course, is the nature of parliamentary procedure, running from amendments, the thousand amendments to a bill, to the great debate on the floor on the general question, where all kinds and shades of implications can be exposed and taken up by others. If a decision is to be taken on a basis of information or education secured by debate, then it cannot be taken by the electorate—and the sovereignty of the people can only be exercised indirectly through a debating chamber. There is an aspect of government as understood in this country that compounds the importance of debate; that is the concept of counsel—and counsel is advice that emerges from debate. The characteristic of English judgment and of English sovereignty, philosophical or otherwise, is that it takes the form of counseling, that there tends to be some form of debate of which the most secret is the cabinet and the most public is the House of Commons, as reported through the media.

DAVID LEA: We have managed to proceed this morning without even mentioning political parties, and that in a purely British context would be inconceivable. Would it be fair to say that in the United States the fact that party platforms are unimportant and the fact that these referendums exist go together? Does it follow that the more referendums are used, the more the credibility of parties is undermined, because people are addicted to fourteen different alliances on fourteen different propositions?

THOMAS FOLEY: Nobody in the United States Congress ever talks about the Democratic or Republican party. I have never heard a member of the Congress ever refer to a colleague and urge a vote for him because he was in the same party. Most Democrats or Republicans could not recall three items on the platform of their party. It is remarkable for us to hear members of the House of Commons asking a minister if this or that pledge in the manifesto will be undertaken. It never happens in the House of Representatives.

DAVID LEA: It is more than a question of what is in the party platform. It is the lack of cohesiveness of the parties more generally.

THOMAS FOLEY: We have 435 parties in the House.

DAVID LEA: The corollary of that is, because one does not have a strong party system, there is never any possibility of putting together a coalition that can change anything fundamental in the economic sense in the United States.

THOMAS FOLEY: That is not true. The absence of party discipline and productivity in bringing about a program is one of the underlying attractions of the initiative and the referendum. How is anything done in the complex pluralism of such a system? Mrs. Thatcher has the capacity with a forty-four seat majority to do something rather dramatic that could not be done in the United States by any president, even with a large party majority in Congress. The interesting aspect of this is that the national initiative is strongly supported by both the most conservative and the most progressive elements of our country's political spectrum. Ralph Nader thinks it is an enormously good idea to break the power of the corporations over Congress and get the people's will imposed on the issues like consumer protection and protection of the environment. Fiscal conservatives, however, are delighted with the prospect of a Proposition 13 at the national level to whip the House Ways and Means Committee into what Mr. Jones and others think they should do and will not do. That is really the foundation of the impulse in America for a national initiative.

We might have more conservatism in taxes than even responsible fiscal conservatives would like to see. Repealing the federal income tax would be one of Mr. Jones's national initiatives. On the other hand, one could completely repeal statutory, not constitutional but statutory, protection of individual liberties and rights; one could repeal the federal civil rights act. The most passionate social questions and the most deeply felt anti-tax feelings are the issues that are likely to be the subject of national initiatives. The highest vote ever recorded on an initiative in Washington state was one that dealt with the lofty question of whether the legislative pay raises of the previous legislative session should be repealed. A furniture dealer started a petition to repeal the modest pay raises the legislature had voted for itself and was sneered at by the administration, which said he could not possibly get 100,000 signatures in thirty days. He got 755,000 signatures, which is half of the total registered electorate in the state. Needless to say, the pay raises were repealed, by a five to one vote.

VERNON BOGDANOR: We need a second essay on how well the legislature in California or other American states works. If one considers the defects of the referendum or initiative and takes an idealized view of how legislatures work, we are naturally going to be critical of the referendum as an instrument of government. If we were to look at the California legislature, we might find that it does not quite conform to the standards laid down by the theorists of representative government; even the British House of Commons may not work as well as it should. There are cases where the government pushes through legislation that MPs hardly understand. There was an education bill, for example, that happily lapsed at the end of the last Parliament in 1979. It dealt with quite an important issue: whether local authorities should be given the power to close schools. One particular clause concerned the reform of the governing bodies of schools: The cost was £5 million. One backbench opposition MP said in standing committee, "I don't think it would cost £5 million; it could cost twice or three times as much. What does it matter? The taxpayer will pay in the end." Then, at a later stage in the bill, one MP revealed by his remarks that he had not understood its basic purpose although it was halfway through standing committee proceedings. That is not a rare event at all; the ignorance is not only on the part of the electorate.

As regards parties, some of us believe that nothing would do more good for British government than to *reduce* their power and authority in the United Kingdom.

DAVID MARQUAND: The British reaction has been a bit too full of horror and consternation. First, on the question that David Lea raised about the weakness in the American party system and the fact that one could not get fundamental changes, when was the last time that really fundamental changes happened in this country? The last time was in the postwar Attlee government. It was possible then because it was based upon a national consensus, which had been built up over a generation of argument and debate, not just in Parliament but all over the country. There was an American president, Franklin Roosevelt, who managed some quite fundamental changes in your system, different though it may be. That was the last time that really fundamental changes were put through in the United States. Structure is not the crucial thing. What is crucial is whether there is a deep consensus in favor of change. If there is, change occurs; if there is not, it does not, irrespective of the political arrangements.

The second point, to be put to the Americans, perhaps impertinently, is a reflection prompted by a most fascinating observation by Enoch Powell. Is it perhaps the case that the American equivalent institution for providing what Enoch Powell called counsel is in fact the Supreme Court? Is the Court really the American equivalent of Parliament in that sense? The biggest difficulty that the British people have in understanding the way the American system works is that the concept that one kind of law can be superior to ordinary acts of the legislature is alien to us. Americans hold that the constitution is a deep and fundamental thing to be interpreted by people who are impartial—we know, of course, that they are not; the Supreme Court follows the election returns—but in principle the Court is supposed to be; that is something which we find difficult to grasp.

I was fascinated by what Dr. Peltason said about the guardians stepping in and correcting the mistakes of the people. In relation to state referendums, I could understand perfectly well how a court would strike down a decision that had been carried by a referendum of the people of a state, if it conflicted with the Constitution of the United States. Dr. Peltason implied that there were other bases, as well, on which the courts could strike down decisions that had been taken in the referendums. What are those other bases?

JACK PELTASON: The constitutional requirements in a state constitution that govern the initiative process can be interpreted to declare a vote ineffective, for example, finding that the petitions to get on the ballot were illegally filed, or that the questions were presented to the voters in an improper manner, or that one initiative approved in a referendum is in conflict with another approved on the same day.

RICHARD SCAMMON: Whatever the referendum has done in the last thirty-five years, it is far less than what the courts have done. The judicial imperium in America has increased its power markedly over people power. In Great Britain, this particular aspect of America's developing postwar government has had almost no attention. The fact, for example, that the schools of the city of Boston were operated by the federal district court, not by the local school authorities, is an example of the growing judicial imperium, which has been much more important than the growth of people power through referendums.

ROBIN DAY: Does that make America more a government of laws or the other way around?

4

The World Experience

David Butler

Referendums are both more widespread and less than most people imagine.[1] Almost every Western democratic country has used them at least once—Holland, Israel, and the United States are the sole exceptions—but only four have had as many as 10 nationwide referendums—France (20), Denmark (14), Australia (39), and, in a quite different league, Switzerland (305).

Most referendums are not designed to decide anything but to legitimize *faits accomplis*. Nondemocratic states seeking to demonstrate their popular support call referendums to endorse the regime or its decisions and usually manage to secure over 99 percent yes; the military regime in Ghana that only got 55 percent (and that by the clumsiest fraud) was, not surprisingly, soon toppled for its administrative incompetence. Even in democratic states, with votes freely cast and honestly counted, overwhelming majorities are the norm rather than the exception. Government-sponsored measures have been rarely defeated, except in Switzerland and Australia. France (new constitution, 1946, and regional devolution, 1969), Ireland (abolition of proportional representation, 1968), Norway (Common Market, 1972), Sweden (driving on right, 1955), and Denmark (lower voting age, 1969) provide almost the only examples.[2]

The subject matter of referendums provides the explanation. They have been called, in the main, to endorse some well-matured constitutional or territorial change and they would not have been put before the people unless there was good reason to suppose they would be accepted. The issues subject to referendum have been limited in range.

---

[1] This short essay draws heavily on the material prepared by David Butler and Austin Ranney, eds., *Referendums: A Comparative Study of Practice and Theory* (Washington, D.C.: American Enterprise Institute, 1978). Above all, it depends on the appendix, which attempts to list all nationwide referendums held up to the middle of 1978.

[2] The miscalculations behind the defeats in France in 1969 and Norway in 1972 ended the rule of the men who proposed the referendums. In Denmark, in 1969, the proposal that was defeated was later carried when put forward more tactfully in a referendum in 1971. The Swedish defeat in 1955 was met by the government later acting unilaterally in defiance of the referendum decision.

The great bulk have been constitutional, seeking approval for a complete constitution or an amendment, for the ending or restoration of a monarchy, or for a change in voting age or electoral system: 55 percent of those in European democracies (excluding Switzerland) fall into this category. A further 22 percent deal with questions of sovereignty—the extension of borders, or participation in an international community. A further 12 percent deal with clearly moral issues, which usually fall outside party politics—prohibition and divorce. Only in Denmark and Sweden have there been referendums dealing with pragmatic questions of government like pension plans and land laws.

Australia and Switzerland

That is, however, to exclude Australia and Switzerland. In Australia, a federal constitution presents jurisdictional problems and her referendums have ranged from the regulation of airlines to the outlawing of the Communist party. Almost all the referendums have involved an extension of federal power and 78 percent of the propositions have been defeated, largely through the whipping up of provincial loyalties. Switzerland is a quite unique case, where almost any issue can be made the subject of a referendum by 50,000 signatures (since 1977, 100,000); just under half of the 297 issues put to referendum up to 1978 received a yes vote. The experience of Switzerland together with that of California and some other American states, mainly in the West, should be studied by anyone who wants to extend popular sovereignty to the everyday issues of government.

The authority of a referendum verdict might be thought to depend substantially on the electoral turnout. Without compulsory voting as in Australia, or semicompulsory as in Italy, people might be expected to go to the polls only when a great issue is at stake. However, although the problem is often masked because the referendum is arranged to coincide with a general election, the record of referendum turnouts is remakably high; few in the major democracies have dropped below 60 percent. In Switzerland, however, where the voters have referendums every three months, the turnout has only passed 50 percent on five occasions of thirty-one between 1968 and 1978; that does not seem to make the Swiss challenge the authority of referendum decisions.

Referendums may be advisory, expressing an opinion for the guidance of the legislature or government, or mandatory, as an essential part of constitutional change. The decision may be by simple majority of those voting—or there may be some more stringent requirement, for example, two-thirds of those voting (Gambia), 50 percent of the qualified electorate (Weimar Germany), 45 percent of the qualified electorate (Denmark until 1953), 40 percent (the Scottish and Welsh referendums of 1979), or 50 percent of those voting in a majority of component states or cantons (Australia and Switzerland). In the vast majority of cases, a simple majority has provided the verdict, although as King Leopold III of Belgium found in 1950, a 57 percent vote is not enough to give acceptance and legitimacy to a constitutional head of state.

Calling the Referendum

In the vast majority of cases, the decision to hold a referendum lies in the hands of the government. In Weimar Germany, in postwar Italy, in many American states, and in the outstanding example, Switzerland, a referendum can be called by enough signatures on a petition.

There does not seem to be anything addictive about referendums. No country, except Switzerland, has let them become habit-forming or turned increasingly to them for legitimation or for problem solving. Equally, the occasional use of referendums does not seem to have subverted parliamentary sovereignty in any cumulative way in the major countries preserving the Westminster model, all of which (except India) have not tried it. World democratic experience suggests various functions:

• *Constitutional.* A referendum may be a convenient check on constitutional change; in some countries the need for a referendum has been, for good or ill, a restraint on politicians who would like to alter the rules of the game.

• *Legitimation.* Basic changes in territorial boundaries, or sovereignty, or structure of government, will be respected more readily when it has been incontrovertibly demonstrated that they command the support of a majority of the voting population.

• *Moral problem solving.* Governments may want to avoid responsibility for some kinds of decisions. Moral questions involving divorce or prohibition may cut across party lines. A referendum can offer a convenient way of dodging the issue by passing it to the public at large.

• *Political problem solving.* Governments divided on central questions of policy can also save themselves from their own divisions by passing on the problem. The EEC referendum of 1975 in Britain provides an outstanding example of a major issue that split the party in power being solved by a popular vote. It is, however, notable that there is no example in any democracy of a specific crisis of authority—like a major industrial dispute—being dealt with by reference to a referendum.

Referendums have largely been a pragmatic device of political management. On the whole, they have been conservative in effect.

Among democratic nations, it is hard to find a single example of a referendum being an instrument of radical change (though California and others could cite examples at a lower level). In a world that is increasingly difficult to govern, referendums have proved a convenient reinforcement of central authority. Except in Switzerland, the calling of referendums has almost always been in government hands. If their initiation moved from governments to people and pressure groups, the experience of California, even more than of Switzerland, suggests that far-reaching changes might result.

Discussion

JÜRG STEINER, *chairman:* The topic for this session concerns "lessons to be drawn from world experience." We have been considering the experience in Great Britain, the American states, and Switzerland. Our purpose now is to enlarge this empirical base and consider the experience of many other countries.

In the Federal Republic of Germany, there is a severe conflict over the nuclear energy issue. In October 1979, there was an informal conference, not much publicized, between Chancellor Schmidt and the prime ministers of the *Länder* in order to reach a compromise. What is interesting is that many of these prime ministers belonged to the opposition parties. Obviously, faced with this difficult issue, the leading politicians were saying that they could no longer play the game of government versus opposition. They had to turn to the "consociational" model, the model of Switzerland, of Holland, and of Belgium.

The question in such a case is, How can there be an opposition? One possibility is that the opposition will come not from other parties but from the people. This is what has happened in Switzerland. We have, on the one hand, all major parties together in a grand coalition, and the people functioning as the opposition through referendums. If we take the West German example, it is clear that there is much doubt about how there can be an opposition when all the major parties cooperate on an issue. Perhaps we can learn from David Butler how some of the continental European countries use the referendum as a substitute for the often lacking party opposition.

DAVID BUTLER: What I want to say is remarkably non-value-ridden, nonideological, nongeneralizable. You have before you the book *Referendums: A Study in Practice and Theory*, which Austin Ranney and I compiled. What I am proudest of in this book is the appendix, the lists of the propositions on which the countries of the world have held referendums and their outcomes.

My father always told his family never to argue about verifiable questions of fact. We had reference books in each room in the house, because one should not waste time squabbling about whether something was true or false, when one could discover it simply by reaching out for a book. Certainly, I have never had that brought home to me more than when, not knowing a great deal about the world's experience of referendums, I tried to compile a list of every nationwide referendum that had ever taken place across the globe. The results are in the book's appendix, which surely is imperfect. I shall be extremely grateful if somebody calls my attention to a missing referendum, perhaps in Nepal or Burundi. Austin Ranney and I hope some day to produce a second, updated, edition and we would be grateful for assistance. Nonetheless, taking our appendix together with the separate lists for Switzerland and Australia, we have included at least 95 percent of the nationwide referendums that have ever taken place. In the literature about referendums and indeed in some of the speeches made at this conference, one finds a sort of abstract animal, a referendum, with properties that are possessed by incredibly few of the referendums that have actually occurred. The actual world of referendums is a different world.

Looking at appendix A, one should think of what is implied by the list of subjects and by the percentage votes. One could focus on the list of democratic referendums in Europe which, omitting the Antipodes, does cover a large proportion of the nationwide referendums in democratic states.

There are myths about referendums. When the British EEC referendum was pending, Michael Steed gave a rather brilliant little talk at the London School of Economics, in which he pointed out how much it was a myth to think that referendums were an addictive thing in the sense that a country tries one and then another, and then continues, until it cannot help having referendums all the time. There has been more than a suggestion of this in some of the comments here. Some have said, or implied, that, if a country moves to having any referendums, it will abolish the whole doctrine of parliamentary sovereignty, and all the normal legislative decisions will be referred to the people. As Michael Steed pointed out, if one took the countries which have had referendums and then measured the length of time between the first referendum and the second, and then the second and the third, and the third and the fourth, one would find that the intervals did not get shorter and shorter but rather longer and longer. Yet, there is a great deal of the literature about referendums that fosters this myth that, once one starts on it, one never knows where it will end.

Perhaps this myth stems from those people who have a cyclical and exponential view of life. One thing that struck me most as an undergraduate was coming across a reference of George Orwell to James Burnham. He said that Burnham suffered from that commonest of intellectual defects—he assumed that whatever is happening now is going to go on happening, only more so. In other words, one spots a trend and expands it exponentially. A few years ago my wife and I were discussing with our children why they treated us so much less respectfully than we treated our parents. They said, quite reasonably, that they did not think it was unfair, because they were sure that their children would treat them even less respectfully than they did us. Then my seven-year-old son looked up at me and said, "When I'm an ancestor, children will eat their parents." My wife and I looked at each other in horror. We suddenly realized we had brought up an Enoch Powell. Here was somebody who actually did Enoch's same trick of taking a trend, projecting it exponentially, and wrapping it up in an epigram!

There is no evidence whatsoever that referendums are addictive. There is no evidence in fact that they are or have been subversive of the ordinary operations of government or governmental responsibility. If one takes all the larger countries with governments operated more or less on the Westminster model, they all, at some time or other, have had referendums. Australia is the only country where there have been many referendums, and that is because of constitutional requirements. The great bulk of issues in Australia are not referred to referendum. Only two or three nonconstitutional referendums have been held, such as the anti-Communist referendum of Robert Menzies that was defeated in 1951. There have been a few issues like that, but, by and large, the Australians have only used the referendum when they really were trying to make a constitutional adjustment.

After Australia, Denmark has had fourteen referendums; it is the only country that gets into double figures with referendums, apart from France, which has only had ten in this century. Otherwise, no country has gone into double figures. There is no reason to suppose that, if it is used in this way, the referendum is a problem. There is, of course, one great exception, Switzerland, which seems to be a genus entirely by itself. It is true that California is larger than Switzerland and that California is in the Swiss mold, as are some other American states. But California is not a nation-state; California is only a part of the federal system. If one takes the nation-states of the world, Switzerland is in a class completely by itself: About half of the nationwide referendums that have ever been held in the world have been held in Switzerland. It is also virtually the only country that has tried the national initiative. There were a couple of initiatives in Weimar Germany; there have been three referendums that had initiative origins in postwar Italy. That is about the lot.

Is the absence of referendums of the California or Swiss type in the rest of the democratic polities of the world explainable by some perversity of theirs, or is it something that comes from an ordinary shrewdness and logic? Because all these countries have tried the referendum, and they have found it to be a good problem solver, they have used it to settle particular difficulties. Belgium is one of the countries that have had just one referendum. They had the problem of Leopold III, the constitutional sovereign, returning after World War II; he— and, more than that, his wife's family—seemed to have collaborated with the Germans and he was not acceptable as a head of state. A referendum produced this paradoxical result: The vote was 57 percent to 43 percent for his return. A general strike followed, led by the Belgian socialists, who argued that a constitutional monarch needs more than a 57 percent majority. Leopold III, who cared about the monarchy, gave up the crown in favor of his son. There has been a perfectly ordinary constitutional monarchy in Belgium since that particular referendum.

One other country that has had only one referendum is Finland, with a vote on prohibition. It is worth noting, when looking at the subject matter of referendums and removing the constitutional issues, that prohibition has been the largest single subject for referendums. It is not happening now, but it was throughout the 1920s and 1930s. The list of Canadian referendums shows that twenty of the twenty-five Canadian referendums at the state level and one of the two at the national level have been on prohibition. That is the kind of moral issue that seems quite sensible to take out of the ordinary routine party political battle, even if one does believe in parties.

Yet, it should be stressed that one of the major reasons why referendums have not been tried in the great bulk of democracies that more or less follow the Westminster model is that referendums are a threat to party authority. Referendums are subversive of party authority; one is encouraging people to think for themselves and not to leave it entirely up to the party to tell them how to think. One encourages them to make an independent judgment; if they have an independent judgment on one thing, they may start wanting to make independent judgments on other things.

PETER SHORE: The question is whether the people or the party leaders are more likely to make *responsible* judgments.

DAVID BUTLER: It is useful to have a member of the Labour shadow cabinet confirming my general view of the attitudes of party politicians.

MICHAEL STEED: I want to take up one or two odd points from David Butler's remarks. I am really fighting a rearguard action on behalf of the continent of Europe, apart from Switzerland, because the spirits of

Switzerland, California, Oregon, and Delaware have dominated our considerations in relation to that of Great Britain. The norm for referendums is not Australia or Switzerland or California, but the countries like Norway, Austria, and Belgium that have used them once, twice, or thrice. Casting my eye over the continent of Europe, which has been grossly undermentioned in this discussion so far, I have two or three random observations, first of all on Belgium.

The key was not actually the 57 percent. The key was that the Belgium referendum result was then broken down into figures that showed that Leopold actually had a minority in the French half of Belgium and a majority in the Flemish half. That kind of division meant that the referendum did not provide an answer. This is of some interest in relation to the question we discussed about the Common Market referendum in Great Britain: Does one count the U.K. as a whole or does one break it up? It was absolutely critical for the Belgium referendum that the results were available at a local level as well as for Belgium as a whole, because they demonstrated that one half wanted Leopold III and the other half did not.

In continuing randomly around Europe, Italy, while its record of government may not be the best in Europe, has perhaps the most instructive use of the initiative. In Italy, the ordinary population can bring something onto the ballot paper, but by a fairly lengthy process, which has resulted in only three actual referendums. If we are looking for possible uses of the initiative, Italy is worth a look. A certain minimum number of signatures is required, either to introduce a new bill or call for the repeal of an existing bill. It then goes to Parliament and Parliament considers what to do about it. If Parliament decides to amend the bill that the petitioners want repealed, that is the end of it; Parliament has been alerted to a popular demand. On abortion, for instance, the initiative in Italy did not lead to the referendum; it led to Parliament taking up the issue. The lobby that wanted to allow freer abortion learned a lesson from what the Catholic Church had done on divorce; Parliament had passed a reform of the divorce law; the church organized a petition to repeal it; their appeal was rejected by the population. Then the anticlerical lobby said, "Aha. We can do that the other way around: There is an ancient law concerning abortion, so let us have an initiative to repeal it." Parliament then did something about it. The initiative in Italy has only been used three times, although it has been attempted many times. The restrictions are fairly heavy. A referendum cannot occur one year before a general election is due or one year after one has taken place, for instance. There are a number of provisions like that to prevent referendums from getting entangled in electoral politics.

If we ever wanted the initiative in Britain, something on the Italian lines, which results in only an occasional referendum, is better than other ways. It is what the Americans call the "indirect initiative," as Austin Ranney described it.

JOHN COURTNEY: In the past, there was a striking similarity among most of the referendums in Canada. They were on matters of great local importance. Twenty or twenty-five referendums have been held on the sale of liquor and three or four have been held on the perennial Canadian problem of daylight saving time. Quebec, in this sense, is rather typical of all Canadian provinces, because in 1980 it will for the first time experiment with the referendum device on an issue of great local importance.

It is really much, much more. It gets to the root of what constitutes Canada without any formal say in the whole process for the rest of the country. In a peculiar way, of course, the subject fits firmly into the Canadian tradition, because it is a local issue, obviously of local importance. This one has far greater consequences for the whole of the country than any previous referendum in Canada.

The only previous referendum even approaching in importance the Quebec one of May 1980 was the national referendum of 1942. That was held on the issue of whether the government should be allowed to retreat from its pledge not to introduce conscription. Because of it, one of the lasting Canadian wartime sayings became, "Conscription if necessary, but not necessarily conscription." The issue in Quebec has become separation if necessary, but not necessarily separation. This is because the subject being debated, that is, "sovereignty association," has been carefully chosen so as to permit a wide range of interpretations by the people of Quebec, even to the extent of permitting some who are opposed to separation to vote yes to the question of sovereignty association, and some who favor separation to vote, incredible as it may seem, no to the question.

RAYMOND WOLFINGER: I have never gone to a conference where somebody at some point has not popped up and shouted, "We are all assuming that so and so is correct and why should we make that assumption?" On this traditional contribution, would Peter Shore tell us why it is irresponsible either (1) to tell people to vote the way they do or (2) for them to be asked to vote?

PETER SHORE: That is perfectly easy: Because they do not have to live with the consequences of their decisions, and they are not responsible for the results of their own votes, and they do not consider the totality of the decisions and the alternatives and the consequences that flow from their particular vote. They are asked to give a judgment on a specific point but not on its context; that is what governments have to do and what Parliament has to do. That is a big difference. When they vote in a general election, they are voting on a program put forward by a party that wishes to assume responsibility for the government and they are able to see the thing in a much broader context. If one puts forward a simple proposition to cut taxes, such as Proposition 13, of course they are going to vote in favor of cutting taxes. If they are asked to consider the wider context of the consequences of that vote, they might feel rather differently; that is a very basic point. What are apparently simple issues, segregated from the general flow of government policy, have consequences of a much more serious kind than the voters have perhaps been presented. That depends on how issues are presented to people in referendums.

I felt somewhat reassured by David Butler's historical, worldwide analysis of the relatively modest use of the referendum. It does not seem that we need only look to the referendum to convey to government, even elected governments, and frequently elected governments, the sentiments of the people on particular issues. I belong to a country and I represent a part of it which has had petitions, petitions of right, petitions of God knows what, for hundreds of years; these petitions have been greatly influential and have even led on occasion to such great disturbances as civil wars. We had a petition of right in 1629, which led to civil war, because the rights were not granted by the Parliament. The way of communicating to the Parliament the deeply felt sentiments of people are there, and they do not have to be institutionalized in the form of referendums.

ANTHONY KING: Do governments pay any attention to petitions?

PETER SHORE: Petitions are important things; when they are presented to Parliament, we take serious notice of them. [Many voices protesting.] There have certainly been substantial petitions, and governments have reacted to them by introducing legislation or making the facilities available for legislation on which they have given a free vote to members of Parliament.

David Butler said that there are four categories in which the referendum has an important function. One is constitutional, the second is legitimation, the third is moral problem solving, and the fourth is political problem solving. It is not a bad classification, only the example is wrong under category four. The EEC referendum of 1975 was not a question of political problem solving. It was a major constitutional problem; it is regrettable that David Butler's perception of what happened at that time and his understanding of the constitution did not lead him to put it under the constitutional category. The general consensus of this particular gathering is rather in favor of using referendums on all kinds of occasions. Their use, however, should be restricted.

Despite George Cunningham's earlier remarks to the effect that there are no principles in the British constitution, there is one principle and that is the sovereignty of Parliament. The only proper role for the referendum in British politics is where an issue clearly affects the sovereignty of Parliament, and there are only two issues unambiguously within that category. One is where we are asked to agree to some major change in the territorial authority of Parliament, as in the question of Ulster, in the question of Scotland, and, to a lesser extent, in the question of Wales. Second, it raises the question of whether and under what circumstances the British Parliament is entitled to give up its powers to other authorities—that was the heart of the question about joining the EEC. We take the doctrine of parliamentary sovereignty seriously, because it expresses the sovereignty of the British people. Was Parliament right to give up not just its right but the rights of the British people to another body, an assembly that claimed powers over Parliament? That is what the issue was all about, and that is how increasingly people are understanding it.

Any future use of the referendum in this country will be confined to just these issues. We shall be hearing more about the question of whether and under what circumstances it would be right to give authority to a European assembly. That, it seems, would raise the constitutional question in its most serious form, just as any reactivation of the Northern Ireland or the Scotland or the Wales issue would raise that question in the same unambiguous form. No other issue would raise it as clearly and unambiguously as that.

Finally, I want to turn to the questions that the chairman put to us, important questions about nuclear energy. I am probably the only person in this room who has had to deal with this problem as a minister. We had to make an important decision about whether we were going to have a nuclear reprocessing plant at Windscale. It would not have been right to put that to a referendum. This is something that Parliament should decide. It is right for it to be decided in a special way. The people have the right to have the fullest possible examination of an issue of this kind. We had, as you know, a special development order procedure; we had a hundred days inquiry, the most substantial cross-examination there has ever been of a planning proposal in this country. We gave the inquiry a carte blanche in terms of the issues to be raised. Anything could be raised: the national interest, whether it was right to do it, what would be its effects, and how they could be dealt with.

85

Then we put the matter to Parliament, basically on a free vote. We had a two-line attendance whip for our members simply to be there because we did not wish the vote to be taken in the absence of parliamentarians, any parliamentarians. Any parliamentarian who objected to it could oppose it without the slightest consequence in terms of his own party. That seems to be right, but it is for Parliament to make these decisions. It is a great mistake to assume that these issues, whether they be nuclear or whether they be other issues, can be sensibly decided simply by a direct appeal to the electorate.

KENNETH BAKER: Probably most of us would say that if one is concerned with the sovereignty of Parliament upward into the Common Market or downward into devolution, those are matters which are rightly the subject of referendums. If the issue is Scottish devolution or Welsh devolution or some arrangement in Ulster, most politicians would assume that any proposals of that sort would ultimately be submitted to a referendum of some sort, at some stage, either at a consultative stage or even possibly just before royal assent. In the Ulster situation, there is an interesting complication in whether it is a referendum just within Ulster or within the entire United Kingdom; we have not quite faced up to this. If, however, one takes Peter Shore's approach about Parliament, then one has to take into account the constituent elements that make up the sovereignty of Parliament, and that means not just the House of Commons but also the Second Chamber. If proposals relating to the power or composition of a second chamber are put forward under Peter Shore's formula, would they also be subject to a referendum?

PETER SHORE: The sovereignty of Parliament is not something abstractly pertaining to Parliament itself, but it is above all the reflection of the right of the people to vote; it is part of their sovereignty. As to the House of Lords, there is considerable doubt about its utility and its function; it has nothing to do with the exercise of the sovereignty of the British people, nothing whatever.

KENNETH BAKER: It does happen to be a constituent part of Parliament as presently defined.

MICHAEL STEED: Maybe the people have tolerated an electoral system that clearly does not fairly reflect them in the House of Commons, on the grounds that the House of Commons is limited by the Lords.

ANTHONY KING: Until Peter Shore used the phrase "free vote," it had not been mentioned. In the United Kingdom, there is something called a free vote in the House of Commons; it is a vote in which the party leaders make no great attempt to get backbench members of Parliament to vote one way or the other. It is widely believed that free votes are held on what are called conscience issues. This view is either tautologous or false, because if one takes matters that are normally thought to be conscience issues, capital punishment, for example, and looks at the record in the twentieth century, most votes in the twentieth century on such issues have been whipped votes, not free votes. On the other hand, if one takes issues that have been free vote issues and asks what has been their character, one finds that some of them have indeed been conscience issues, such as abortion and capital punishment, but many others have been on such issues as (on the Conservative side) the Common Market. The view is almost universally held in Britain that there is a neat one-to-one fit between what are called conscience issues and free votes. There is, in fact, no such fit. The simplest theory to explain what issues are put to a free vote in the House of Commons is that they are issues that the government of the day wants to get out of the cabinet room so that somebody else will decide them.

If one wishes to predict when there is going to be a government-initiated referendum, it will be when there is a big issue that a government cannot control and wants to get rid of. If one wants a simple sort of predictive theory, of when one is going to have referendums, leaving constitutional theory aside, leaving initiatives aside, that is what it is all about; the free vote issue in the British context and the referendum issue should be assimilated as having the same political character.

ROBIN DAY: David Butler says that the EEC referendum of 1975 in Britain provides an outstanding example of a major issue that split the party in power being solved by a popular vote, and he puts that under the category of political problem solving. He is absolutely right. When Peter Shore said that this was not the issue, I challenge him to take a referendum of all British members of this conference and ask whether any have a doubt whatever that the reason we had this referendum was because the Labour government was split and Harold Wilson could not keep his party together. Harold Wilson had sworn under no circumstances would he ever have a referendum, but he had a referendum because it was the only way he could solve the problem. Peter Shore does himself an injustice by trying to rewrite history.

Second, Kenneth Baker asked about the question of a referendum on abolishing the House of Lords; Peter Shore said that issue had nothing to do with the sovereignty of Parliament, and nothing to do with the sovereignty of the people. That makes my point even more strongly, because, if the House of Lords were abolished, there would be

87

nothing to stop the temporarily elected Commons majority from abolishing elections altogether. Therefore, the sovereignty of the people would be fundamentally affected by the abolition of the Second Chamber.

PETER SHORE: Robin Day is right about Harold Wilson's motives in relation to the Common Market. That was not necessarily the motive of a number of us who opposed the Common Market. We felt it was a fundamental constitutional question that the people ought to decide directly.

ROBIN DAY: I don't doubt your sincerity in putting that argument. But the reason for the referendum was the issue.

PETER SHORE: The proper reason for the referendum, not the actual reason, is the concern. The other point on the Lords is questionable. If Parliament were to prolong its stay other than in conditions of war, that would be indeed a proper subject for a referendum because it is precisely these constitutional issues where it does seem that a referendum is absolutely crucial. That would not be the case in altering the status of the House of Lords.

5

Regulating the Referendum

Austin Ranney

When a polity first decides to hold some kind of referendum, it soon learns, as the United Kingdom learned in 1974–1975, that many decisions must be made about its conduct.[1] Among the most critical questions to be answered are these:

• Who may initiate a referendum: The government? Some specified number of citizens signing a petition? Either?
• Can a referendum be held on any issue of public policy, or are certain matters placed beyond reach—for example, the privileges and immunities of certain specially protected minorities?
• Who shall determine the wording of the proposition to be decided? The government? A special commission? The initiators of a popular petition?
• What regulations, if any, shall govern the organization, conduct, and financing of the campaigns for and against the proposition?
• What number or proportion of votes shall be required to pass the proposition? A simple majority of those voting on it? A specified proportion of all eligible voters?
• What shall be the effect of a proposition's victory? An expression of public opinion which the government may follow or ignore as it wishes? A mandate requiring the government to act in a certain way?

A polity's answers to these questions are bound to have major consequences for the role referendums play in its governing process and for the shape of its public policies. This conference is concerned with all of these questions and more, but this essay focuses on questions of how the organization and finance of campaigns for and against referendum propositions are, and should be, regulated by law. I shall begin by outlining the principal similarities and differences between campaigns for candidate elections and campaigns for referendums.

---

[1] For an account of how the United Kingdom made those decisions in 1974–1975, see David Butler and Uwe Kitzinger, *The 1975 Referendum* (New York: St. Martin's Press, 1976), chap. 3.

Candidate and Referendum Election Campaigns

Every democratic polity holds relatively frequent elections among candidates for public office, but only Switzerland and a dozen or so states of the United States hold as many or more referendums.[2] It is not surprising that most of the legal regulations governing campaign organization and finance in most democracies apply largely or entirely to candidate elections, not referendums, and that most of the scholarly literature analyzing campaign regulation deals almost entirely with candidate elections.[3]

In many respects, the two kinds of campaigns are similar. The contestants, whether party or candidate organizations or groups advocating or opposing referendum propositions, need to keep the voters on their side from straying to the opposition. They are glad to detach as many supporters of the other side as they can, although the difficulty of such "conversions" keeps them from being a prime campaign objective. Above all, the contestants need to stimulate and activate their supporters sufficiently to induce them to vote.

The methods used by the two kinds of campaigns are also quite similar. Increasingly, both kinds are designed and directed by professional "election consultants," whose training and approach is rooted in commercial advertising, not partisan politics. These professionals make increasing use of the "new politics" technology of public opinion polling, television advertisements, computerized direct-mail solicitation of funds, and the like.

There are, however, enough significant differences between candi-

---

[2] The data in David Butler and Austin Ranney, eds., *Referendums* (Washington, D.C.: American Enterprise Institute for Public Policy Research, 1978), Appendix A, pp. 227–237, show that until 1978 a total of twenty-one democratic countries had held at least one nationwide referendum. Switzerland had voted upon by far the largest number of propositions, a total of 297 in 187 different elections, followed by Australia with 39 propositions, France with 20, and Denmark with 10. Only the United States and the Netherlands had held no nationwide referendums at all.

In addition, twenty-one of the states of the United States have made extensive use of popularly initiated referendums. Between 1898 and 1976, a grand total of 1,224 propositions were voted upon in those states; the leaders were Oregon (207 propositions), California (159), North Dakota (137), Colorado (119), and Arizona (117); ibid., pp. 76–77.

[3] The scholarly literature on campaign regulations for candidate elections is far too voluminous to be noted here. In this essay, I have relied heavily on Alexander Heard, *The Costs of Democracy* (Chapel Hill, N.C.: University of North Carolina Press, 1960); Herbert Alexander, *Money in Politics* (Washington, D.C.: Public Affairs Press, 1972); Arnold J. Heidenheimer, ed., *Comparative Political Finance: The Financing of Party Organizations and Election Campaigns* (Lexington, Mass.: D. C. Heath Co., 1970); and Herbert Alexander, ed., *Political Finance* (Beverly Hills, Calif.: Sage Publications, 1979).

date election campaigns and referendum campaigns to warrant the special attention the latter receive in this essay. For one thing, political parties are usually much less active and prominent in referendum campaigns. This creates something of an organizational vacuum; it also removes the party labels that for most voters in most candidate elections are the most powerful indicators of which contestants merit support. For another, the special nature and requirements of the mass communications media, particularly television, make it more difficult to portray the pros and cons of propositions than candidates' records and personalities. For yet another, the absence of party labels in referendums deprives them of much of the structure and continuity that usually characterize candidate elections. This, in turn, makes it more difficult to inform and activate voters in referendum campaigns. Finally, referendums offer much less opportunity than candidate elections for direct and secret quid pro quo payoffs by the winners to their financial supporters. A heavy contributor to a winning candidate may expect and receive a number of more or less secret payoffs in the form of government contracts, special tax advantages, ambassadorial appointments, or places on an honors list. A heavy contributor to the winning side in a referendum can expect only whatever general benefit may come from the victory or defeat of the proposition—a benefit he shares equally with all those on that side whether they contributed to the campaign or not.

Accordingly, the principal issues in the regulation of campaign organization and finance for referendums are similar, but not identical, to those most prominent in candidate elections.[4]

The Issues

Public Disclosure. Probably the most widespread regulation of campaign finance in candidate elections in modern democratic countries is the requirement that candidate organizations and/or political parties make periodic financial reports to designated public officials.[5] These reports may then be read by any citizen and published by any newspaper or other mass medium. They usually include the names and addresses of all contributors, the amount contributed by each, and the amount, purpose, and recipient of each expenditure.

---

[4] The most comprehensive reviews of the issues for candidate elections are Heard, *Cost of Democracy*, and Alexander, *Money in Politics*, chap. 13.

[5] At least fourteen countries have such requirements; see table 7.1 in Khayyam Zev Paltiel, "Campaign Finance: Contrasting Practices and Reforms," in David Butler, Howard R. Penniman, and Austin Ranney, eds., *Democracy at the Polls* (Washington, D.C.: American Enterprise Institute for Public Policy Research, forthcoming).

Some commentators oppose public disclosure requirements on the ground that they are bound to have a "chilling effect" upon financial contributions and therefore upon one important form of political activity. Ralph K. Winter, a professor of law at Yale University, puts the point thus:

> [Public disclosure laws] in effect require that political acts of individuals be registered with the government and publicized. Such legislation thus might subject potential contributors to the fear that persons with different views or political affiliations, for example, clients, employers, officials who award government contracts, might retaliate. The effect, therefore, might be to "chill" or deter political activity.[6]

Several countries—notably Denmark and Norway—have rejected disclosure and reporting requirements on precisely these grounds.

In addition, the task of gathering, recording, verifying, and reporting all this information is demanding, especially when there are many small contributors. The costs of producing the reports often consume a good deal of the resources that would otherwise be devoted to advancing the organization's candidate or position on the referendum.

The proponents of full public disclosure reply that whatever slight chilling effect the requirement may have is far outweighed by its benefits. One benefit claimed is that disclosure satisfies the public's right to know all the facts relevant to any political contest it is called upon to decide; only thus can truly informed votes be cast. Another benefit claimed is the highly desirable chilling effect it has on efforts to "buy" elections by financing lavish campaigns for one side. After all, disclosure proponents say, it is much harder to buy an election if everyone knows the effort is being made; grossly excessive contributions and expenditures may well provoke backlash among the voters and cause them to vote the other way. Hence, the argument concludes, full publicity is one of the best guarantees available against the excessive influence of money on election outcomes.

My reading of the literature on this point suggests that both sides produce much plausible and even eloquent rhetoric but little hard evidence to demonstrate either the claimed beneficial or harmful effects of public disclosure. Its main effect is that of facilitating the enforcement of other regulations, and it should have a part in the regulation of referendum campaigns, providing that the minimum size of the contributions whose donors must be individually listed is set high enough to keep the reporting and enforcement burdens minimal.

---

[6] Ralph K. Winter, *Campaign Financing and Political Freedom* (Washington, D.C.: American Enterprise Institute for Public Policy Research, 1973), p. 20.

Expenditure Ceilings. After public disclosure, the next most common campaign finance regulation in democratic countries is the setting of upper limits on the total amount that may be spent by, or on behalf of, a particular candidate or list of party candidates. These ceilings are sometimes expressed as specified sums of money and sometimes as amounts proportional to the number of registered voters or the number of persons who voted in a preceding election.

There appear to be three main arguments for expenditure ceilings: (1) They keep costs within manageable limits for all contestants; (2) they ensure that disparities in expenditures among the contestants will be kept within "fair" bounds, that is, no contestant will be permitted to buy the election by putting on a far more lavish and effective campaign than his opponents can afford; (3) as a result, expenditure ceilings increase public confidence in the fairness of the contest and therefore in the legitimacy of the result.

Expenditure ceilings, however, are more heavily criticized than any other form of regulation. Their critics make two main charges. First, the limits are almost always set far below what is necessary to mount even what most campaign organizers feel is a minimum campaign. They are, therefore, all but impossible to enforce; they are widely violated, and everyone knows it. While expenditures by large national organizations can with some effort be monitored and limited, those made by small, local, ad hoc groups or individuals can be recorded and monitored only by impracticably large and expensive enforcement agencies. Hence, the limits tend to become something of a joke; this increases public cynicism and apathy toward the election process.

Second, the more effectively expenditure ceilings are enforced the more they favor the incumbent in candidate elections and the status quo in referendums. Other things being equal—for example, the size and quality of campaigns—voters are likely to reject the novel in favor of the familiar; thus, a formal equality becomes an actual bias in favor of one side.

Prohibitions of Certain Contributors. One quite common regulation prohibits all contributions from certain types of persons and organizations. Most commonly outlawed are contributions by trade unions, business corporations, civil servants, persons or firms doing business with the government, and foreign persons and organizations. The purpose of such regulations is to prevent the purchase of undue influence by persons or organizations most likely to make direct financial gains from the victories of particular candidates or parties.

Even as applied to candidate elections, these restrictions receive a good deal of criticism. The most compelling is the argument that contributing money to a favored candidate or party is one way a citizen can take action to express and advance his or her political preferences —a way that is comparable to and every bit as legitimate as talking to a neighbor or making a speech or writing a letter to a newspaper. It therefore deserves the same protection against abridgment. Preserving freedom of political action for everyone has a higher priority among democratic values than does preventing undue influence by a particularly affluent person or organization.

These objections to prohibiting certain contributors are convincing in the context of candidate elections, and even more persuasive in the context of referendums. As already noted, whatever may be the opportunities for unfair and improper payoffs to large contributors in candidate elections, they are almost nil in referendums, where the desired outcome *is* the payoff, equally available to all who favor it whether they have contributed to the campaign or not. Accordingly, there is no benefit from excluding certain persons or agencies from contributing to referendum campaigns that justifies the unavoidable abridgment of their rights of political expression.[7]

Restrictions on Contributions. A few countries, notably New Zealand, Japan, and the United States, put ceilings on the amounts individuals and organizations may contribute to a particular candidate or party. Under the American Federal Election Campaign Act amendments of 1974, for example, an individual is allowed to contribute a maximum of $1,000 to a congressional or presidential aspirant's campaign for his party's nomination and another $1,000 to a congressional candidate in the general election campaign. An organization, such as a political action committee, can contribute a maximum of $5,000 to a single candidate in a single campaign. In the prenomination campaign, however, the federal government is allowed to match with public funds only contributions of $250 or less, and so gifts of that size are eagerly sought.

The dispute about restrictions on contributions closely resembles those about expenditure ceilings and prohibiting certain contributors. Restricting how much persons or organizations can contribute to a candidate or a cause is clearly a limitation on their ability to express and support their political preferences. It is not as severe a limitation as prohibiting them from making any contribution whatever, but it is a significant abridgment nevertheless. Some commentators feel that it is

---

[7] A much debated issue in the United States is whether a corporation may legitimately use corporate funds to support or oppose a referendum proposition it feels directly affects its ability to do business; see "Corporate Contributions to Ballot Measure Campaigns," *University of Michigan Journal of Law Reform*, vol. 6 (1973).

a price worth paying for the benefit of preventing wealthy persons and organizations from buying elections but, like many other critics, I remain unconvinced that the benefit, if any, is worth the cost.

Expenditure Floors and Public Subsidies. In recent years, a growing number of commentators have argued that the major need in regulating campaign finance is not to put ceilings on excessive expenditures but rather to put publicly funded floors under inadequate campaign resources so as to guarantee that every contestant's case will receive at least adequate presentation to the voters.[8] Eleven countries provide some form of assistance to parties and/or candidates in candidate elections, and the case for such aid seems even stronger for referendums. As we have seen, the absence of parties and party labels in referendum campaigns means that the voters enter the campaigns with less information and fewer guideposts than in candidate elections, and the campaigns are therefore significantly more important as suppliers of the information and arguments that make for interested voters and informed votes. Accordingly, the prime object of government regulation of referendum campaigns should be to ensure that both the proponents and opponents of each proposition should have enough resources to make at least adequate presentations of their cases.

This guarantee can be provided in one or more of several ways. One is for the government to make direct subventions to the campaign organizations of each side and let them spend the public money and any additional money they raise on any campaign activity that they choose.[9] Another is for the government to print and distribute to all voters some kind of pamphlet containing the pro and con arguments as written for it by the contending organizations and/or by the government itself.[10] Still another is providing each side with an equal amount

---

[8] Among the leading expositions of this view are Dick Leonard, *Paying for Party Politics: The Case for Public Subsidies* (London: Political and Economic Planning, 1975); and Alexander, *Money in Politics*, pp. 230–243. For a review of the different subsidies provided by democratic countries, see Khayyam Zev Paltiel, "Public Financing Abroad: Contrasts and Effects," in Michael J. Malbin, ed., *Parties, Interest Groups, and Campaign Finance Laws* (Washington, D.C.: American Enterprise Institute for Public Policy Research, 1980).

[9] Note that this can be accomplished only if the government officially designates one organization as the umbrella agency for each side, an agency that will assume all responsibility for compliance with the law and will receive all subsidies for its side of the issue.

[10] In the campaign before the 1975 British referendum on continuing membership in the European Economic Community, for example, the government designated Britain in Europe as the umbrella organization for the yes side and the National Referendum Campaign as its counterpart for the no side. The government invited each to submit a statement of its case, wrote a statement of its own position, and published each of the three cases in a pamphlet circulated to all

of free time on television and radio, as seventeen countries now provide for the parties in candidate elections.

Some commentators argue that there should be no public subsidy whatever for any political campaign, including those for referendums. They argue that such a subsidy constitutes unwarranted government meddling in what ought to be entirely free action—or inaction—by citizens and citizen groups. If the advocates and opponents of a particular referendum proposition cannot muster enough enthusiasm for their cause to raise money for an adequate campaign, then they should take their chances in the psephological marketplace.

More persuasive is the argument that, if one accepts the basic idea of the referendum—the proposition that voters should be able to vote directly on at least some issues of public policy—then it follows that all voters should have equal access to at least minimum amounts of information about the pros and cons of each proposition put before them. That condition is most likely to be met if government makes sure that those minimums are provided; the contending sides should be free to mount any campaigns above the minimums that their size, enthusiasm, and resources permit. Ceilings no, floors yes.

Whatever may be the merits of restricting, limiting, and closely regulating contributions and expenditures in campaigns for candidate elections, the case for restrictive regulations of campaign finance for referendums is weaker. The values of free speech and free political action are at least as strong, if not stronger, in referendums. The opportunities for secret and corrupt payoffs to contributors to the winning side are much smaller in referendums. There is evidence to suggest that money is not an absolute political weapon in either type of election and that the biggest and most expensive campaigns do not carry the day in referendums any more than they do in candidate elections.[11]

Our considerable experience with campaign finance in candidate elections strongly suggests that the least defensible of all forms of regulation are ceilings on expenditures. They almost invariably are set well below the amounts needed to mount what the contestants feel is even a minimally respectable campaign. Hence, there are strong pressures to evade them and they are extremely difficult to enforce, particularly where politics is decentralized and many unknown and unsupervised local contributions are made to national causes. Not surprisingly, they

---

voters from one to two weeks prior to the balloting; Butler and Kitzinger, *1975 Referendum*, pp. 290–304. Most American states distribute similar pamphlets, although some prepare the pro and con statements on each proposition themselves rather than leaving it up to the partisans of the contending sides.

[11] In one of the few empirical studies of the matter, Eugene Lee reports that in sixteen referendums in California between 1972 and 1976 the side spending more money won only eight contests; Butler and Ranney, *Referendums*, pp. 104–105.

are—and are known to be—widely evaded, a situation that does little to bolster public confidence in the institution of referendums or in democratic processes in general.

Full public disclosure and reporting of contributors and their contributions has severe costs. It requires a great deal of expensive recording, tabulating, and reporting; it unquestionably has a chilling effect upon the political activity of at least some potential participants. Yet, its costs may be a necessary price for maintaining public confidence that referendum campaigns are open, aboveboard, and fair, and that referendum results are legitimate and accurate expressions of the popular will.

For reasons already given, the most desirable of all campaign finance regulations, especially for referendums, is the provision of sufficient government subsidies to each side on each proposition to ensure that its case will be at least adequately presented to the voters. Beyond that, each side should be free to mount any additional campaign it can afford.

A Model for Referendums

Given these views, it seems that the regulations used by the United Kingdom for its 1975 referendum on remaining in the European Economic Community provide an excellent, though not flawless, model for other referendums. The principal items were the following:

1. The official designation of one national "umbrella" organization for each side—Britain in Europe (BIE) for the promarketeers and the National Referendum Campaign (NRC) for the antimarketeers. Each organization served as the recipient of all public monies and as the agency responsible for observing campaign regulations.

2. A direct treasury grant of £125,000 to each side for campaign expenses

3. Full public disclosure of all receipts and expenditures and of the names of all persons contributing £100 or more

4. No ceilings on either contributions or expenditures

5. The printing and circulation to all voters of three pamphlets: One prepared by BIE setting forth its case for a yes vote; one prepared by NRC setting forth its case for a no vote; one prepared by the government information unit setting forth the government's reasons for recommending a yes vote.[12]

It can be argued, to be sure, that this system was heavily biased in favor of the promarketeers. NRC was able to raise and spend only

---

[12] For the preparation and texts of the pamphlets, see Butler and Kitzinger, *1975 Referendum*, pp. 59, 94, 110, 163, 290–304.

£ 10,000 over its government grant of £ 125,000. BIE, on the other hand, spent a total of £ 1,481,600—nearly eleven times as much as NRC and more than any party has ever spent on a general election.[13] Yet, there is no reason to suppose that BIE bought victory for the yes side. Polls taken throughout the campaign showed consistent majorities for remaining in the EEC, although their size increased in the campaign's last week. The leading studies of the referendum all agree that the campaign clearly did not convert an initial no majority into the two-to-one yes majority produced by the election. At most, it enabled the promarketeers to retain the advantage with which they began.[14]

On balance, then, it seems that the reasons for minimizing restrictions and maximizing publicly guaranteed floors are even stronger for referendum campaigns than for candidate election campaigns. Whether democratic countries are in fact moving in that direction is less clear.

---

[13] Ibid., pp. 85–86, 95–96.

[14] Cf. ibid., p. 96; Anthony King, *Britain Says Yes: The 1975 Referendum on the Common Market* (Washington, D.C.: American Enterprise Institute for Public Policy Research, 1977), pp. 123–127; and Philip Goodhart, *Full-Hearted Consent* (London: Davis-Poynter, 1976).

Discussion

MICHAEL RYLE, *chairman:* There are two ways of looking at the ground. One can look at it from the air and focus on the terrain's large features, or one can see what it looks like from below, one can get down to the dirt, the nitty-gritty. This is what Austin Ranney's essay deals with, and this is what we shall discuss. We are going to turn our attention from constitutional theory and look at some of the practical problems of actually running referendums.

AUSTIN RANNEY: My essay is *not* concerned with the basic question that, quite properly, dominates our discussions: Should a democratic country and/or a parliamentary democracy ever allow its citizens to vote directly on a question of public policy, and, if so, on what kinds of questions in what circumstances? My essay takes its departure from the premise that *if* a country decides that it is going to hold a referendum, there are a number of decisions that have to be made about how the referendum will be conducted. They are, to be sure, decisions on practical matters, not directly on the great questions of political theory, but many of them touch upon the great questions.

My essay focuses upon one set of those practical questions: What regulations, if any, should govern the organization, conduct, and financing of the campaigns for and against referendum propositions. Since some here have been saying that Britain has a six-word constitution, I shall sum up my essay in four words: ceilings no, floors yes.

TAM DALYELL: I read Austin Ranney's essay with great pleasure, but it did not mention television. In the United States, it would be expected that each of the factions would take what they could get on television; there is not the system of party political broadcasts that we have. Speaking for myself and my colleagues in the Labour Vote No Campaign in the devolution referendum, one of our most uncomfortable moments came when we had to decide whether to take court action against the independent television companies in terms of the Independent Television Act for restraint upon a situation where they would have shown four or five yes broadcasts to one no broadcast. It was quite unacceptable to those of us in the Labour Vote No Campaign. The court action did take place, and the high court did find in our favor. More vexation was caused by the decision to go to court, "against the party" as it was portrayed, than by any other single event in the devolution argument.

AUSTIN RANNEY: There should be enough broadcasts to present *each* side adequately. Both the yes and the no sides ought to have those broadcasts either directly provided by state television, as in your country, or free time provided or money provided to purchase it. Beyond that floor, however, if either side is able to muster sufficient support to put on two or three additional programs, they ought to be allowed to do so.

It is wrong to think of money and what money can purchase as some kind of absolute weapon. We have Eugene Lee's testimony that in California referendums the side spending the most money has won only about half the time. Then, too, there was an episode in Oregon last year that may interest you. Of all the referendums that were held in the American states in 1978, the one that had the highest turnout, nearly 70 percent of the voters—a fantastically high turnout in American elections for anything—was on a proposition allowing persons other than licensed dentists to fit false teeth. Why did such a peculiar issue produce such a high turnout? The answer is that when small and poorly financed groups put the proposition forward, the Oregon dentists put on a lavish television campaign with commercials and speeches and billboards. Their campaign backfired. The voters became so sick of the dentists' ads and so disgusted with their effort to buy the victory that they turned out in large numbers to beat the dentists. As long as both sides have an *adequate* chance to present their case, I would not be worried about one side having more broadcasts than the other side.

ROBIN DAY: It does seem to be absolutely clear that if we are going to move toward greater use of the referendum in this country, even on an ad hoc basis, and particularly if we are going to have any kind of referendum act to enable them to be introduced, we have to solve the problem of access to television. Perhaps our American friends are unaware of this, but in our referendums on the Common Market and on the Scottish and Welsh devolution, totally different considerations applied. We found both sides all right in the Common Market campaign because there were two umbrella organizations there. They were cross-party organizations that got together and agreed to do a broadcast; it was not difficult to give equal time in terms of what we call broadcasts that are free to the parties.

AUSTIN RANNEY: Did they control the content?

ROBIN DAY: Yes, subject to the laws of libel, they controlled the content, as the parties do in what we call party political broadcasts. In the Scottish devolution referendums, the whole thing came to pieces; Tam Dalyell did a great public service by going to court. Tam, did the court ban the broadcasts or did they have to do them in a fairer way?

TAM DALYELL: In effect, the broadcasts were banned because the Independent Broadcasting Authority (IBA) was going to have five broadcasts yes and one broadcast no; in the end, there were no broadcasts at all, as the BBC felt it had to follow the court decision.

ROBIN DAY: The BBC followed suit reluctantly, so, in other words, although Tam Dalyell got his unbalanced programs banned, in fact there was a lack of proper referendum broadcasts in Scotland. It seems that we have to work out the rules clearly on this and have something equivalent to the Representation of the People Act provisions for the coverage of television. The BBC was annoyed that this court action came up; the BBC did not actually come under the relevant act because there is no act covering the BBC. Then, in the end, the BBC thought it ought to comply with the court decision and the government was annoyed with the BBC for doing that.

On the question of Quebec, Mr. Ranney mentioned that the decision had not been made as to wording the question. The referendum must raise the question clearly and at the same time win the vote. I was in Montreal a few weeks ago, and I was told that the question was going to be, "Are you in favor of the Quebec government seeking to negotiate with the federal government the terms of sovereignty association?" That is going to be the question, or words to that effect. This, of course, is not asking the real question—"Are you in favor of breaking up the Canadian federation?"—because that would lose.

DAVID MCKIE: It seems that the great difference between the European referendum and the Scottish referendum was precisely the one that Mr. Ranney covered in his first point: Everybody was floundering in the Scottish case because of the lack of umbrella organizations. It not only affected television, it also affected the leaflets. When I was going round in Scotland, people were saying, When is the government leaflet coming out?

DAVID BUTLER: The Quebec Act provides that there shall be two umbrella organizations and that no money shall be spent except by the two umbrella organizations. If one is for Quebec separation, one has to work within the proseparation umbrella organization dominated by the Parti Québécois members of the legislature; if one is against separation, one has to accept total Liberal domination of the antiseparationist group by Liberal members of the legislature. In the original draft of the bill, it would be illegal for an ordinary citizen against separation to spend even a few pounds on having a public meeting.

One should not concentrate exclusively on television as the major means of communication, as the study suggests. One important question about television communication is the form it takes: Is it done by fifteen-second or thirty-second slots in short ads? I would not mind seeing a worldwide rule that no party political material may be televised in relation to elections or candidates that does not last at least two minutes. In Britain, the broadcasting organizations have persuaded the parties to come down from the old-fashioned twenty-five-minute speech to ten-minute or five-minute party political broadcasts. Neither on television nor on radio in this country, have we got below that particular time.

I am less upset than some people by the bogusness of the question that may be put in Quebec. There was a good deal of talk in Britain about the wording of the question in the 1975 referendum, and there was a poll study that asked the question hypothetically in eight different ways, with major differences in responses to the different formulations. People were upset at this. The wording of the question about entry into the Common Market or the European Community did not matter. At the end of an election campaign, where things had been discussed fully, people knew perfectly well what they were doing. They were voting yes or no. Nobody went to the ballot box and actually read the words. There had been quite adequate publicity in advance. By the end of the campaign in Quebec, people will have reached a decision not on the question as officially stated but on a general sense of what is really at issue. What is said in an ordinary neutral news program has much more impact than what is said in a party political program on behalf of the Labour party, for instance, or on behalf of a no campaign.

One angle of this, touched on by Tam Dalyell, is the question of the role of the umbrella organization. Umbrella organizations raise real difficulties, but if a party wishes to impose a number of regulations upon total expenditures by one side or the other, upon contributions, and upon accounting, it is difficult to see how that can be done effectively without an umbrella organization. Here, we have a choice, a tradeoff that has to be made between two good things, or, if you will, two bad things. If one has mandatory umbrella organizations, one may threaten freedom and diversity of opinion. If one does not have umbrella organizations, one inevitably will have much less effective enforcement of the expenditure limit, contributions, and accounting. That may be a price one should be willing to pay.

RICHARD SCAMMON: If one gets involved in the referendum as a continuing function, the tendency is, at least in the American states, to hold referendums periodically, at specified times. One must remember that, in America, 80 to 90 percent of the referendums are on incredibly trivial questions ("Shall the county be permitted to expend $4,500 to build a new bridge across the Wapus-Wapus Canal?"). These votes are required by the present statutory and constitutional arrangements. While one thinks about nuclear power and prohibition as the normal kinds of issues, one also gets down to the regulation of the massage parlors.

TAM DALYELL: Yes, but there is the particular problem of what seems to be irrevocable. In both the EEC referendum and the Scottish/Welsh referendums, there was in practice little chance of altering the decision once it had been taken. We had set a juggernaut in motion, we were on a moving escalator, and we almost certainly could not get off. This is a bit different from the situation in Richard Scammon's county, where presumably either the matter is trivial or it can be changed if people do not like it.

THOMAS FOLEY: Whether it is irrevocable or not, when our British friends talk about the issues, they talk about significant issues—whether a nation joins the Common Market or does not join, whether one devolves powers to Scotland and Wales or whether one does not. I am going home next week to vote on six referendum issues. One is whether we should mandate a charge of five cents on every container of beer or soft drink sold and distributed within the state. It is a tremendously important issue as far as the aluminum industry is concerned, but it is hardly of the quality of the British association with the EEC. Our public would not tolerate much free television time being given in most states to a balanced discussion of those issues. They would simply switch it off. The question of why we have so many thirty-second ads is a technical one. We have rapidly developed remote control, quick-switching television sets in the United States. We are getting shorter ads because we have fourteen channels, and the viewers are not going to sit and listen to anyone talk about five-cent containers. We cannot have maximum limits on expenditures without having a constitutional problem. We cannot mandate the television people to show programs of any weight or significance without losing audiences. We are stuck at our level of rather mundane issues with letting private financing of the budget take most of the burden.

PETER SHORE: It is true that British referendums have concerned only issues of major significance, although that is not to say that they are irrevocable decisions. Nevertheless, they are major decisions, and the rules and conditions under which the referendum is to be held is therefore as important as the arrangements for a general election. That imposes great obligations of care on the organization of the referendum and the whole question of expense; indeed, Tam Dalyell suggests that there was a flaw in not putting a ceiling on the umbrella organizations. There was a marked disparity, of course, in the expenditures by the two sides in that referendum. That, in itself, is not the really decisive factor. The decisive factor is the part played by television and the press because they are the ways in which people are really reached. It is true that we had on television and on radio equality of time as between the different organizations, but really that is quite secondary in the British context for the conduct of elections in terms of print, television, and radio coverage. The factor that matters is the balance of how different items relating to that election are handled. We have all kinds of rules to ensure that independent television and the BBC give equality of treatment quite outside the limited number of directly controlled television and sound broadcasts that the two umbrella organizations are given. It seems, on the whole, that these rules of behavior in the actual period of the referendum campaign were fairly observed. We had the rather unique situation in Britain where, unlike general elections, all the national newspapers were clearly committed to one side or the other. Insofar as people are influenced by the views of the papers that they read, then they had, with one minor exception, a unanimous national press recommendation for a yes vote.

MICHAEL STEED: First, I agree totally with David Butler on this question about the formulation of the proposition. It seems that it is the campaign that defines what the question means. Second, despite Austin Ranney's comments, it would be a tragedy if we allowed money to play the part in British politics that it has come to play in American politics.

On umbrella organizations, from some of the earlier discussions of the shambles that was the coverage of the Scottish and Welsh campaigns, there was a sense in which people thought, "Aha, how well we did it in the European campaign; wasn't it a good thing we had these two clear umbrella organizations between which media coverage was balanced and so forth." There was a degree of distortion in recognizing those umbrella organizations. The National Front was totally excluded from the anti-EEC umbrella organization. As it happens, all the British here, indeed everybody here, would be grateful for anything that prevented that particular cancer from growing in British society. Nonetheless, in principle was it right that a political party that polled around 3 percent of the vote in the previous election, that was the largest party in England united against the Common Market—was it right in principle that it should have been excluded because we did not like their views on other matters? If one starts on that slippery slope, one is only a few steps away from what has been done in Quebec.

Another worry is illustrated by comparing the British umbrella organization with what happened in Norway in the Common Market referendum. In Norway, a people's campaign, organized to present the anti-Common Market viewpoint and led by nonestablished politicians, managed to turn that referendum into something of a contest between established party leaders and people who said, "We are against what this establishment wants; we don't think people really want what big business and the party leaders tell us." In Britain, with all respect to Enoch Powell, Peter Shore, and one or two others, like Barbara Castle, the no campaign consisted of a few familiar faces. By recognizing two organizations that essentially were led by established politicians, the British EEC referendum was turned into a contest between two sets of established politicians; therefore, the channeling of money and the recognition that the BBC gave created an entirely different impression of what the contest was about than was the case in Norway. What happened in Norway could have happened in Britain. The fact of recognizing established leaders of umbrella referendum organizations can produce a different result from letting things happen freely.

HENRY DRUCKER: Michael Steed is absolutely right about the kind of disaster we would get if we were to force people into umbrella groups. It is fair to say that, in the case of the Scottish referendum, it was precisely because a number of politicians felt there had to be umbrella groups that they jumped the gun. Three MPs jumped the gun and formed their own yes campaign without the support of any party; that actually made it impossible for the yes people to get together, whether or not that affected the noes. Life would be intolerable if they were forced into campaigns together; this is going to be one of the important differences between referendum campaigns in the United Kingdom and those in the United States. People do not want to compromise their party positions by their positions on a particular referendum.

PHILIP GOODHART: I do not see any future referendums in this country in which one will be able to get two umbrella organizations as in the

European referendum. It will be impossible. It will, therefore, be impossible for the government to send out official communications to all the voters concerned. The problem of access to television is going to be the most important one we face in Britain. In the Scottish and Welsh referendums, the broadcasting authorities discussed the question with the chief whips in the normal party political forum, and clearly they got it wrong and came up with a disgraceful balance. Given that viable umbrella organizations will be rare, what can one do? It would be right to establish a referendum commission of distinguished independent people who, when a referendum occurs, will be able to meet and see that fair play is done. They can discuss with the BBC and Independent Broadcasting Authority exactly what the balance is going to be and all the other problems that develop. Let us get the commission established quickly so that people can accept the idea.

JÜRG STEINER: In regard to Switzerland, we have discovered in recent research the "package effect," meaning that it matters what the other issues on the ballot are when a particular measure is voted on. It affects the size of the turnout and therefore can determine the fate of a particular measure.

Contrary to all the nice suggestions of Austin Ranney, in Switzerland, we have absolutely no rules, everyone spends just what he wants, and there is no public disclosure. Like the Swiss banks, we also have secret things about the referendums. Yet, there is no movement to introduce any regulations. There is not even a movement for public disclosures; how much is spent on a particular referendum is one of our best-kept secrets.

MARTIN KARMEL: Regarding the regulation of campaign finance, I envisage a group of organizations putting up posters in 11,000 branches, all in fine type and absolutely free without any expenditure or contribution on their part, and 11,000 managers being briefed to speak to all their customers, again without expenditure on anybody's part.

AUSTIN RANNEY: If there were a referendum involving the regulation of savings accounts in banks, and a religious sect put up a poster on a building saying "Jesus Saves," might that be regarded as a campaign document? The question Mr. Karmel raises is one debated at great length and in minute detail by our Federal Election Commission, as it affects our presidential campaigns. The reason is that the commission considers a "contribution in kind" to be the same as a contribution in money. They have to inspect everything closely to see whether it is a contribution in kind. There are severe legal limits on how much money can be spent in a presidential campaign. There is one form of expenditure, however, on which there is no limit, and either party and any candidate can spend as much money as they can raise on it. That item is lawyer's fees, because in order to make sure that they are obeying the laws they must hire a lot of lawyers to advise them at every step. The problems that you pose are difficult. The more complex the laws, and the more severe the limitations, whatever else will happen, the richer the lawyers will get.

ANTHONY KING: "Ceilings no, floors yes" was first applied to money and then to something that Robin Day said more specifically applied to television. Austin Ranney said that each side assumed that every other side should be given a certain amount of time, but he thought there should not be any ceilings on their television exposure. Is that not, in fact, a United States–specific observation? In how many countries in the world can political organizations buy time on television for political purposes?

KENNETH BAKER: I endorse Philip Goodhart's statement that, if we were to use referendums on an ad hoc basis in the United Kingdom, it may well be unlikely that umbrella organizations will emerge. The reason why umbrella organizations emerged in 1975 and 1978 was that each of the two major political parties was divided within itself on the issues. There were significant minorities in both parties that were at odds with their party's majority, and therefore umbrella organizations were the most suitable and convenient means for conducting and financing the campaign, certainly in the EEC referendum. If we use referendums on an ad hoc basis in the United Kingdom, it may well be on big issues that divide the parties, such as the issue on the future of the Second Chamber. If a bill is taken through by a government to abolish the Second Chamber, one would take it through the House of Commons, and, before it got to royal assent, there might well be a referendum. At that stage, the parties would be clearly divided. That raises interesting problems, because when a bill has reached that stage in our system, there is the implication that it is government policy; that, in itself, has enormous implications. The government of the day may well consider it to be so important as government policy that it will, in fact, use its considerable weight to argue its case. Therefore, there is a lot to be said for the proposition that, before we indulge in a national referendum on that sort of issue, we should work out the ground rules carefully indeed; to that extent I support what Philip Goodhart was saying.

DAVID MARQUAND: It seems that this discussion has shown that those who feel that it would be a mistake to try to have legislation on referendums in advance are wrong. There are some fundamental problems, however. If the whole purpose of the referendum is to give a legitimate result that is not available from the normal parliamentary process, that will not happen if the result is at all close. If the party that lost feels it was robbed because there was not proper prior discussion about what the ground rules ought to be, the result will not have legitimacy.

I disagree with Kenneth Baker that there would be a great problem if the government were divided from the opposition; that would be rather an easy thing to handle. Most referendums are going to be on issues the ordinary party divisions cannot cope with, and that is going to be the whole reason for having them. Therefore, almost by definition, there will be divisions within the parties. If there are no umbrella organizations, how on earth can one avoid the problems that arose in Scotland, which Tam Dalyell had to go to the high court to solve? It seems that they are insoluble unless there are umbrella organizations to which time can be allotted. It is a vicious circle.

On money, it is perturbing to see the kind of mood that seems to come through both from those talking about American states and from Professor Steiner talking about the Swiss experience. Those two sorts of experience may not be relevant to the kind of situation that might exist in this country if there were another referendum. I played a fairly active part in the Britain in Europe campaign and was quite heavily involved in the television side of that campaign. We had money pouring out of our ears. We had so much money we did not know what to do with it. The result would not have been any different if, in fact, there had been less expenditure by our side. As someone on the winning side, it did bother me a bit that there was such an enormous disparity in campaign money. In leaving aside the rather special case of referendums on not terribly central issues like dentists in Oregon, can those who have done research on this topic prove that money is not important in affecting the outcomes of referendums? The American and Swiss examples are not terribly convincing. A substantial body of evidence would have to show that money does not talk in referendums before I would be prepared to accept this and to accept Austin Ranney's slogan of no ceilings.

AUSTIN RANNEY: If one side campaigns not at all because it has no money and the other side puts on an excellent campaign because it has a lot of money, the side that puts on no campaign will not always win. There are many instances in which the side that spent the most money on campaigning nevertheless did not win. In other words, money in campaigning is not unimportant. If one has enough money to put on the minimum necessary kind of campaign, one does not get an increment of success for every increment of money spent. In that sense, money is certainly not an absolute weapon.

RAYMOND WOLFINGER: One reason is that there are substitutes for money, which usually come down to organization of one sort or another. Precinct work—that is, door-to-door canvassing—can be quite persuasive, particularly in low-turnout elections. This sort of campaigning cannot usually be procured by the expenditure of money. Instead, it results from certain kinds of groups, like labor unions, that have the capacity to mobilize and direct campaign workers. Groups based on intense emotions, such as a desire for peace in Vietnam or opposition to abortion, often can achieve this sort of organization. Similarly, there are local situations in which a network of ideological activists combined with a particular sort of environment, like a large university, produce a formidable political force that needs virtually no cash expenditures to generate a lot of votes. This, incidentally, is the situation in my home town of Berkeley.

This leads to the observation that since it is impossible to figure out in advance all the different kinds of advantages that one side or the other might enjoy and since legitimacy is important in referendums, then it is best not to pile on too many regulations of electoral efforts. The more regulations there are, the greater the risk that the losers will believe that they lost because all the rules imposed an unfair handicap.

GEORGE CUNNINGHAM: If we are going to use referendums often, it would be highly desirable to have a code of practice that governs them. The difficulty is that when one turns to individual requirements in that code, such as minimum numbers, the difficulties seem to be quite insuperable. We have discussed, for example, the difficulty about whether umbrella organizations are relied upon to the point where we really see that it is highly desirable to rely on umbrellas. Yet there are circumstances, which Tam Dalyell has described well, where some people will find it counterproductive to be mixed up in the umbrella and that will tend to be when the rebels in the party are a small minority. If differences merely halve the party, then one can go in with the umbrella organization. When the rebels are a small minority in a party, then it is counterproductive for them to be associated with the 95 percent of the other party.

The umbrella matter is not the only one where it is difficult to foresee what rules to make in advance. One of the problems we had in the devolution campaign was that people said, "Look, why have you

109

got the 40 percent rule in the devolution campaign when you didn't think of putting forward such a rule in the EEC referendum?" It was difficult to answer that. There is a case for having a minimum rule like that in some referendums but not in others. There will be some questions in which the ayes and nays are about equal and one must do something. It might not be the case when one is changing the status quo, needs a big majority to change it, and should not change it without this authority. But in a case where the balance is much more equal, where one must do something, a majority of one ought to suffice. There will be other situations, such as the abolition of the House of Lords, where people would say it would not be right to abolish the House of Lords unless a significant majority of people supported the proposition. On that question too, it is difficult to see how one can prejudge what the code ought to be.

THOMAS FOLEY: In the United States, corporate money has sometimes made an equal debate on the issue possible, particularly with initiatives. Many existing groups are organized to push the initiative, they have a network of volunteers, and only the advertising brought on by aluminum or steel companies has enabled the public to make a judgment. Otherwise, it would have been a one-sided issue. I am a little nervous when some of my British friends say money is always bad. In many cases, corporate money has made a serious judgment possible.

ROBIN DAY: I am shocked to hear Philip Goodhart speaking on behalf of a government dedicated to the reduction of public expenditure to advocate another "quango" [quasi-nongovernmental organization] to deal with the question of time on television. The commission would consist of the same sort of people who have already informed the government and the BBC and the members of the IBA; it should decide the question of time. Any legislation we have, whether George Cunningham is right or not, to try to work out the ground rules for referendum campaigns should say that the BBC and the IBA have a duty to provide not only spare time within their own coverage of things, but also free time for both sides. Tam Dalyell will agree that it would be perfectly simple for any sensible broadcasting executive to work out five free broadcasts on each side and give them to relevant people on each side without any reference to umbrella organizations.

Second, I am surprised to hear Philip Goodhart say that he does not expect any umbrella organizations in the future. It was he who forecast earlier that we might get referendums, perhaps even from this government, on the subject of legislation dealing with trade unions.

Does he not think that umbrella organizations will grow from that? I will tell him what they are now.

TAM DALYELL: There is no quarrel with David Marquand's logic. The political reality is that, if George Cunningham and I had gone to the gates of the Govan shipbuilders or a joint shop steward's committee at Leyland or wherever under an umbrella organization, we would have had a different result than the extremely satisfactory and successful result we actually had. It comes back to something that my friend Henry Drucker said. He said that it would compromise the party position by taking an attitude on referendums, and this is perhaps one of the great differences between the referendums that we have had and the referendums on the other side of the Atlantic, where party complications have not been quite so delicate. When the prime minister came to the big meeting on the devolution referendum in Glasgow, the chairman of the party that supposedly wanted devolution above all talked about everything from the French Revolution onwards, but not about the case for voting yes. The chairman, Mrs. Janey Buchan, like many others, was going to vote no. Many party officials and their wives said they would vote no, even though it was counter to the party's position. That is why there was a deathly silence and that is why in many cases one will inhibit in some way what party activists say about the merits of the case for the referendum under discussion when their party political position is implicitly at stake.

AUSTIN RANNEY: We have been discussing the most basic of all of the issues about the referendum device because clearly, if satisfactory rules are not developed, then whatever else can be said about high democratic principles, there cannot be a useful referendum. The price is too high.

What should the rules be? David Marquand has made a most important point. Fundamentally, the desirability of the referendum rests more than anything else upon its claim to legitimacy—on the belief that a decision made by the people directly without any distortion by any kind of intermediating organization is democratically the most authentic decision that can be made. David Marquand has well reminded us that one can have that kind of legitimacy only if the rules are widely accepted as fair and regular. If you in Britain are thinking about using referendums in a bigger way, you had better have a set of rules that will be widely accepted, not different rules drummed up ad hoc from one issue to the next.

Many people here have expressed the worry that something that works reasonably well in some American contexts will work much less well in the British context because of the strength of the parties, because of the difficulties of getting umbrella organizations, and the like. It would have been interesting if someone had spoken of the Australian experience, where there are strong parties and extensive use has been made of referendums.

In the British case or in any other case, if the practical difficulties in the way of holding referendums by fair rules are too grave, the difficult decisions that lie ahead will be made without referendums.

6

Referendums and the European Community

Anthony King

It does some violence to the truth, but probably not very much, to say that there are six and only six considerations that lead to the holding of referendums.[1]

First, someone may advocate the holding of referendums because he believes in direct democracy; that is, he believes that as many decisions as possible should be taken by the whole people, or at least by as many of them as care to participate. In a small community, like a village or small town, direct democracy may take the form of a village or town meeting; in a larger community, like a state, province, or country, direct democracy is almost bound to involve the holding of referendums. It is the widespread belief in direct democracy in Switzerland that leads to the holding of so many referendums in that country.

Second, someone may not believe in direct democracy as a general proposition but may nevertheless feel that certain distinct classes of issues should be settled by the people as a whole rather than via the usual representative institutions. These issues might be issues of conscience like divorce, abortion, or the closing of pubs on Sundays; or they might be constitutional issues—decisions concerning how and by whom future political decisions shall be taken. The constitutions of several countries in Europe allow for the holding of referendums on constitutional issues. In Britain, referendums were once held only on a narrow range of conscience issues, such as Sunday closing in Wales, but more recently they have been held to determine constitutional issues, such as whether governmental powers exercised centrally in London should be devolved onto regional assemblies in Scotland and Wales.

---

[1] The rest of this essay draws heavily on David Butler and Austin Ranney, eds., *Referendums: A Comparative Study of Practice and Theory* (Washington, D.C.: American Enterprise Institute, 1978). Another useful source is the March 1976 issue of the *European Journal of Political Research* (vol. 4, no. 1) entitled "Referenda in Europe." The constitutions of the various European states were obtained from their embassies in London. The writer does not claim to be an expert on all nine of the present member states of the European community, let alone the three applicant countries, and some of the information in the paper is based on conversations with journalists and embassy officials.

Third, someone may not hold strong views about direct democracy one way or the other but may hold very strong views about a particular issue and may advocate the holding of a referendum on that issue because he objects to what is taking place via the normal representative processes and believes that, if the question is put to the people as a whole, the outcome will be different, that is, will be the one that he personally favors. In other words, he is prepared to regard the people as a sort of court of appeal, an alternative forum in which, with any luck, he and his friends can get their way. Such a person will be in favor of referendums that he thinks he can win, against referendums that he thinks he may lose.

Fourth, someone may not hold strong views either about direct democracy or about the particular issue at hand but may advocate the holding of a referendum in order to strengthen his own political position or that of his regime. Suppose that, as between courses of action X and Y, a political leader prefers X. But suppose further that he knows that he is perfectly capable, using the normal constitutional processes in his country, of ensuring that X is adopted. He may nevertheless believe, if he is confident that the people at large also support X, that it will be worth his while to hold a referendum in which the position of him or his regime and the fate of X are linked together. If X wins, so does he.

Fifth, someone may want a specific decision to be irreversible. The right decision from his point of view may have been reached via the normal constitutional processes, but he may fear that this decision is in danger of being reversed by means of these same normal constitutional processes. He may therefore advocate the holding of a referendum on the issue in order that, if the referendum produces the right result from his point of view, the issue will be settled once and for all. In other words, he wants a vote of the whole people in order to legitimate a decision that might otherwise be called in question.

Finally, of course, a referendum may be held in a country on an issue because, in that country on that issue, a referendum has to be held; the holding of a referendum is required either under the constitution or by law. In Ireland, for example, proposed constitutional changes have to be approved in a popular referendum; in Denmark, proposed constitutional changes must be approved by the people, and, in addition, one-third of the Danish parliament can demand a referendum on any bill.

Of the six considerations listed, clearly the first two are, in some sense, principled or conscientious (they raise large questions of political theory), while the next three are purely tactical: One advocates a referendum not because one believes in referendums as such but in order to achieve the outcome that one wants on a specific issue. In circumstances where the holding of a referendum is not required by law, it goes without saying that someone may advocate the holding of a referendum for several reasons at once. One may, for example, have a general disposition in favor of direct democracy and at the same time believe that, on a given issue, a vote of the whole people would produce the result that one wants.

For brevity's sake, let us give each of these six considerations a label. The first we shall call the "direct democratic," the second the "qualified direct democratic," the third the "alternative forum," the fourth the "prestige," the fifth the "legitimating," and the sixth the "legal." How have these various considerations been related to the holding of referendums on the European Community so far? How might they be so related in the future?

The Record So Far

The original six—Italy, France, West Germany, Belgium, the Netherlands, and Luxembourg—came together to form the European Economic Community in 1957. None of the six countries held referendums at that time, and indeed in none of the six was it seriously argued that a referendum should be held. Referendums were neither legally required nor sought on political grounds. The reasons for the lack of interest in holding referendums when the community was launched appear to have been twofold. In the first place, more or less by chance, the original six countries were not ones in which the holding of referendums was usual: even in France, although referendums were allowed for in the constitution, none was held between the time the constitution was ratified in 1946 and the fall of the Fourth Republic twelve years later. In the second place, the events leading to the signing of the Treaty of Rome in 1957 were not politically salient or especially controversial in any of the six countries. Most European politicians, apart from the Communists, were in favor of greater European integration. In addition, the long-term political and economic significance of the setting up of the EEC was widely underestimated.[2]

Matters had changed, however, by the early 1970s when the time had come to enlarge the community. No one now was in any doubt

---

[2] It is striking that two standard political histories of postwar Europe hardly bother to discuss the internal politics within each of the original six countries concerning the establishment of the EEC and do not mention the possibility that referendums might have been held. See Richard Mayne, *The Recovery of Europe: From Devastation to Unity* (London: Weidenfeld and Nicolson, 1970), especially chap. 10, and Roger Morgan, *Western European Politics since 1945: The Shaping of the European Community* (London: B.T. Batsford, 1972), especially chap. 9.

about the importance of the community, and, in three of the four countries seeking to join, the issue of membership was highly controversial. In the event, referendums were held in all four countries—the United Kingdom, Norway, Denmark, and Ireland—and also in one country that was already a member, France.

The United Kingdom became a member of the community on January 1, 1973. Its referendum, however, was not held until two and a half years later. The Conservative government of Edward Heath, which took Britain into the Common Market, never intended to hold a referendum on the issue. No national referendum had ever been held in Britain before, and the Conservatives saw no reason to set a precedent; they were (or claimed to be) opposed to the holding of referendums in principle, and they were more than satisfied with the passage by Parliament in the usual way of their European Communities Bill. The Labour party, however, was divided on the issue. One faction was in favor of Europe and against holding a referendum; the other was against Europe and in favor of holding a referendum. The anti-European faction won a struggle for power inside the party and committed it to holding a general election or referendum on the issue once a Labour government had renegotiated the terms on which Britain had entered the EEC. The anti-Europeans believed, or at least hoped, that the British people, acting as an alternative forum, would reverse the decision taken by Parliament. Their hopes, however, were dashed. A referendum was held in June 1975. The pro-Europeans won it easily.[3] (For the results of all the referendums held on Europe so far, see table 1.)

In the British case, there was no constitutional provision for the holding of referendums, but it was always open to Parliament to decide that a referendum should be held in any particular case. The same was true in Norway. But in Norway it seems to have been tacitly understood from the beginning that the results of any negotiations with the community should be placed before the Norwegian people as a whole. This seemed to many Norwegians an issue that should be settled by means of direct democracy. Moreover, both the pro- and anti-Europeans were in favor of such an appeal to the people. The pro-Europeans believed that the Norwegian people would vote yes and saw the referendum as a means of legitimating Norway's Common Market membership. The anti-Europeans, like their opposite numbers in Britain, hoped

---

[3] On the British referendum, see Anthony King, *Britain Says Yes: The 1975 Referendum on the Common Market* (Washington, D.C.: American Enterprise Institute, 1977); David Butler and Uwe Kitzinger, *The 1975 Referendum* (London: Macmillan, 1976); and Philip Goodhart, *Full-Hearted Consent: The Story of the Referendum Campaign—and the Campaign for the Referendum* (London: Davis-Poynter, 1976).

that the Norwegian people would vote no and saw the referendum as the only way of reversing a decision that they did not like. The result was a substantial triumph for the anti-Europeans, and the Norwegian referendum of September 1972 closed the issue in Norway for the foreseeable future.[4]

In Denmark, as we saw earlier, one-third of the national parliament can demand the holding of a referendum on any piece of legislation before it. At the time of the Danish elections in 1971, it seemed almost certain that enough anti-Europeans would be elected to parliament to make the holding of a referendum on the issue inevitable. Believing a referendum to be inevitable in any case, and seeking to avoid a party split on the issue, the Danish Labour party, the largest single party in Denmark, agreed that a referendum should be held even if none were legally required. It thus set an example for the British Labour party to follow. The Danish referendum was held in October 1972, a month after the Norwegian, and produced a 2-to-1 majority in favor of Denmark's joining the EEC. The issue was not entirely closed by the result, however, and Denmark's community membership remains an issue in Danish politics—much more so than in either Norway or Britain.[5]

The Irish referendum was the most straightforward of those held in the 1970s. Before 1972, the Irish constitution vested all legislative power in the Irish parliament. Since membership of the community meant that some legislative powers had to be transferred to the community, it followed that the Irish constitution had to be amended; and in Ireland amendment of the constitution requires a referendum. It seems doubtful whether a referendum would have been held otherwise, since both major political parties in Ireland, Fianna Fáil and Fine Gael, were in favor of Ireland's joining the EEC and since an overwhelming

---

[4] On Norway, see Henry Valen, "Norway: 'No' to EEC," and Ottar Hellevik and Nils Petter Gleditsch, "The Common Market Decision in Norway: A Clash between Direct and Indirect Democracy," both in *Scandinavian Political Studies*, August 1973 (Beverly Hills, Calif.: Sage Publications, 1973); also Henry Valen, "National Conflict Structure and Foreign Politics: The Impact of the EEC Issue on Perceived Cleavages in Norwegian Politics," *European Journal of Political Research*, vol. 4 (1976), pp. 47–82; Henry Valen and Willy Martinussen, "Electoral Trends and Foreign Politics in Norway: The 1973 *Storting* Election and the EEC Issue," in Karl H. Cerny, ed., *Scandinavia at the Polls: Recent Political Trends in Denmark, Norway, and Sweden* (Washington, D.C.: American Enterprise Institute, 1977). A useful short essay is Johan Jørgen Holst, "Norway's EEC Referendum: Lessons and Implications," *World Today*, vol. 51 (March 1975), pp. 114–120.

[5] On Denmark, see Nikolaj Petersen and Jørgen Elkit, "Denmark Enters the European Communities," in *Scandinavian Political Studies*, vol. 8 (1973); Ole Borre, "Recent Trends in Danish Voting Behavior," in Cerny, ed., *Scandinavia at the Polls*; and Peter Hansen, Melvin Small, and Karen Siune, "The Structure of the Debate in the Danish EEC Campaign: A Study of an Opinion-Policy Relationship," *Journal of Common Market Studies*, vol. 15 (1977), pp. 93–129.

majority of the people of the country were evidently of the same view. The result of the referendum, held in May 1972, was something of a foregone conclusion, with more than 80 percent of those who went to the polls voting yes.

If the Irish referendum was straightforward, the referendum in France was bizarre. There had been no referendum in France when France itself joined the community, and the constitution of the Fifth Republic certainly did not require a referendum on the occasion of other countries joining. President Pompidou, however, decided to hold a referendum in order "to indicate the extent of national consensus on a major policy," "to restore the prestige of the regime," and to reassert his own authority.[6] In fact, Pompidou's referendum, held in April 1972, backfired. The question was whether Britain, Norway, Denmark, and Ireland should be admitted to the European Community. The answer was as expected, but the French electorate "bristled with indifference," the turnout was low, President Pompidou's authority was marginally diminished rather than enhanced, and no referendum has been held in France since.[7]

From the experience of the 1970s, two lessons can be drawn. The first is that, if membership in the European Community is a highly contentious political issue within a country, it is likely, though by no means certain, that a referendum will be held on it. If the opponents of entry are in a minority in Parliament but believe they are in a majority in the country, they will press for a referendum on "alternative forum" grounds. Under the same circumstances, those in favor of entry are likely to be prepared to concede the holding of a referendum on "legitimation" grounds: They will fear that, if a referendum is not held, the issue will remain contentious and the opponents of entry may succeed sooner or later in reversing the original decision. In addition, of course, the fact that referendums were held in all four new member countries in the 1970s will make it just that much more difficult for future applicants not to follow suit.

The second lesson of the 1970s is that referendums are dangerous things. The Norwegian Social Democratic party concurred in the holding of a referendum in the belief that the Norwegian people would vote yes; instead they voted no. The anti-Europeans in the British Labour party made exactly the same mistake; the 1975 referendum tied Britain

[6] Vincent Wright, "France" in Butler and Ranney, eds., *Referendums*, pp. 149–150. See also Jack Hayward, *The One and Indivisible French Republic* (London: Weidenfeld and Nicolson, 1973), pp. 246–248; and Claude Leleu, "The French Referendum of April 23, 1972," *European Journal of Political Research*, vol. 4 (1976), pp. 25–46.

[7] Wright, "France" in Butler and Ranney, eds., *Referendums*, pp. 143–144.

even more securely to Europe. Finally, Pompidou held a referendum that he need not have held in order to increase his prestige; instead, the outcome had the effect of diminishing it.

Referendums and the European Future

What bearing do the referendums of the 1970s have on likely developments in the 1980s?

Three countries are currently seeking admittance to the European Community: Greece, Spain, and Portugal. It seems improbable that a referendum on community membership will be held in any of them. The Greek constitution explicitly allows for the holding of referendums, and the main opposition party, the Pan-Hellenic Socialist Movement (PASOK), which is opposed to Greek membership in the EEC, has followed the example of the British Labour party in calling for a popular vote to settle the issue. So far, however, the Karamanlis government has had little difficulty in resisting the pressure from PASOK, and only if PASOK were to win an early election is it likely that a referendum would be held.

As far as Spain and Portugal are concerned, the constitution of neither country requires the holding of a referendum on an issue like community membership, and so far political pressure for a referendum has not developed in either country. The main reason is that, in both Spain and Portugal, opinion is strongly, some would say passionately, in favor of membership. In Spain, every party including the Communists favors entry; in Portugal, only the Communists are opposed. If a referendum is held in either country, it will be either for purposes of legitimation or because at some time before the conclusion of the negotiations some political upheaval gives anti-European political groupings far more influence than they have now.

What about the existing member countries? When the time comes for one or more of Greece, Spain, and Portugal to join the community, is it likely that any of the present members will follow President Pompidou's example of 1972? To pose the question in that form is already to suggest the answer. It seems extremely unlikely that any government that has already agreed in the Council of Ministers to the accession of one or more of the applicant countries will want to risk both its own prestige and the successful enlargement of the community by holding a referendum when it has no need to do so. Certainly, none of the present nine members' constitutions makes a referendum on such an issue even remotely mandatory. Moreover, the holding of even one referendum could lead to serious dislocation in the community. Suppose that one of the present nine decided, for any reason, to hold a referendum on the admission of Greece, for instance; and suppose that the referendum quite adventitiously turned into a sort of plebiscite on the record of the governing party or coalition in that country. The result could be that Greece is excluded simply because of the unpopularity of the governing party or coalition in question. President de Gaulle at least had specific reasons for wishing to exclude Britain; the scenario just envisaged would result in the exclusion of Greece more or less by accident. Of course, parties hostile to the community might advocate the holding of referendums on the admittance of new members precisely for the purpose of causing disruption of this kind. One can easily imagine the British Labour party and also the anti-European parties in Denmark behaving in this way.

A larger, more important, and more difficult question concerns any constitutional changes that may be proposed for implementation within the community itself, in particular the transfer of powers from the council of Ministers to the now directly elected European Parliament. It is hard to see how such changes, if they were to be meaningful, could take place without substantial revisions to articles 137–154 of the Treaty of Rome. For that reason, if for no other, they seem unlikely to take place in the foreseeable future. If they were to take place, however, the case for the holding of referendums would be strong. Today any national government can, in practice, veto any proposal it dislikes, provided it dislikes it enough and is prepared to incur the inevitable political costs; but presumably, if powers were transferred from the Council of Ministers, controlled by national governments, to the European Parliament, national control in this form would cease. Europe would have become significantly more "European."[8]

None of the present or applicant members of the community would be legally bound to hold referendums in the event that such radical changes were proposed, but the pressure to put the issue before the people would certainly be considerable in several of them. The pressure would come from those hostile to the community in principle (many in the British Labour party, for example) but also from those (for example, the French Gaullists) who accept the community but do not wish it to develop along supranational lines. The pressure for the holding of referendums would probably come mainly from the opponents of change, since it seems unlikely that national governments,

---

[8] The reference in the above paragraph is to formal changes of the kind that might lead to the holding of referendums; but, of course, as David Marquand quite rightly points out (session VI, pp. 6–9), constitutional change in the European community is less likely to proceed via this route than by means of a gradual shift of powers within the terms of the existing Treaty of Rome. Under these circumstances, the whole question of holding referendums becomes academic.

having agreed to the changes themselves, undoubtedly with much difficulty, would want to put them at risk in this way. In other words, the main consideration in the minds of those advocating referendums would be the one labeled "alternative forum" earlier. The slogan would be "The politicians are trying to take away your rights. *You* must stop them."

Those using such arguments would, of course, be doing so on purely tactical grounds; they would not want referendums to be held on any proposal to *increase* the Council of Ministers' powers at the expense of the European Parliament. Nevertheless, those advocating referendums would also be able to make out quite a strong case in principle. Any substantial strengthening of the European Parliament would have the effect of changing not merely the community's constitution but the constitutions of its member states as well. The powers of national governments and national parliaments would be diminished, possibly quite significantly. Anyone believing that major constitutional changes should be put to the people would be bound in conscience to support the holding of a referendum in his country even if he himself supported the changes and feared that in any referendum the voters would throw them out. Under these circumstances there would, of

TABLE 1

REFERENDUMS ON THE EUROPEAN COMMUNITY

Country	Date	Issue	Voting Yes (%)	Turnout (%)
France	April 23, 1972	Admission of Denmark, Norway, Ireland, United Kingdom	67.7	60.7
Ireland	May 10, 1972	Join community	83.1	70.9
Norway	September 24–25, 1972	Join community	46.5	77.6
Denmark	October 2, 1972	Join community	63.3	90.1
United Kingdom	June 5, 1975	Stay in community on renegotiated terms	67.2	64.5

SOURCE: Butler and Ranney, eds., *Referendums,* tables 1–3, pp. 11–13.

121

course, be many to argue that the proposed changes were really not so "major" after all.

Given the tactical pressures that would be brought into play, and given the strong arguments in principle, it is hard to believe that a community of nine—let alone a community of twelve—could revise its constitution without at least a few of the member states holding referendums. This probability constitutes yet another obstacle in the way of creating a Europe significantly more integrated and supranational than it is now. The United States of America was created in an age that, for all its liberalism, was still predemocratic. The United States of Europe is being created in a world that is far more democratic in temper. Democracy may not prevent major changes in Europe, but it does seem likely to slow them up.

Discussion

DAVID MCKIE, *chairman:* Several people have suggested that this conference should have a referendum of its own. So we are circulating a ballot to each of you on the question, "In the next ten years do you wish to see the referendum play a larger part in your national political life?" You should check either the yes or no box and, to enable a little comparative analysis, you should also check the U.S. or U.K. box. Hand your marked ballots to the chair, and the results will be announced later.

I shall now ask Tony King to talk to us about his essay on referendums and the European Community.

ANTHONY KING: I have before me, insofar as they are written down, the constitutions of the twelve countries most concerned with the future of the EEC. There are six countries in which, for all practical purposes, the referendum is not mentioned. These are the United Kingdom, the three Benelux countries, Portugal, and West Germany. There is a brief reference in the German basic law to referendums, but they are only to be held on the subject of changing the boundaries of the various *länder*. The possibility of holding a consultative referendum is explicitly mentioned in the constitutions of two countries, both applicant countries to the EEC, Spain, and Greece.

In several countries, the constitution requires that a constitutional change be ratified by a popular referendum. Those countries—and the significance of this will emerge later—are Spain, Ireland, France, and Denmark. In one other country, Italy, there is the option of a constitutional amendment being put to the people under circumstances specified in the constitution. Altogether, five countries of the twelve make some provision for the use of this device in amending their constitutions.

Finally, with regard to statutes, in three countries it is open to a minority of the legislature, and/or to the government, to require that, before a statute is formally promulgated, it must be approved in a referendum. Those countries are France, Ireland, and Denmark. The French position, as Vincent Wright well knows, is rather complicated. All by itself, as Michael Steed said, is Italy. In Italy, once an act has been passed by the legislature, it is possible for half a million voters to petition to have that act stricken from the statute book. In the case of abortion, for example, if one wanted to vote yes to abortion, one had to vote no on the initiative measure proposing the repeal of law providing for abortion.

Looking again at some of these constitutions, which are in some cases quite bulky documents, I did find the sort of provisions in some that people were talking about with horror when they appeared in American state constitutions. My favorite single passage comes in the constitution of the Italian republic, title 2, article 30, which provides that the law shall lay down rules and limitations for ascertaining paternity.

Notice that if one is talking about the future of the European Community, one is talking about two classes of questions: What will happen, and what should happen? One is also talking about two issues: the enlargement of the community, and the possibility of a transfer of power from the existing Council of Ministers possibly to the European Parliament. One is talking about all these questions in the context of twelve different countries. A little bit of arithmetic suggests that to do this job properly, one must have the answers to forty-eight different questions. Obviously, neither in the essay nor in these remarks can I do anything remotely like that, so let me take the two issues, one after the other, first enlargement of and then a change in the internal constitution of the community, and say something briefly about each.

It seems unlikely that referendums will be held in more than, at most, two or three countries about the enlargement of the community. It is always open for the French president to do what Pompidou did in 1972, but precisely for that reason it is unlikely to happen. None of the constitutions requires a treaty or a domestic act of parliament to enable the community to be enlarged; and no constitutional provision requires that issue to be put in a popular referendum. The question then really is: In any of these countries, either the existing nine or the applicant three, is there likely to be considerable internal political pressure, which a government might not be able to resist, for the holding of a referendum?

In the applicant countries, there probably is not. In the case of Spain, although a referendum could be held, the fact is that practically the whole of the Spanish political community, including the Communist party, is in favor of Spanish entry into the EEC; political pressure for a referendum is unlikely. In the case of Greece, there is some internal political pressure from the Papandreou-led left-wing party, which does not want Greece to enter the EEC. It has already petitioned the president under the Greek constitution to have a referendum on that issue and he has turned it down; short of the left becoming the government, it seems that a referendum is unlikely. The Portuguese constitution makes no provision whatever for the holding of referendums, and in Portugal the degree of consensus on joining the Common Market is almost as high as it is in Spain, though in Portugal the Communists are against it.

In the case of the existing countries, the one possibility seems to be that some of the persons who wish that their country were not in the community might want to seize the opportunity provided by the proposed addition of three such different countries to throw something of a spanner in the works, to reopen the question of community membership within their own country. The two most obvious candidates for such a move would seem to be those in Britain, chiefly, though not solely, in the Labour party, who might want a referendum on enlargement as a means of reopening the whole question of British membership and likewise the very substantial anti-Common Market forces in Denmark. The aim of such an exercise would be not so much to prevent the enlargement of the community, though that might be considered a valuable byproduct, but rather to put the issue of their own country's membership back on the political agenda.

Should referendums be held about enlargement? Unless one actually had some political purpose in so doing, the case in abstract constitutional theory for having a referendum is not a strong one. The position differs, though, if one raises the second issue, which is the transfer of powers to the European Parliament or to some other genuinely supranational body. I might remind our American colleagues who do not follow European Community affairs closely that, at the moment, decisions of any consequence are taken in the Council of Ministers, which is simply a meeting of people from the member governments. The European Community is only in a limited way a supranational institution.

If there were a proposal to make Europe in some sense a genuinely federal state, with a supranational, directly elected assembly with powers, then it seems that two things would follow immediately. First, this would require substantial revision of the Treaty of Rome; even a quick glance through the treaty indicates that one cannot make that kind of change without renegotiating the whole exercise. Second, it seems, in reading the constitutions of quite a number of the countries, and even considering their unwritten political rules, that such a change in the balance of political power within the institutions of the community would raise constitutional issues not merely for the community

125

but for each of its constituent members—sometimes formal constitutional questions, sometimes informal ones.

The question then is, Is it likely that referendums will be held if such changes are ever proposed? The constitutions of Denmark, Ireland, and Spain probably would require the holding of a referendum; on political grounds it is hard to believe that the balance of political forces is not such in the United Kingdom, France, and possibly Italy as to make it difficult for the government of the day in any one of those countries to propose such major constitutional changes without referendums being held. In other words, if any major changes of this kind are proposed, there will be referendums in Ireland, Denmark, Spain, the United Kingdom, and France at least, and possibly in a couple of the other countries.

The other question in this connection is, Should referendums be held? That turns straightforwardly on beliefs about whether, if constitutional changes are proposed within a country, the people of that country should be consulted about them and asked to say yea or nay to them. It seems that if one believes that the answer to that question is yes, that the people do have a right to pronounce upon things as important as their constitutions, if one cleaves to Peter Shore's line that in the British case anything that would derogate further from the sovereignty of Parliament is something that should be referred to the people, then one cannot really—consistently or in good conscience—say no to the idea of having a referendum on the issue of the transference of power to a European Parliament.

There are at least forty-eight questions. I hope I have said enough to give a sense of the complexity of this question and the really rather large quantity of both information and theory that one needs to bring to bear in order to discuss these matters sensibly.

DAVID McKIE: David Butler said that referendums, on the whole, have been conservative in effect and that in quite a lot of cases it has been fear of the unknown that has been the dominant factor. On the basis of Tony King's analysis, it appears that in five countries it might be necessary to have a referendum. Would that probably work against that sort of development of the European Parliament?

ANTHONY KING: Yes. Given the tactical pressures that would probably be brought into play and given the strong arguments in principle, it is hard to believe that a community of nine, let alone a community of twelve, could revise its constitution without at least appeals in the member states to hold referendums. This probability constitutes yet another obstacle in the way of creating a Europe significantly more integrated and supranational than it is now. Democracy may not prevent major changes in Europe, but it does seem likely to slow them up. That is to say, it seems that there is some nontrivial probability of a no vote on these matters in at least one and possibly several of these countries that would have the effect, as things now stand, of preventing a transfer of powers within the community. If I were either a Labour anti-marketeer or a French Gaullist, I would campaign for the holding of the referendum in the belief that if I lost I would be no worse off than I am now, while if I won I might be able to prevent the creation of a supranational Europe.

DAVID MARQUAND: It seems that the argument is based on a misunderstanding about the present nature of the community, about the nature of the Rome treaty, and about the nature of likely future developments within the community. If, tomorrow or next year or the year after that, a proposal were made to make a massive and fundamental change in the whole nature of the treaty, then probably the consequences that Tony King has discussed would result. This is such an unlikely state of affairs as to be not worth discussing at all. What we ought to be discussing is how the community might develop in practice in the reasonably foreseeable future. If it were to acquire a more supranational role, what kind of role would that be, and would it involve the sorts of consequences Tony King described? The biggest single step which the community could take towards becoming more supranational would be to implement the treaty commitments on majority voting in the Council of Ministers. That is a commitment into which they have already entered. The treaty commitments on majority voting in the Council of Ministers are not being operated because of the Luxembourg compromise in the middle 1960s, when de Gaulle refused to allow those commitments to be carried out. The present procedures of the Council of Ministers are not those that were set out in the treaty.

How could it be argued that the constitutions of the signatories of the treaty would require referendums to be held in order to implement provisions to which they have already agreed and which have already been ratified? That would do more than anything else to make the community supranational. Regarding the powers of the European Parliament, it is true that, both in the United Kingdom and in France, the legislation enabling direct elections to be held included a provision making it illegal for the powers of the European Parliament to be increased unless the two national parliaments concerned agreed. Let us look at what is in fact the most likely way in which the European Parliament might increase. By far the most probable way is through an increase in the size of the community budget. The community budget is in a state of incipient crisis. Within the next year or two, its ex-

127

penditures will exceed its revenue, and there will be a crisis in the community, which will have to be settled somehow. If the community budget increases in size, the powers of the European Parliament will automatically increase, because the new expenditures will almost certainly belong to that category of expenditure over which the Parliament has the last word. It cannot really be argued that an increase in the community budget, for example, by big new spending on regional policies or social policies, would necessitate the holding of referendums of the kind Tony King has been talking about in any of the member states. Yet, that is the most likely way in which the power of the European Parliament might increase.

As one last example, in the last year and a half, a European monetary system has been established, in which all member states except the United Kingdom participate. It is intended, by some of its proponents at any rate, to be a move toward monetary union. Full-scale monetary union would obviously change the character of the community substantially and would entail a fundamental transfer of functions from the national level to the community level. The constitutions of the member states do not require referendums to be held even on that. In this country, opponents of any British membership of the community might be able to insist on a referendum on the question of whether Britain should join the European monetary system, although no antimarketeer is proposing that a referendum should be held on it. If Britain did join the European monetary system, and if the European monetary system then developed in a way that a lot of us think it ought to develop, we would be on a moving escalator, and there would never be a point at which it would be obviously appropriate and right to stop the escalator by having a referendum. Those are some of the reasons why Tony King's analysis of the constitutional facts of the case is not entirely congruent with the community situation.

ROBIN DAY: As a distinguished ex-Eurocrat, could David Marquand say whether, if we actually went over to majority voting as the treaty says, there is a great deal of difference between majority voting in a community of six or nine and majority voting in a community of twelve or thirteen? Does it not raise a totally new situation of majority voting, and would that not call for a referendum? A lot of people might say they would take a different view of majority voting in a community consisting of all sorts of strange countries halfway across the world compared with the little nucleus of European countries.

DAVID MARQUAND: One could argue that. Do not forget that the system of majority voting is not straightforward. The rules laid down in the

Treaty of Rome provided for an incredibly complicated system of weighted voting, which meant that the big countries could not have been outvoted by the little ones. Each country had a weighted vote, depending on its population and size, rigged in a complicated way. When we joined, the weights were so distributed as to make it impossible for a couple of big countries to be outvoted by all the others.

ROBIN DAY: Wouldn't you want to know the exact weights and then vote on it?

DAVID MARQUAND: Yes, I would, but I am not making a moral judgment, I am making a factual judgment. The constitutions of member countries would not require referendums to be held, even in this case. There might be political pressures for a referendum in some of the countries—there might well be in France, for example. A large section of French opinion is against the admission of Spain, and there may well be a referendum in France on that issue.

JÜRG STEINER: Let us think about the question of what the European community would look like in twenty or thirty years, what kind of political system it could be. Maybe looking so far ahead, we will decide that we do not want it. The experience of Switzerland might provide some clues. Switzerland has had to deal for centuries with the basic questions that are confronting Europe today, namely how to integrate different national groups into the same political system. It was not easy. If Europe is integrated, it may have the same kind of problems that we had in Switzerland for so long.

What is the real solution? It is not the government-versus-opposition model. We have developed in Switzerland a different model, the consociational model. We have learned from long experience that one can keep these different national groups together only if all of them participate in the executive on a regular basis. There is no other solution for Europe in twenty or thirty years, if indeed it is going to integrate. The solution is not a Westminster model where large segments of Europe would be excluded from power for a long time.

If we had only the representation of all major groups in the executive, that would be a bad system of an elite cartel with little participation for the people; this is exactly the critique that one hears against EEC. If the European Parliament got real power and appointed the cabinet, and the cabinet were composed of all major political forces, then participation in the European parliamentary election would not be so meaningful, because one could not replace one set of leaders with another. Consequently, one would need other means for the people to

129

express themselves, and one means would be the referendum. Maybe all this is frightening. Maybe what was feasible in Switzerland, a small country, is not feasible in Europe. If one wants to go in the direction of more European integration, one must choose the consociational model and supplement it with the referendum. It is a difficult, slow process.

GEORGE CUNNINGHAM: David Marquand's remarks are interesting, because he is really saying that for the future development of Europe there is no point along the path where it would be appropriate to say, "Here is the watershed; this is the point at which we should submit future developments to the test of a referendum." That is right, because, having once decided to go in, it is arguable that one should at least have foreseen that all the rest would follow. I remember talking a few months ago to a British judge, who is a member of the Court of Justice of the European Community. I said to him, "Assume that you are in the House of Lords, as a court, the supreme court of Britain, sitting as a British judge. An issue comes up where there is a point of clear community law that such and such is the case, but the British Parliament has passed an act that says that, notwithstanding community law, nevertheless the law of Britain is hereby declared to be as follows. Would you hold in favor of the community law or in favor of the British law on that point?" He said that, as a British lawyer, he would hold in favor of community law, that he would not take account of the "notwithstandings," and he would say that since Parliament has not taken us out of the community, he would hold that community law is superior. That is just to illustrate the way in which progressively, and insidiously, the process of unification goes on, without there ever being a natural point at which one can say: This is the fork in the road.

TAM DALYELL: It would be impertinent to talk about South Down or Tower Hamlets or Beckenham or Islington, but if I went to the electors of West Lothian in some kind of a referendum on Greek admission to the EEC, on the size of the community's budget, I would be met by ribald bewilderment. The constituents would say, "What on earth do we pay you for as a member of the British Parliament if not to take on our behalf difficult decisions on such matters?" No, the truth is that if there is to be a referendum of this kind, it would not only have to be on a point of cataclysmic importance, but the turning point would have to be obvious to the whole nation. If we were to hold a referendum on a seemingly trivial issue, we would get a derisory percentage voting and a great deal of ribaldry.

VINCENT WRIGHT: First, when we look at the recent experience of Western Europe with referendums, one has granted divorce in Italy, one settled peace in Algeria, and one confirmed British entry into Europe. Those seem to me to be radical proposals indeed, and, in contrast to David Butler, I think one *can* affect radical measures by referendums.

Second, to return to what seems to be one of the fundamental issues at stake in the entire conference, if there is any degree of popular initiative in starting the referendum process, one might well have referendums on the evolution of the European Community. The Labour party, particularly in the middle of a miners' strike, could want a referendum on a European monetary union. In other words, if the opposition has the ability to exploit propitious political circumstances by launching a referendum, it might well grasp at it. No government in Europe has any interest at all in holding a referendum on the evolution of the European Community, either because it would be received as totally superfluous, because there is a great deal of consensus in the country in question, or because it would be highly divisive and politically dangerous to the government in question.

DAVID LEA: The Euro-fanatics, who are often also referendum fanatics, have been careful not to put their two logics together. Take the question of the enlargement of the EEC, and one can see why. Why don't they advocate a Euro-referendum? The answer is that they know very well that referendums do not convey legitimacy. If we had a referendum in each of the countries about enlargement, and France voted no and Britain voted yes, people would say, "Oh that's very difficult, what do we do now?" Someone might say, "Well, let's just take the Euro-referendum result in the aggregate." Let us say that if it produced a Euro-vote of 58 percent yes and 42 percent no on enlargement, would this somehow convey legitimacy and be accepted in the countries that had voted no? It would not. Why is it that people are evading the Achilles heel of their argument and declining to talk about Euro-referendums?

ENOCH POWELL: In the preceding session, Peter Shore commented to the effect that referendums should be held on proposals which derogate from the sovereignty of Parliament.

PETER SHORE: Which derogate from the sovereignty of the people *and* Parliament.

ENOCH POWELL: If I might take the proposition without the intrusion of the difficult word "people," and if I might make a further amendment—no one should cavil at "derogate from the sovereignty of the Crown in Parliament," which is the correct description—then my proposition is that one can settle no such question by a referendum. One can only settle it by civil war or, in the relevant case, by international war. One cannot settle it by referendum because a referendum can only be held and can only be given effect, negatively or positively, by the Crown in Parliament, there being no other way of doing it. The proposition that one should derogate from the sovereignty of the Crown in Parliament is a revolutionary proposition, and no revolutionary proposition can be dealt with by voting. The only thing one can do if there is a move to transfer authority in the nation from the Crown or the Crown in Parliament to some other authority is to resort to force. This does not logically apply to the question of the extent of the limits of the jurisdiction of the Crown in Parliament. The same would not apply if the question were whether Cornwall should be part of the United Kingdom of Great Britain and Northern Ireland. That could be settled intelligently and logically by a plebiscite in Cornwall. I am referring to the sovereignty exercised over any nation.

Similarly, the proposition that authority should be transferred to an external source of power can only be settled physically, because it is essentially a violent assertion, it is essentially the substitution of one order of thought for a different order of thought. Such substitutions do occur, but they are mediated by power, by force. We deceive ourselves if we suppose that a referendum is a means of peacefully securing the transfer of power from the Crown in Parliament to some other domestic authority or from the Crown in Parliament to an external authority. This was confirmed, in a sense, by Her Majesty's government in relation to the referendum of 1975, when they asserted that if the answer were yes, our continued membership would nevertheless depend on the continuing assent of Parliament, thus admitting that every day in Parliament the Crown in Parliament decides the question that was purported to be dealt with by way of referendum.

VERNON BOGDANOR: This issue of the European Community illustrates one of the fundamental dilemmas of the referendum, one which was well understood by liberal opponents of democracy in the nineteenth century. It is this: The more power one gives to the people, the harder it is to secure change or progress. Many in the nineteenth century thought, correctly, that if one has democracy, one cannot in the long run avoid the referendum. It is worth asking how many of the arguments against the referendum that we have heard are also arguments against democracy. Liberals in the nineteenth century believed, rightly, that progress comes from minorities and that therefore the more one extends power to the people, the less progress one gets. This is the dilemma in which people like Peter Shore find themselves. People on the left believe instinctively in popular sovereignty, but they also know instinctively that the more power they give to the people, the more difficult it is to secure the kinds of changes which the left wants, not only in social and economic policy but on moral issues also.

David Marquand wants Europe to advance but he feels instinctively that, if it could advance only through popular referendums, it would be at the least a slow process. It seems that David Lea has it the wrong way around. It is not the Euro-fanatics who are the referendum fanatics: The Euro-fanatics do not want to have much to do with the referendum. David Lea is a conservative on the Europe issue and so he ought to be a referendum fanatic. He does not want Europe to advance, and the way to stop it from advancing is to use a referendum, to use the weapons of democracy and popular sovereignty.

RONALD BUTT: Nobody has taken any account of the possibility of the general election as an alternative to the referendum on the question of European enlargement. I take Vernon Bogdanor's point about the problems raised by demands for progress. In the not-so-distant past, it was almost a constitutional practice, when there was any issue that seemed to have some kind of national importance (for example, protection), to hold a general election and put it to the people, if the government felt it lacked authority or a mandate from the previous election. If that were done today, it would solve the problem of referring important questions to the people. It also would solve the sort of problem that Tam Dalyell mentioned when he spoke about the laughter that a referendum on this sort of issue would produce in his constituency. There are not many single issues on which it would be practicable or desirable to hold a general election specifically—but there are some, and the EEC could have been one of them. Of course, it might have split the parties, but so what?

NEVIL JOHNSON: Following what Vernon Bogdanor said, it is important to distinguish between consent and initiation in a democracy. Surely it is beyond dispute that what he says is generally true, that is, initiation and innovation on the whole do not proceed from the broad mass of the electorate; they proceed from persons and minorities who take initiatives of one sort or another. In contrast, consent can be given by the people en masse, as it were. In Britain, we have the problem of unrepresentativeness and inflated claims to authority in a fairly acute form. For example, the last Labour government's mandate and its claim to use parliamentary sovereignty for realization of this supposed mandate rested on the direct approval of 29 percent of the electorate; similarly, the mandate so vigorously claimed by the new Conservative government in fact rests on the consent of no more than 33 percent of the electorate. Those figures point to a real problem in Britain about the conditions of democratic consent, the unrepresentative electoral system.

AUSTIN RANNEY: Vernon Bogdanor has raised a truly basic point, and more ought to be said about it. It is implicit in almost everything we have said about referendums, whether about the expansion of the EEC or continued British membership therein or whatever, that referendums are a logical extension of the idea of democracy and that democracy itself is a fundamentally conservative, antiprogressive system, that all change comes from minorities. Therefore, logically, people who do not want change ought to favor democracy and therefore referendums, and people who do want progress and change ought to take the opposite view. There are two questions here, one logical and one empirical. The logical one is about definitions; all change is not progress and all progress is not change. It is important to make that distinction.

David Butler said that referendums tend to favor the status quo, because voters tend to fear the unknown. That is an empirical statement. The concluding chapter of *Referendums* reads as follows:

> Is the referendum in effect a conservative or a progressive device—that is, does it usually produce outcomes pleasing to the right or to the left? This is usually the first—and often the only—question political activists ask about referendums, and it is not without interest to scholars as well. The evidence set forth in [various of our chapters] is too patchy to justify a definitive answer. But our preliminary verdict would be that the referendum is a politically neutral device that generally produces outcomes favored by the current state of public opinion. Public opinion is seldom left or right on all questions at any given moment, nor is it consistently left or right on any question through all time. For example, [the chapter on the American states] shows that in the 1960s and 1970s, [public opinion] was generally liberal on questions of government spending and conservation of natural resources and generally conservative on questions of taxation and regulation of morals. In Switzerland in the same period . . . referendums have approved both liberal measures ([for example] compulsory unemployment insurance, wage and price controls) and conservative measures ([for example] mandatory balanced federal budgets); and they have also defeated both liberal measures (free abortion, higher taxes on upper incomes)

and conservative measures (reducing the number of resident foreigners, reducing the tax system's progressivity).

Such evidence inclines us to believe that partisans of either left or right would be well advised to examine carefully and in advance the state of public opinion on the issues that most concern them before they embrace the referendum as the sure pathway to the policies they want. We also believe that such considerations explain why in most polities adherents of both left and right are found among both the advocates and opponents of holding referendums.

That applies to this conference as well.

ANTHONY KING: In returning to the important and interesting points raised by David Marquand and George Cunningham on the referendum in this country in 1975, we were assured by many of the people who wanted us to vote yes that, whatever else we were doing, we were not entering a supranational community. We were told again and again by all sorts of people on the pro-European side that we were voting to enter a Common Market in which the British government would have a veto on most everything more or less in perpetuity. Now we are told, with some pleasure by David Marquand and with some anguish by George Cunningham, that the world is not like that. That comes as no great surprise to many of us; there is either taking place a gradual evolution toward a generally more supranational Europe or, on the contrary, an evolution by stealth; in any event, the process is going on. It is difficult to see how a referendum could be fitted into this kind of continuing, higgledy-piggledy, slow, evolutionary process. Let us suppose that I were a British Gaullist, let us suppose that I did not mind the Common Market but I did not want it to become a supranational government, and let us suppose that I believed I had been misled back in 1975. The practical question is, What is a crucial turning point, or moment, at which one could try, if at all possible, to decelerate it? I am rather Marquandite on this issue, I actually rather like the process; I rather hope that George Cunningham and people who agree with him do not find a way of doing this. It seems to be a reasonable thing for them to want to try to do. The question is, Is it possible, and, if so, how?

ROBIN DAY: I was working this out when trying to decide how to fill in my ballot, and I filled it in yes mainly on the ground that we must have referendum at some stage on progress toward European unity and federation. The question is, What is the practical test of this? Any major move toward either political or economic union to which we are not already wholly committed by the treaty should be put to a referendum in the United Kingdom. This should occur, for instance, if greater powers are to be given to the European Parliament. Another instance would be a supranational, if not a federal, state.

RONALD BUTT: There could be a general election.

ROBIN DAY: A general election raises all sorts of problems, and we all know what they are. First, the single-issue general election is difficult to have and it is difficult to remember one since 1909 on the House of Lords. Second, Prime Minister Heath tried it and look what happened to him. Third, suppose one had something on the powers of the European Parliament and one wanted to test the people's opinion. It might be totally impossible for one reason or another to have a general election at that particular time because it might not suit the government that there was a crisis in Northern Ireland or something. It is an interesting point but easily destroyed.

In case of a move to a stronger European Parliament, would Enoch Powell's dislike of referendums be overcome by his dislike of the EEC and would he welcome such a referendum on such a development? Would Peter Shore regard that as one of the cases where the sovereignty of the people should be made effective through a referendum?

PETER SHORE: I am profoundly unsympathetic to the idea of referendums. I do not like them at all and therefore do not wish to use them. We are only considering the referendum in this quite exceptional circumstance of Parliament deliberately entering into arrangements to subordinate itself to another legislative authority. This obviously has never appeared on the agenda of British politics before. It is so inconceivable that people like myself have to consider what is in a sense the curious defenselessness of the British constitution and of the British people, namely, that any Parliament can make a decision that actually changes profoundly not only itself but the rights of the British people that are exercised through Parliament. The sovereignty of Parliament is always there and cannot be permanently abandoned. It is just there, and that is the strength of Enoch Powell's position. We cannot challenge that. The question is—What are the conditions under which we should put substantial parts of that sovereignty of Parliament on loan to others?—because that is really what it is, it is on loan and it can always be recalled.

I would add that I think George Cunningham is entirely wrong about the judges. It is instructive to look back in our history at one similar experience. That occurred in our relations to the authorities of the papacy over a large part of the civil law and many other aspects of law in this country in the sixteenth century. Parliament found it possible to abolish all such external jurisdiction in a matter of six years and in three acts of Parliament. It has been done and therefore it can be done again. As for the judges, they have each taken an oath of loyalty to the Crown under pain of instant execution or a period in the Tower. There is no question, no doubt whatever, that the power can be reclaimed, if the will is there to reclaim it.

ROBIN DAY: What is your answer on the point of the referendum? Would you favor a referendum in those circumstances?

PETER SHORE: I am not moving into the question of a referendum. I dealt with the question of whether Parliament can cease to be sovereign, and I am saying no as strongly as I can. About Parliament loaning part of its sovereignty, clearly the question of the referendum depends on the magnitude of what is involved. Is it a significant and major step? If it is, then it seems that one has a duty to one's own people and to all the other people with whom one is entering into these arrangements, as one government follows another, one saying yes, the other saying no, with all the disruptive consequences that flow from that. Only in those circumstances in which a significant delegation of Parliament's rights on loan is about to be made should a referendum be used.

ENOCH POWELL: On every point except one, I agree with what Peter Shore has said. It is a spectacle that foreigners ought to note to hear an ex-Socialist cabinet minister and a high Tory whose high Toryism prevents him from being a Conservative speaking with the same voice and with the same emotion on this subject. I disagree with his view that a loan can be recalled. Most experience is contrary to this proposition. A loan can sometimes be recovered, though the article loaned is not always in the same condition as when it was lent out. Above all, power, a subtle and difficult commodity, is a tricky thing to loan even for a minute; every minute that ticks by when that power is in somebody else's possession diminishes the prospects of recovering it intact. In the last resort, I would not object to a referendum provided it were on the same basis as the last one, namely, that if the answer were yes— or if the answer were what one did not want—our continuing membership, our continuance of the loan, would depend upon the continuing assent of the Crown in Parliament.

ROBIN DAY: In other words, you are prepared to protect parliamentary sovereignty by a referendum that you nonetheless believe undermines parliamentary sovereignty.

ENOCH POWELL: I would not propose it. Even though it were a weapon that had a recoil, I would still try it against the enemy.

7

Referendums and Separatism I

Philip Goodhart

While the recent surge of interest in the holding of referendums on tax reform and balanced budgets seems to have opened a new era in the history of referendums, it is clear that the most important referendums are those that directly affect the sovereignty of countries or regions.

The argument about the desirability of self-determination has gone on intermittently in Western Europe since the days of Erasmus, but the first formal plebiscite affecting sovereignty followed hot on the heels of the French Revolution. The aftermath of that revolution produced outbreaks of sporadic violence in the papal territories of Avignon, which had been ceded to Pope Clement VI more than 400 years before. The revolutionary leaders who controlled the neighboring French departments wished to annex the papal territories; in 1791, the assembly in Paris, by a majority vote, rejected proposals for annexation on the ground that there was not sufficient firm evidence about the real wishes of the local population.

Three commissioners were then dispatched by the assembly to try to restore order and conduct a formal poll. The electoral machinery was crude. All males over the age of twenty-five who were not in domestic service and who paid taxes worth 10 pence or more a year were allowed to take part. An announcement that the poll was due to take place was usually given by the town crier one day before the election meeting, which was normally held in the commune's largest church. After a short speech, the presiding officer, who was usually the local mayor, put the question to the meeting in his own words: Those who wanted union with France should stay in the church, while those who wanted to continue with papal rule should go into the chapel, or vice versa.

Of the ninety-eight separate communes, fifty-two voted for France and nineteen for the pope. Of the remaining twenty-seven communes, ten refused to vote at all; seventeen said they had voted for France at earlier meetings and refused to meet again because of the pressure of work at harvest time. The population of the fifty-two communes voting for France was twice the size of all the other communes put together. There were arguments about intimidation; after an angry debate, the

French assembly passed a law of union absorbing the Avignon communes on September 14, 1791. The result of the first modern exercise in self-determination by referendum was implemented.

In the next few months, there were further crude plebiscites on sovereignty in Savoy, Nice, and Geneva. It was in Italy that self-determination referendums had their finest hour. In 1848, 561,000 of 661,000 qualified voters in Lombardy voted for immediate union with the kingdom of Sardinia; in 1870, 68,466 Romans voted for inclusion in modern Italy. Between these two polls, referendums were held in Tuscany, Emilia, Sicily, Naples, Umbria, and Venetia. It is fair to say that the modern state of Italy was built by a series of referendums in which overwhelming majorities turned out to vote for the unification of their country. The process was directed by the Italian statesman, the Conte di Cavour, who claimed that "the Dukes, the Archdukes and the Grand Dukes have been buried under the pile of ballots deposited in the electoral urns of Tuscany and Emilia."

Referendums and Separatist Movements

Today, over a century after Cavour and his colleagues completed the building of modern Italy through the use of plebiscites, the referendum device clearly has a role to play in controlling and containing the swarm of separatist movements that affect so many of the most advanced industrial and democratic nation-states. In some countries, notably Canada, the demand for a referendum has been a weapon brandished by the separatists. In most other democratic countries afflicted with vociferous separatist movements, however, the call for a referendum has generally come from those who are most anxious to preserve the unity of their country. This certainly has been true in the United Kingdom.

In the years leading up to the First World War, the arguments about Irish home rule led directly to the first demands for constitutional referendums in the United Kingdom. At Westminster, as Liberal governments became increasingly committed to implementing home rule, the Conservative opposition could argue that a major constitutional change was being pushed through a reluctant Parliament because the Liberal cabinet of the day needed the continuing support of Irish nationalist members. Sixty-five years later, critics on both sides of the House could also point out that the Labour government's enthusiasm for pressing ahead with devolution legislation in Scotland and Wales increased in direct proportion to its dependence on the votes of the nationalist members. It was not surprising, therefore, to find Arthur Balfour, then leader of the Conservative party, formally proposing in 1911 that any bill establishing a national parliament, assembly, or national council with legislative powers in Ireland, Scotland, England, or Wales should not be presented to the monarch or receive the royal assent until it had been submitted to a poll of the voters and approved at such a poll.

It is, after all, only natural that any politician anxious to preserve the unity of his country should wish to provide unusual opportunities for both consultation and second thoughts before finally putting any separatist legislation onto the statute book. In theory and in practice, it is difficult for any separatist leader to argue the case against a special referendum for any length of time. The whole case in favor of any system of devolution generally depends upon the presumed desire of the people concerned to achieve an increased measure of home rule. Nor is it easy for separatists to resist a referendum on the ground that such a poll infringes parliamentary sovereignty.

While everyone may be forced to agree that the wishes of the people should be consulted, there is room for protracted and often violent argument about *which* people should be consulted. Are the Bretons the only people who should be asked about the future of Brittany? Should the Scots be the only people to have a direct voice in shaping the constitution of Scotland?

Limiting the Electorate

Advocates of home rule, autonomy, or devolution have always sought to limit the size of the electorate within the region concerned. The size of the electorate can clearly be a matter of life or death: The argument about whether self-determination in Northern Ireland should be settled on a six-county or a thirty-two-county basis has cost nearly 2,000 lives in the last ten years.

In practice, those who wish to check the spread of local home-rule movements seem in recent years largely to have abandoned the argument for a nationwide constitutency in return for provisions requiring a certain minimum proportion of yes votes in the area concerned. Clearly, the 40 percent amendment to the Scottish devolution bill, which was introduced by George Cunningham and which required a yes vote from at least 40 percent of the registered voters in Scotland, dramatically altered the whole shape of the referendum contest in Scotland and Wales in 1979. Particularly after the result in Scotland, it will be more difficult to argue against the use of the 40 percent barrier in any future devolution referendum. If the final word is to be left with the people of a particular province or region, it is perfectly sensible to argue that the inhabitants of that area should be required to show active interest rather than passive acquiescence.

There is little to be said, however, for changing the rules late in the game. Home-rule movements and home-rule legislation inevitably provoke feelings of alienation and ill will. It is important, in order to minimize the inevitable residual sense of bitterness—after all, few separations or divorces are really amicable—that everyone should know beforehand exactly what hurdles have to be jumped by the separatists, and exactly how high those hurdles will be. It is perfectly possible that some future British government will turn its hand once again to drafting and presenting a devolution bill. It would be as well to try to achieve some form of consensus now, when emotional fires are banked, on the general desirability of including a 40 percent hurdle in any future referendum on a measure for home rule.

In recent years, the wing of Northern Ireland's Social Democratic and Labour party, which believes in severing the link with Great Britain in favor of union with the Irish Republic, has strengthened its position against those members of the SDLP who are more interested in power sharing. If it is becoming increasingly clear that the 40 percent hurdle will be part of any future home-rule referendum, it is plain that the hurdle involved in any legislation leading directly or indirectly to full independence should contain even higher hurdles. As a decision in favor of outright separation would have direct effects on all the citizens of the United Kingdom, it is plain that there would be an overwhelming case for consulting voters throughout the kingdom. Here the case is strongest for using the referendum as a safety belt to ensure that parts of the country do not casually drift away. If it is right to argue that the hurdle for home rule should be a yes vote by 40 percent of those on the electoral register, then it must be right to say that at least 50 percent of all those on the register in the region where independence is sought must give positive approval before an independence bill is put into effect.

A Second Vote

The same hurdle need not be applied in all parts of the country during a nationwide referendum. If a majority of those on the electoral roll in Scotland, let us say, were to vote in favor of independence, and a simple majority of voters in Northern Ireland, Wales, and England also voted yes, there would be little point in imposing further delay. If a majority of the voters in Northern Ireland, Wales, and England voted against independence for Scotland, however, while a clear majority of those on the electoral roll in Scotland voted in favor, there would be a strong case for providing time for second thoughts. In such circumstances, it is arguable that it would be right to hold a further poll in Scotland alone, where the 50 percent hurdle would still apply. If a majority of the Scottish people voted twice for full independence—with a reasonable time

141

gap between the polls—it would be difficult for the British electorate to restrain them. The integrity of the United Kingdom, or any other democratic state, is worth the effort and expense of holding two, or even three, tests of public opinion.

As far as the United Kingdom is concerned, all that is plainly far in the future. Some students of the Northern Ireland political and demographic scene believe that if present trends continue there could be a natural majority in favor of breaking the link with the rest of the United Kingdom toward the end of the first quarter of the twenty-first century. That is still a long way away, but it should be made plain now, when the prospect of change is remote, that no alteration in the status of Northern Ireland, or any other part of the United Kingdom, could be contemplated until an absolute majority of those entitled to vote had positively recorded their wish for a change.

Again, it is plain that the constitutional machinery involved should be outlined well in advance of any crises, so that orderly procedures come to be accepted by those most actively concerned. The promise of a well-conducted referendum cannot defuse the heat, the passion, and the threats of violence, which are inevitably associated with independence movements, any more than sensible laws can eliminate quarrels in unhappy families. The referendum, far more than an ordinary general election, ensures that both a safety valve and a safety strap are at hand.

NOTE: The discussion at the end of the next chapter covers chapters 7 and 8.

8

Referendums and Separatism II

Vernon Bogdanor

But democracies are quite paralysed by the plea of Nationality. There is no more effective way of attacking them than by admitting the right of the majority to govern, but denying that the majority so entitled is the particular majority which claims the right. [Sir Henry Maine, Popular Government, 5th ed., 1897]

Where there is conflict over the allegiance of a territory, or over the proper boundaries of a state, a referendum or plebiscite (the terms are used interchangeably in this essay) is frequently seen as the best means of resolving the dispute. Indeed, it may seem to be the only method through which the irreconcilable creed of nationalism can be rendered compatible with popular government. Until 1914, large, dynastic, multinational empires could be held together through the authority of the emperor, so that the boundary of the state was determined by the extent of his power. The forces of democracy and nationalism destroyed imperial authority, and the will of the people seemed to be the only force capable of holding the state together. It was for this reason that the plebiscite was invoked after World War I by the victorious Allies, seeking to create new states based upon the principle of self-determination. More recently, with the growth of ethnic nationalism, the referendum or plebiscite is again coming to be used as a weapon aimed at defusing national animosities. How effective a weapon is it?

We can seek an answer to this question by examining first the use of the plebiscite to resolve territorial conflicts after World War I, then by looking at the problems posed for the United Kingdom by the conflict in Northern Ireland and considering whether the referendum offers a means of resolving them, and finally by examining the use of the referendum in the recent debates over devolution to Scotland and Wales. It will be shown that the referendum can indeed be of value in resolv-

NOTE: I would like to thank Dr. R. A. C. Parker of The Queen's College, Oxford, Dr. Peter Pulzer of Christ Church, Oxford, and Mr. P. M. Williams of Nuffield College, Oxford, for their helpful comments on an earlier draft of this paper.

ing territorial disputes in certain clearly circumscribed situations, but it cannot provide the will to agreement where none exists. It can articulate a submerged consensus but cannot create one. The referendum, therefore, is an instrument of limited value, but within these limits it can be politically indispensable.

Referendums after World War I

Their victory in the First World War gave the Allies an excellent opportunity to use the plebiscite to arbitrate between the territorial claims of the Central Powers—Germany and Austria-Hungary—and the subject nationalities of these disintegrating empires. To this end, the Allies arranged for eight plebiscites to be held under League of Nations auspices in 1920 and 1921. Two of these plebiscites—those in Schleswig and in Upper Silesia—raised problems of a kind that were to become familiar in later years.

Schleswig, a province lying between Germany and Denmark, was annexed by Prussia in 1867 and absorbed into Bismarck's Reich. By 1920, it still had an overall majority of Danes, but there was a German majority in the southern zone. Germany, in accepting the Allies' proposal for a plebiscite, asked that the vote be taken in communes, and only in those communes containing "more than 50 per cent of Danes in unbroken territorial integrity," thus minimizing German losses.[1] The Danes, on the other hand, asked for a plebiscite in the north as a whole, but commune by commune in the southern zone. Faced with this response, many Germans living in Schleswig then indicated that they would prefer arrangements under which the *whole* of Schleswig would return to Denmark, thus preserving the unity of the province and with it the possibility that the German population of Schleswig might at some future date start a separatist movement that would recover the province for Germany.

The Allies decided to divide Schleswig into two zones, a northern and a southern zone, and to take the vote in each zone as a whole. North Schleswig opted by a predictably large majority—75.4 percent—for union with Denmark, while South Schleswig to the surprise of many, chose by a larger majority—80.2 percent—to remain part of Germany. This result was accepted amicably by both sides, and the new frontier between Denmark and Germany was not a matter of contention during the interwar period.

Upper Silesia was a far more contentious territory, however, and the conflicting claims of Germany and Poland were exacerbated both by

---

[1] Sarah Wambaugh, *Plebiscites since the World War* (Washington, D.C.: Carnegie Endowment for International Peace, 1933).

the economic importance of the region and by a deep-seated and emotional hostility between the two nationalities. After considerable disagreement at Versailles and a number of violent disturbances in the region itself, a plebiscite was held, commune by commune. A majority of the communes, although not an overwhelming one, declared for Germany; in all, 59.6 percent of the voters declared for Germany and 40.4 percent for Poland. It was decided, however, that Upper Silesia should not remain as a whole with Germany but should be partitioned, the line of partition being drawn so as to coincide as far as possible with ethnographic divisions and so as to take into account economic factors, with roughly 60 percent going to Germany and 40 percent to Poland.

Plebiscites were not held, however, in all the areas ceded by Germany after World War I. Indeed, the Allies came to a decision that there were certain territories where plebiscites ought *not* to be held. The German government demanded a plebiscite in Alsace-Lorraine, "which the conscience of France rejects as an outrage against truth and a challenge to justice," because for Frenchmen it was an indissoluble part of France that had been stolen by Bismarck in 1871.[2] Furthermore, according to the French government, more than half a million Frenchmen had emigrated from the area since 1871; during the First World War, Germany had colonized it and deported French citizens. The Allies accepted these arguments and refused a plebiscite.

In other territories, a plebiscite was deemed inappropriate because it would call into question areas of strategic or economic importance to new states such as Poland and Czechoslovakia. A plebiscite was refused in Danzig so that Poland could be assured of an outlet to the sea. The Austrian request for a plebiscite in the German parts of Bohemia and Moravia was rejected since the Czechs claimed that these areas were part of the "historic Czech lands," a claim based upon "the arguments of historic right and geographic unity," and the need to make the new state viable.[3] It is significant that it was precisely those territories in which plebiscites were refused (with the exception of Alsace-Lorraine)—Danzig, the Polish corridor, and the Sudetenland—that were the subject of revisionist claims by the Nazis in the 1930s.

On the other hand, the frontiers that were fixed by plebiscite could not easily be undermined. In the case of Schleswig, "the plebiscite was so fair and excellently administered that the Schleswig Question, which caused three wars in the nineteenth century and rent the councils of Europe for some seventy years, has ceased to exist."[4] Admittedly, many

---

[2] André Tardieu, *The Truth about the Treaty* (London: Hodder & Stoughton, 1921), p. 238.

[3] Wambaugh, *Plebiscites*, p. 23.

[4] Ibid., p. 98.

Germans refused to accept her eastern frontiers as more than temporary; some believed, indeed, that the wishes of a minority of Germans were more important than that of the Polish majority. Even before Hitler, German leaders such as Stresemann and Schacht laid claim to the whole of Upper Silesia. There was no shared desire for a settlement; the Upper Silesian plebiscite could not *settle* the issue. On the other hand, the fact that a plebiscite had been held made it far more difficult for German politicians to use Upper Silesia as a "grievance" in front of world opinion; even where a plebiscite cannot settle an issue, it can *defuse* it by isolating extremists. Although the Upper Silesian plebiscite did not produce an agreed and lasting settlement, it served to weaken German claims to the whole territory in the eyes of liberal opinion elsewhere.

It would have been difficult, therefore, for Germany to have appealed to liberal opinion in other countries for the return of the Polish portion of Upper Silesia, as she did in 1938 over the Sudetenland. Perhaps, therefore, if the Allies had insisted upon plebiscites in the German-speaking areas of Poland and Czechoslovakia, the Nazis would have found it more difficult to secure their foreign policy successes.

Issues in Plebiscites: The Case of Ireland

The plebiscites held at the end of World War I were not without their problems. In particular, they showed how difficult it is to answer the question, What should be the size and delimitation of the territory to be consulted in the referendum? In the case of Schleswig, a different result would be obtained according to whether it was treated as a whole, divided into two, or divided on a commune-by-commune basis. How far should strategic or economic requirements or considerations of viability be allowed to weigh against the principle of self-determination? Difficult judgments need to be made if these questions are to be answered satisfactorily. They are judgments involving a balance between different principles; they cannot be answered on the basis of the principle of self-determination alone. They therefore contain great potential for conflict.

Similar issues arise, of course, in considering the claims of contemporary separatist movements. If Quebec has a moral right to declare its independence from the rest of Canada, do the English-speaking residents of Quebec have the right to form an enclave declaring allegiance to Ontario? If Scotland has the right to separate from the rest of the United Kingdom, do the Orkney and Shetland Islands have the right to separate from Scotland? In the 1975 referendum on whether the United Kingdom should remain in the European Economic Com-

146

munity (EEC), should Scotland have been granted the right to decide her future independently from the rest of the United Kingdom? Considerable embarrassment would in fact have been caused if Scotland had voted for withdrawal while the rest of the United Kingdom voted to stay in.

These questions are of importance since the decision to hold a referendum on separation of a part of the state implies that only that part has the right to determine its future, irrespective of the wishes of the rest of the country: a right that has been granted to Northern Ireland, and possibly to Scotland and Wales also (in the sense that a British government would probably not stand in the way of a majority demand for independence in Scotland or Wales) but not, for example, to Cornwall or the Isle of Wight. Some nations have refused, of course, to accept that any part of their territory has the right to determine its future on its own. That was the attitude taken by Abraham Lincoln to the Confederacy and by General Yakubu Gowon towards Biafra.

In the modern world, Ireland poses the most difficult of the problems concerning the proper delimitation of the area that is entitled to self-determination, because there is no way of satisfying the conflicting national claims of Catholics and Protestants. In the nineteenth century, Unionists opposed home rule because they feared that under any system of devolution of power, minority interests would suffer—whether Anglo-Irish landowners and Northern Protestants in a united Ireland or Northern Catholics in a partitioned Ireland. According to Lord Salisbury, "Out of every five persons in Ireland three are anxious for measures which are inconsistent with the rights of the other two. The only hope of reconciling the just claims of both parties is to merge them in a larger whole, in which they will be controlled by a greater number who are strangers to the passions of both parties."[5]

Ireland was partitioned in 1920; Northern Ireland was created by carving out of Ireland six counties of the historic province of Ulster. Its boundaries had no particular ethnographic rationale; they were drawn so as to ensure that the new unit was large enough to be viable but small enough to retain a large Protestant majority determined not to be coerced into joining the newly created state in southern Ireland.

In 1948, Ireland became an independent republic outside the commonwealth, and section 1 (2) of the 1949 Ireland Act, recognizing Ireland's republican status, affirmed that Northern Ireland would not cease to be a part of the United Kingdom without the consent of the parliament of Northern Ireland (Stormont). Northern Ireland thus became the only part of the United Kingdom whose allegiance was conditional

---

[5] Lord Salisbury to H. Smith, August 12, 1893 (Salisbury MSS, Christ Church, Oxford).

upon the will of its population as interpreted by its parliamentary representatives, a situation reflected perhaps in the official title of the British state, the United Kingdom of Great Britain *and* Northern Ireland.

With the dissolution of Stormont in 1972, the British government had to find some alternative means of ascertaining the will of the people of Northern Ireland; Edward Heath as prime minister promised that "a system of regular plebiscites" would be held for that purpose.[6] Only one plebiscite has so far been held in Northern Ireland—the border poll of 1973—and the debate in the House of Commons on the border poll bill on November 21, 1972, showed the limitations of the referendum in so complex a situation.

Should the voting in the poll be on a province-wide basis, or should it be on a county-by-county or even district-by-district basis? The government favored the first alternative, which would probably show a majority, on the order of 2 to 1 for remaining in the United Kingdom. Paul Rose, a Labour backbench supporter of Irish unity, moved an amendment calling for the count to be made county-by-county. This would show that two counties—Fermanagh and Tyrone—had Catholic majorities; it would constitute a prima facie case for ceding these counties to the republic.

In support of his amendment, Rose could argue that Northern Ireland had been carved out of Ireland without regard to the homogeneity of its population or to the history of Ulster as a unit; he could also claim that in the 1920 Government of Ireland Act Northern Ireland was defined not as a unity, but in terms of the six counties. Why then should it not poll on a county-by-county basis?

To both the Conservative and Labour front benches, however, the repartition of Ireland was anathema, a solution that might well lead to the collapse of Northern Ireland as an entity separate from the republic. If repartition were not contemplated, the result of a poll on a county-by-county basis would offer a peculiar signal to the voters of Fermanagh and Tyrone. If they voted against the link with the United Kingdom, they nevertheless would be in receipt of a message from the British government that they had to remain with Northern Ireland whatever their wishes. The government therefore rejected the Rose amendment, but this meant that a voter who wished to see Northern Ireland continue to exist, but as a four-county, rather than a six-county, unit, had no way of expressing that view in the border poll.

The Irish Republic refused to accept the validity of a referendum held in a single part of Ireland. To the government of the republic as to liberal home rulers such as Gladstone and Asquith, Ireland was one

---

[6] House of Commons, vol. 833, col. 1862, March 24, 1972.

nation, not two, and Northern Ireland was as indissoluble a part of the national territory of Ireland as Alsace-Lorraine was of France. The opponents of the border poll claimed that it was a propaganda exercise designed to convince other countries that Britain was not holding down the population of Northern Ireland by force. It was hardly needed in order to discover the opinion of the majority in Northern Ireland; as long as the majority was Protestant, it would be inconceivable that the province would opt to join the republic. In fact, the result of the poll was predetermined by the way in which the boundary was drawn between the north and the south in 1920. In these circumstances, a referendum cannot do much to unite a fundamentally divided society that must be governed "without consensus."[7]

Wording the Proposition in Separatist Referendums

Political choices in the modern world are not as simple as they once were; the choice facing ethnic nationalists today is rarely the either/or of independence or submission to a central authority. Indeed, the meaning of independence must be severely qualified in a world in which multinational corporations, intergovernmental organizations, and demands of economic interdependence are taken into account. The EEC in particular fundamentally alters the context within which nationalist movements in Western Europe operate, for the independence of a territory within the EEC is a very different matter from independence outside it. If the process of European integration were to continue with functions at present exercised by ministers in London, Paris, et cetera, being transferred to Brussels, ethnic nationalism might come to be seen as offering a necessary balance to remote government from Brussels.

Economic interdependence imposes clear limitations upon the degree of autonomy that an independent country can enjoy. An independent Scotland or Quebec, for example, that retained economic links with England or English Canada respectively, would be in a far better position to safeguard its economic future than an independent Scotland or Quebec that did not retain such links. In the case of Scotland, any appraisal of the possibilities of independence would have to include an analysis of Scotland's likely share of North Sea oil; in the case of Quebec, the reaction of the oil-rich province of Alberta would be as important as that of the federal government in Ottawa.

Solutions to such problems, if they emerged at all, would be likely to do so only as a result of long, complex, and probably tortuous nego-

---

[7] This is the title of an influential book on Northern Ireland by Richard Rose: *Governing without Consensus: An Irish Perspective* (Boston: Beacon Press, Inc., 1971).

tiations. Can a referendum that demands a blunt yes or no answer embrace the ramifications and subtleties involved in the modification of traditional constitutional ties? Is it not all too easy for the result of a referendum to be misused by one side or the other in the negotiations that follow?

In Quebec, the separatist Parti Québécois (PQ) came to power in 1976, promising a referendum before any declaration of independence. This enabled it to win the votes of those opposed to the previous Liberal regime in Quebec but opposed also to independence. Fearing massive defeat, however, in a vote on independence, the PQ opted for a gradualist approach through the idea of sovereignty association. The referendum held in 1980 asked only that the Quebec government be given a mandate to enter negotiations on sovereignty association with the federal government.

Sovereignty association is hardly a concept familiar to political scientists, let alone to the educated layman. Its implication is that Quebec be given full sovereignty over its own affairs, while retaining economic links—association—with the rest of Canada. What can full sovereignty mean in such circumstances? Must it not imply some restrictions upon the economic policy that a Quebec government might otherwise wish to pursue? What restrictions would it need to accept if it were to enjoy the benefits of association with the rest of Canada? Upon what terms would the association be negotiated? If the Parti Québécois believed that it need not restrict the economic autonomy of a sovereign Quebec, while requiring concessions from the rest of Canada, was it not in the position of a man who, having divorced his wife, asks her to become his mistress?

It seemed that 38 percent of those Quebeckers who had heard of the coming referendum were unable to define sovereignty association. Nearly one-third of those questioned in an opinion poll conducted by the Toronto *Globe and Mail* believed that under a regime of sovereignty association Quebec would continue to send MPs to Ottawa.[8] Indeed Morin, minister for intergovernmental affairs in the Quebec government, claimed that the referendum was merely a *bargaining* tactic to force English Canada to negotiate a new constitution and thus "renew federalism."[9]

Prior to the 1980 referendum, there were at least five constitutional options facing Quebec—the status quo, a special status for Quebec within the Canadian confederation, "renewed federalism" (although this might turn out to mean the same as special status), sovereignty

---

[8] Toronto *Globe and Mail*, March 26, 1979.

[9] Ibid., March 14, 1979.

association, and complete independence. It is not to be expected, of course, that these complicated constitutional options will have more than a shadowy existence in the public mind. It would have been difficult to know what interpretation to put upon a yes answer to the question asking for a mandate to negotiate sovereignty association. Among Anglophones in Quebec, 64 percent said that they were opposed to sovereignty association, but this percentage fell to 49 percent when sovereignty association was interpreted to mean the retention of links with English Canada.[10] In a speech in October 1978, Claude Ryan, the leader of the Liberal party in Quebec, called Lévesque's proposed referendum a deception. Sovereignty association depends upon the willingness of other provinces to form an economic union with a sovereign Quebec. Since several of the provinces of English Canada had already rejected such a proposal, a sovereign Quebec must reach an economic agreement with the rest of Canada on a completely new basis, with no guarantee that the rest of Canada would accept Quebec's proposal. The only choice remaining would be continued membership of the federation or independence. In the event, however, the PQ was denied its mandate since the referendum resulted in a clear victory by the noes.

The Border Poll

Similar complaints were made that the two questions asked in the Northern Ireland border poll—"Do you want Northern Ireland to remain a part of the United Kingdom?" and "Do you want Northern Ireland to be joined with the Irish Republic outside the United Kingdom?"—were by no means exclusive of the possibilities, even if the option of independence for Northern Ireland was ruled out. When the border poll bill was debated in the House of Commons, Merlyn Rees, the shadow Northern Ireland secretary, requested that a third question should be asked: "Do you want eventually to live in a united Ireland brought about by free consent of the peoples of Northern Ireland and of the Republic of Ireland?"[11] It was the aim of the leading opposition party in Northern Ireland—the Social Democratic and Labour party (SDLP)—to secure a united Ireland through such free consent, but it was prepared meanwhile to accept the constitutional status quo. The SDLP, therefore, might be able to answer yes to both of the questions— yes to membership of the United Kingdom in the short term, but yes also to membership of the Irish Republic in the long term. The Alliance party, a small nonsectarian party attempting to bridge the gap between

---

[10] William P. Irvine in the Montreal *Star*, May 15, 1979.

[11] House of Commons, vol. 846, col. 1100, November 21, 1972.

Protestants and Catholics, was also subjected to embarrassment since in its view the poll would polarize its supporters rather than unite them; it faced the dilemma of advising its supporters how to vote.

In the view of the Alliance party, it was "meaningless to ask people to vote for the link with Britain without making clear the terms under which the link is acceptable to the House."[12] Prime Minister Heath had recently hinted in a speech in Belfast that the rest of the United Kingdom would continue to support Northern Ireland only if two conditions were met: that there were safeguards and an assurance of greater political influence for the minority and that, within the context of the EEC, the majority in Northern Ireland would accept that it would be unrealistic to seek to prevent the growth of closer links between Northern Ireland and the rest of the EEC, including the Irish Republic; that is, the "Irish dimension" to the Northern Ireland problem would have to be recognized.

If Northern Ireland's membership in the United Kingdom were to depend upon her acceptance of these conditions, then some members of the minority community who would otherwise favor a united Ireland, might well be prepared to support the link with Britain. If, on the other hand, a restoration of Stormont, or any other constitutional device placing greater power in the hands of the majority Unionists, were in the offing, members of the minority community would be that much less likely to opt for continued membership in the United Kingdom. Were the terms under which Northern Ireland was to remain part of the United Kingdom those set out by Mr. Heath in Belfast, or were they to be those of the majority in Northern Ireland whose Unionist representatives held the balance of power at Westminster for much of the period 1974–1979? The votes of many members of the minority might turn upon the answer to that question. Yet the white paper setting forth the British government's view of Northern Ireland's constitutional future was not published until after the poll, so that the ballots were cast in ignorance of what that future might be.

Moreover, the two questions asked in the Northern Ireland border poll did not include all the options, even when the above qualifications are taken into account. Some might hold that Northern Ireland ought to be governed as a condominium, as proposed by Richie Ryan, a member of the Fine Gael Opposition in the republic, or that a confederation of the British Isles as proposed recently by Garret FitzGerald, the leader of the Fine Gael party, might be an appropriate solution, at least in the long term. Yet clearly the border poll would be an unsuitable instrument for elucidating the degree of detail and subtlety of argument

---

[12] Quoted by Merlyn Rees, ibid.

needed to determine Northern Ireland's constitutional future. In such a situation, the referendum is a very blunt tool indeed.

In any event, the SDLP and the other parties supported by the minority advised their supporters to boycott the poll, since "neither of the two questions posed represented the point of view held by most anti-Unionists in Northern Ireland" (SDLP statement). The poll was therefore "an empty exercise."

The result of the poll was as follows:

- Turnout: 58.6 percent
- For remaining within the United Kingdom: 591,820 (57.4 percent of the electorate)
- For joining with the Irish Republic: 6,463 (63 percent of the electorate).

The poll may have assisted British politicians and diplomats who wished to emphasize to the representatives of other countries that the majority in Northern Ireland genuinely did wish to remain a part of the United Kingdom. It certainly did nothing to "take the border out of politics," nor did it assist the growth of nonsectarian parties in the divided province. Unless the poll is to be held at periodic intervals, it cannot be regarded as settling for all time the constitutional status of Northern Ireland. If it is held periodically, the issue becomes intensified each time the referendum approaches. If there were to be a swing of opinion in the province such that a majority came to favor the link with the republic, it is surely fanciful to argue that a referendum would be required to register it.

The 1979 Referendums on Devolution in Scotland and Wales

When the question at issue is devolution rather than independence or separation, even more complex problems came to the fore. Devolution is, after all, a rather peculiar constitutional category; some would not regard it as a genuine constitutional category at all, lying as it does somewhere along the spectrum between the unitary and the federal state. To most electors, no doubt, the concept is a quite meaningless one. Nor were the actual proposals offered to the people of Scotland and Wales by the Labour government in March 1979 straightforward examples of the genre. In fact, different models were proposed for Scotland and for Wales, Scotland being offered legislative devolution and Wales executive devolution, a subspecies of the genre whose intricacies even the most devoted student of constitutional documents would find difficult to explain. Moreover, both schemes were examples of what has been called a minimalist approach to devolution, in that they conceded as little as possible to the devolved administrations, hedging the transfer of power with a complex collection of central checks, as opposed to a maximalist approach, one that transfers such major powers as the instruments of economic planning and the right to levy taxes.

Polls taken in Scotland since 1974 seemed to show that opinion was divided fairly evenly among a number of different options. Roughly 20 percent favored the status quo and 20 percent favored independence, but the 60 percent who supported devolution were divided between those favoring an assembly indirectly elected via the local authorities, an assembly on the lines proposed by the government, and an assembly of a maximalist kind. As far as Wales was concerned, it seemed from polls taken by BBC Wales on February 8 and 28 (the referendum being on March 1) that an assembly as proposed by the government was less popular than either a legislative assembly of the type proposed for Scotland or complete self-government (although there was a strong majority in Wales against devolution).

It is not surprising, therefore, that there was considerable confusion among the yes and no camps in the referendum campaign. Among the no voters in Scotland were those who rejected constitutional change of any kind, but the official position of the Conservative opposition was that it was opposed to the Scotland Act but not to the principle of devolution itself. The party's spokesman on devolution, Francis Pym, presented "four viable options" to the Scotland Act, ranging from a mild tinkering with the Westminster committee system to full-fledged federalism. After the referendum, however, the high no vote was in fact interpreted as a rejection of devolution in any form.

Among the yes voters, the divisions were even wider. Hardly anybody seemed to want the Scotland Act for itself. The bulk of the Scottish Nationalist party (SNP) saw it as a step to separation, the Liberals as a step to federalism, and enthusiastic devolutionists, such at the late John Mackintosh and Alick Buchanan-Smith, supported it as a step toward the maximalist approach that they favored. Thus, the Yes for Scotland group led by Lord Kilbrandon, which veered toward the SNP, presented a yes vote as a vote for separation, while the Alliance for an Assembly led by Mr. Buchanan-Smith presented a yes vote as a vote against separation.

Amid all this confusion, the no camp held the advantage, since they could attack a specific scheme, admitted by many of its supporters to be flawed and defective, compared to which the status quo must have seemed tolerable even if not positively desirable. Indeed, the no camp held the same advantage in 1979 as the yes camp had enjoyed in the EEC referendum of 1975—they represented the status quo while their opponents had to contend with fear of the unknown.

154

In retrospect, if the Labour government were seriously concerned to secure devolution on the statute book, it might have done better to have held a consultative referendum on the *principle* of devolution before introducing a bill into Parliament. Then, if there were a yes majority, Parliament might have acted as a genuine council of state, devoting its energies to producing the best bill possible, the most suitable means to an agreed end. Instead, MPs opposed to devolution had little incentive to improve the Scotland or Wales bills, for that would only enhance their credibility in the referendum. A consultative referendum admittedly would have been subject to all the disadvantages attached to the Northern Ireland border poll or the 1980 Quebec referendum in that the question would be asked in abstraction from any specific proposals. It might nevertheless have proved a lesser evil than the procedure actually adopted, in that it would have shown whether Scotland or Wales actually favored devolution. If there had been a no vote in a consultative referendum, a good deal of parliamentary time would have been saved.

The Argument for a Second Question

One of the main disadvantages suffered by the yes campaign was its association with the SNP and with separatism, an option that, as we have seen, only one-fifth of the Scottish electorate (at most) supports. It was for this reason that the argument for a second question on independence in the referendum was urged by Labour MPs such as Norman Buchan and by Conservative devolutionists such as Lord Home. The second question would have demarcated the devolutionist position from the policies of the SNP, and if, as seems likely, the vote were no to independence, the SNP "would be given notice that they should not abuse the terms of whatever devolution bill is passed into law" by using the assembly as a staging post to independence.[13]

The government, however, rejected this argument, claiming that the introduction of the second question would give the independence option a credibility that it would otherwise lack and perhaps also because a multi-choice referendum, rather than clarifying matters, would have added to the confusion. This, as we have seen, prevented the case for devolution as a barrier to separation from being effectively presented.

The result of the referendum in Scotland did little to clarify the situation. It was:

- Yes: 1,230,937 (51.6 percent of the vote; 32.85 percent of the electorate)

---

[13] Lord Home, House of Lords, vol. 389, col. 1217.

- No: 1,153,502 (48.4 percent of the vote; 30.78 percent of the electorate)

The yeses, although technically winning the referendum, failed to reach the 40 percent threshold that Parliament had indicated as necessary for the Scotland Act to be implemented. It was generally agreed, even by supporters of devolution, that the majority was too small to justify embarking on so novel a constitutional experiment. For the first time in British politics, it was formally accepted that a special majority was necessary to ensure passage of constitutional legislation, a landmark in our constitutional evolution and one whose consequences may well be wide-ranging.[14]

It is, however, doubtful whether the referendum settled the constitutional issue in Scotland; many believe that the SNP might again threaten the hegemony of the U.K. parties in Scotland. Even in Wales, it has been argued, where the Wales act was rejected by a vote of 4 to 1, the vote did not finally settle the issue.[15] It is always possible for supporters of devolution to argue that a simpler and cleaner bill, or one presented in a different political atmosphere, could have secured majority support. Many devolutionists will continue in their attempt to convert opinion in Scotland and Wales.

Similarly, although there was a 2 to 1 majority for the United Kingdom to remain in the EEC in the 1975 referendum, that did not settle the issue for all time. On the day that the results of the EEC referendum were declared, Tony Benn, a leading antimarketeer, said:

> I have just been in receipt of a very big message from the British people. I read it loud and clear. . . . By an overwhelming majority the British people have voted to stay in and I am sure that everybody would want to accept that. That has been the principle of all of us who advocated the referendum.[16]

Yet five years later, the argument over the EEC continues as it was bound to do; it is perfectly possible to imagine a British government taking Britain out of the EEC following a second referendum. The complexity of the issues and the wide range of constitutional options in the modern world make it far more difficult to secure permanent decisions on questions such as allegiance to the EEC or devolution

---

[14] See Vernon Bogdanor, "The 40 Percent Rule," *Parliamentary Affairs*, Summer 1980.

[15] J. Barry Jones and R. A. Wilford, *The Welsh Veto: The Politics of the Devolution Campaign in Wales* (Glasgow: Studies in Public Policy, University of Strathclyde, 1979).

[16] David Butler and Uwe Kitzinger, *The 1975 Referendum* (London: Macmillan 1976), p. 273.

than to the comparatively more straightforward territorial conflicts after World War I. It is easier in a referendum to answer with some degree of finality the question—"Do you wish to belong to country x or y?"—than it is to evaluate complex constitutional alternatives.

Yet, it would be wrong to dismiss entirely the use of the referendum in dealing with the challenge of separatism. It was far better, surely, that the Wales Act should be rejected by the electorate than defeated in Parliament when the nationalists would have claimed that the voice of the Welsh people was being ignored or alternatively imposed upon Wales by a political elite against the wishes of the majority, which would have considerably increased popular alienation from government. Even in Scotland the inconclusive result did at least show that, contrary to the claims of the SNP, the Scots were hardly straining at the leash for a devolved assembly. It therefore has helped to defuse the issue if it has not settled it.

The Labour government's devolution proposals as originally presented to Parliament made no provision for referendums since, according to Michael Foot, the minister responsible for devolution, the government, through its manifesto commitment, enjoyed a mandate for devolution. It is unlikely, however, that more than a small minority of the electorate were even aware of this manifesto commitment. It is hard to believe that more than a small minority intended their vote to be interpreted as giving a "mandate" for devolution. When the House of Commons forced the government to promise referendums as the price for getting the legislation through Parliament, it was reasserting, therefore, the principle of the popular control of government and downgrading the shadowy committees, whether in transport house or central office, that make policy when their party is in opposition. The result of the referendums showed the absurdity of the mandate theory of government. Far from being an attack upon parliamentary government, therefore, the referendum is a powerful weapon against the oligarchs and wire pullers who create the condition described by Lord Hailsham as "elective dictatorship," the attempt by a government elected by a minority to make "major changes in the constitutional patterns of major institutions" without seeking popular approval for them.[17] The referendum, therefore, makes it possible to ensure that such changes occur only where there is a popular consensus behind them—a significant modification of the adversary pattern of British politics.

We must, of course, accept the argument that the referendum cannot provide a final solution to constitutional problems; it is not as if there is any alternative instrument available that could solve such

[17] Philip Goodhart, House of Commons, vol. 926, col. 382, February 15, 1977.

questions once and for all. As Benjamin Disraeli noticed, there is no finality in politics, and least of all over issues involving the volatile and sensitive emotions aroused by ethnic nationalism. One should not expect, therefore, to discover an instrument which can achieve finality in a democratic state. When that point is understood, then the referendum becomes, to paraphrase Winston Churchill, the worst possible instrument to resolve territorial disputes—except for all the others.

Discussion

AUSTIN RANNEY, *chairman:* The ballots in the Ditchley Park referendum on referendums of October 28, 1979, have been counted and verified. The official results are as follows:

- United Kingdom: Yes, 13; No, 12
- United States: Yes, 2; No, 5
- Stateless: Yes, 2; No, 0
- World Grand Total: Yes, 17; No, 17

This result may not constitute a clear popular mandate, and I doubt that it will appear in the appendix of the second edition of *Referendums*, but the Chair declares that it well and truly reflects the consensus that has emerged from our discussions here.

The next business of this session is concerned with the papers by Philip Goodhart and Vernon Bogdanor on referendums and separatism.

PHILIP GOODHART: For a variety of reasons, there has been a rash of separatist movements affecting the advanced democratic states in the postwar world. In recent years, ethnic separatist terrorists have killed people in Austria, Belgium, Canada, France, Italy, the Republic of Ireland, Spain, the United Kingdom, and the United States of America.

When faced with a separatist movement, it is only natural that any politician who is anxious to preserve the unity of his country should want to provide unusual opportunities for both consultation and second thoughts before putting any legislation dealing with the matter on the statute book. The referendum is quite clearly a device that provides unusual opportunities for consultation and second thoughts, and thus many people, up to and including Peter Shore, who do not really like referendums are willing to concede that the referendum is useful in these circumstances and that a referendum should be used before home rule or other form of independence is conceded to any province or area.

The question then is, Can one devise any form of ground rules

---

NOTE: This discussion covers both chapter 7 and chapter 8.

that are going to help us to carry through these referendums and get the maximum amount of acceptability? Quite clearly, a referendum could end in the breakup of a union between people who have been linked for a thousand years. A referendum on that kind of question is of an entirely different nature from a referendum to decide on whether a bridge should be built in Calhoun County, Georgia, or whether the false teeth of the people of Oregon should be fitted by dentists, or even whether this particular conference is in favor of referendums. Clearly, different rules have to be applied.

This country owes an enormous debt to Tam Dalyell and George Cunningham for the work they did on the Scottish devolution referendum and the efforts that, in Tam Dalyell's words, they made to stop this particular juggernaut. The efforts that George Cunningham made to introduce the 40 percent rule to the Scottish devolution referendum are possibly the most important initiative taken by a backbencher in the House of Commons since the end of the war. George Cunningham himself has admitted that he felt some embarrassment at the way in which this particular hurdle was pulled onto the track at the last moment. It is important, if one believes in the possibility of further devolution problems arising in the United Kingdom, that one should try to get a consensus as early as possible as to what the ground rules should be. Clearly, the 40 percent hurdle that George Cunningham dragged onto the track is the right one as far as devolution itself is concerned. One could argue, however, that when a referendum comes to Northern Ireland, it might not be applicable there, because the question would be one of powers that have been granted in the past and taken away rather than one of establishing an entirely new system.

It is possible that an independence movement will gain ground in parts of the United Kingdom in the years to come. It is right that, at an early stage before the situation reaches a crisis, we should agree on the height of the hurdle that is going to be dragged onto the track. It seems that it would be unthinkable to contemplate independence for any part of the United Kingdom, or indeed independence for any province in any advanced Western country, unless 50 percent of those entitled to vote actually turned up and voted in favor of this drastic step. In other words, one wants to have a high hurdle indeed.

Finally, I would quarrel with Vernon Bogdanor's idea that it would be possible, indeed desirable, to have a consultative referendum on the principle of devolution before introducing a bill into Parliament. It seems that it is impossible really to think of an abstract principle of devolution, and there are an infinite number of models of devolution that one can devise and play with. It seems that any referendum on this should follow the debate in Parliament and the taking of counsel that Enoch Powell refers to rather than preceding it.

JÜRG STEINER: In Switzerland, we recently have had a complicated situation involving the use of the referendum in a separatist situation that might have some lessons for other countries. This was not a question of separation of any part of Switzerland from the confederation, but of the separation of part of the canton of Bern from that canton. Bern is the second largest canton in Switzerland; about 17 percent of its population are French-speaking. Some of the French-speaking people are Catholic and some are Protestant; the area the French-speakers live in is called the Jura.

There was agitation in the Jura, mainly by the French-speaking Catholics, to leave the canton of Bern and form a new canton of their own. A referendum was held in the entire canton on the question of whether this was permissible, and it passed. This is something you have not done in Great Britain; you have not asked the whole of the British people whether there should be a referendum in Scotland or Wales on devolution. Parliament made that decision for them. In the Bern canton, the whole Bernese people voted to allow a referendum to be held among the people of the Jura to see whether they wanted to secede from Bern and form a new canton of their own.

The second referendum was then held in the Jura, and the answer was yes, but just barely; there was a large minority in opposition. The French-speaking Protestants in the three southern districts, unlike the French-speaking Catholics in the three northern districts, wanted to remain in Bern.

Another referendum was held in the three southern districts, and they decided that they would not join the new canton but would remain in Bern. It was even more complicated than that. Each local community at the border between the south and the north was allowed to vote on the question; some decided to stay in Bern and others voted to join the new canton.

On January 1, 1979, a new canton of Jura was established consisting of the three northern districts. That did not end the troubles; in fact, they have become quite serious. There was a dispute over who could vote. Some said that people who have immigrated into Jura from the old canton should not have the right to vote in the Jura referendum; others said that people who had lived in Jura but moved elsewhere should have the right to vote. Some people in the new canton of Jura are saying that they will never accept that the southern districts can remain in Bern.

It is a difficult situation. There was some violence recently; while no one was killed, no one knows where it is going to end. So if one tries to organize a referendum on an issue of separatism and the parties are not in agreement on the ground rules, it can make for an impossible situation.

TAM DALYELL: Vernon Bogdanor said that, in retrospect, if the Labour government were seriously concerned to place devolution on the statute book, it might have done better to have held a consultative referendum on the principle of devolution before introducing a bill into Parliament. Then, if there were a yes majority, Parliament might have acted as a genuine council of state devoting its energies to producing the best possible bill, the most suitable means to an agreed end. At that point, I burst a proverbial blood vessel, because—it is an unpleasant word to use —what Vernon Bogdanor is recommending is at best a pig in a poke and at worst a calculated deception. It is to the credit of the Labour cabinet that, though some of them might have thought that such a ploy would be convenient, on principle they refused to do this and they were right. It is monstrous that it should have even been suggested that one hold a referendum on a vague notion and then somehow, when one has the acceptance of a proposition that two and two make five, one tries to set up a subordinate parliament in part, though only part, of a United Kingdom, which many of us know is impossible. The idea of having referendums on vague propositions so that one can come to the nitty-gritty and the difficulties and the rocks on which one may perish after the event seems absolutely monstrous. In 1974, the question was put forward whether the Scots wanted more say in their own affairs. Who is going to say no to that kind of bland proposition? It was only after five years of the House of Commons educating itself that it became apparent to a great number of my fellow countrymen that the thing was impossible and that the real question was—Do you want the breakup of the British state?—which is a wholly different proposition. With all the violence and vehemence that I can summon, I disagree with Vernon Bogdanor's proposition.

EUGENE LEE: Sometime in the next five to six years, the two congressmen here may well be asked to resolve the status of Puerto Rico. It appears to be national policy, as expressed by the President and by congressional leadership, that "we will support the will of the Puerto Rican people." Our discussions here have been relevant to what we mean by this policy. One question is, How do we define the Puerto Rican people? Are they only the 3 million on the island, or do they also include the 1 million in New York City? What do Congressmen Jones and Foley have to say about that?

JAMES JONES: It all depends on how we develop the whole process of the referendum and see whether that takes hold first. The President would negotiate holding a plebiscite, Congress most likely will go along with that, will adhere to it, and will take the results of it. Congress will not develop any clear set of rules in advance of that.

THOMAS FOLEY: I served for a while on a Puerto Rican status commission. The problems are as complicated in Puerto Rico as they are in Northern Ireland. Every subject, every social grouping, every matter of social convenience is arranged around the status question, and there is a whole series of words that announce which side you are on. To hold a mandatory referendum on this question would be insanity and productive of violence, an impossible situation for the United States to permit. Suppose, for example, that 51 percent of all the eligible voters in Puerto Rico voted for statehood, 40 percent voted for continued commonwealth, and 9 percent voted for independence—*but* the 9 percent and part of the 40 percent were determined to resist by force the imposition of an irrevocable political relationship with the United States. We would be asking for civil war. Whatever the judgment made upon Puerto Rico in a plebiscite has to be reviewed by Congress in the light of the subtle and difficult problems that exist in that area.

The one thing that referendums do not do is measure intensity. They give a general reaction to a situation. The majority may be placid and rather casual about it, while the minority may say, "Never! we will raise an army, we will use violence." Only a political body—a legislative body, a council, or a cabinet—has the capacity to make the judgments of how intensely the various positions are held. Using referendums in some areas of constitutional change is extremely dangerous, unless one considers the precise circumstances.

As for Puerto Rico, if a substantial majority there voted for independence in a referendum, it would clearly be honored by the American Congress; there would be no desire to hold onto Puerto Rico in a relationship which it did not want. The statehood question is a problem in two ways. First, it would shackle Puerto Rico with a political relationship that would be irrevocable. Second, one of the traditional requirements of statehood is that the state have some capacity to support the federal union. Puerto Rico is clearly an economically dependent area that enjoys great privileges. It is allowed to keep for local purposes all the federal taxes raised in Puerto Rico and all the excise taxes on all its products. If New York had that rule, it would be the Garden of Eden.

RICHARD SCAMMON: In questions of devolution, home rule, self-determination, or whatever, the referendum has value but only limited value. Our British friends, for example, will remember the frustration of the original government of Ireland Act caused by the activities of the Currah camp just before World War I. They will also recall that, in the general election of 1918, no referendum was held in Ireland, but the Fenians announced in advance that they would regard this election of members of the Westminster Parliament as, in effect, a referendum on independence for Ireland. Some seventy-five or so Fenian members were returned for Irish constituencies. A referendum is not needed to accomplish this. Most often such questions devolve to the gun in so many parts of the world. Thomas Foley raised the question about the potential for violence in Puerto Rico. What do we do if the vote is 90 to 10 against independence but the independentistas have the bombs?

How does one handle this kind of problem? If one gets to this point, one essentially has destroyed the reality of the consensus. There are real problems that relate to the administration of elections in non-consensus areas. Puerto Rico possibly will become one. Northern Ireland may well be one. Ireland in 1918 was certainly a prime example. The lack of consensus may lead to a political solution to which the referendum may contribute. It is just as likely to lead to the gun, and the decision will be finally dependent upon the will of the people who shoot and bomb. What would have happened in the United States in 1861 if the referendum had been as developed then as it is now?

ENOCH POWELL: What has been said about Puerto Rico is relevant indeed and illuminating in regard to Northern Ireland. It has been said that a referendum cannot give one intensity. There is another thing a referendum cannot do: It cannot debate. Unlike Puerto Rico, Northern Ireland does return at present twelve, and will in the next Parliament return seventeen or eighteen, members to the House of Commons. The constituencies are, and will be, as impartially drawn in Northern Ireland as in any other part of the kingdom, because they are drawn by the same authority. That will provide much more reliable guidance and illumination to those who, in the United Kingdom, have to decide the future of Northern Ireland than the results of any referendum could possibly do. That is because there will be people there, representing the different points of view and roughly numerically proportionate to the different points of view, who will be obliged, in front of those who sit in judgment—the House of Commons, and Parliament as a whole—to explain, to argue, and to deal with specific propositions. The Puerto Rican case has revealed the great advantage that parliamentary representation, even on matters of this sort, can have over the numerical outcome of a referendum.

MALCOLM RUTHERFORD: It seems that we are not discussing the merits of referendums as such but their application to particular cases and issues. It is striking that many of the people around this table who seem to dislike referendums must have been most prominent in grasping at them as a last resort to defend particular ideas. Tam Dalyell argues with such conviction that, had devolution gone through, Scotland would inevitably have broken away from the United Kingdom. It is so difficult to prove that argument that it is scarcely an intellectual argument at all. It might have happened; I would not have minded if it had. It is unclear why an Independent Scotland is wrong. It would come to terms with the rest of the United Kingdom. In any case, one cannot simply accept this certainty that it would have gone, or that, if it had, it would necessarily have been a bad thing.

Equally with sovereignty—why should one be against the diminution of British sovereignty? I am rather in favor of it, but I return to the point that people who are against referendums have embraced them most enthusiastically when it was the last thing that they could do. The questions that we should be talking about might be put like this: Is there some way in which we want to give people a bigger say than they now have in the running of their lives and the environment around them? We are looking for new ways of making a political system more responsive to, or at least more aware of, what people want. A referendum is only one possible way. Peter Shore, for example, has been involved in many forms of quasi-referendums. The widening of the planning appeal, or the appeal against planning permission, the Windscale enquiry, are all examples of giving people a bigger say. We did not proceed that way a few years ago. It seems right and an improvement that we should proceed that way.

Some of us might like to go further. We make a mistake to say that we are confining our discussions to the so-called bigger issues. In the view of persons outside this room, are what we call the bigger issues truly the bigger issues? Somebody was amused about the high turnout in the Oregon referendum on false teeth. Is that such a small issue? It seems that people are actually quite concerned about that. Some people said that the British Labour party has never recovered from its own argument on the subject of how much people should pay for teeth. Equally, the last British government spent five years arguing about devolution and got nowhere. It spent five years arguing about the subject of industrial democracy and got nowhere. We should link these things together. The pursuit of industrial democracy is an attempt to give people a wider say. The fact that we have not yet found a satisfactory solution does not mean that the problem has gone away. Like the problem in Scotland, it will recur. What this means in the end is that we should see referendums simply as one of several ways of improving the political system (I speak mainly of Britain), making politics more human, and giving people a larger say. It has nothing to do with ideology, what are supposed to be left- or right-wing views, nor an artificial division into big or small issues. If we could see referendums in this wider context, we then could move on to establishing ground rules and variants.

HENRY DRUCKER: Philip Goodhart put forward two principles that are entirely reasonable and should be adopted. First, whatever rules we have for referendums will be clear rules well known in advance. Second, on questions of devolution and separatism, we have a high hurdle for acceptance.

However, such rules should not include a 40 percent rule as in the referendum on Scottish devolution. That rule was not an effective way of achieving a high hurdle. It is entirely possible, for example, that one would get 40 percent yes and 38 percent no. That would pass the 40 percent rule, but it would not achieve the purpose of a high hurdle. It would not achieve the purpose of ascertaining that an overwhelming majority of the Scottish people were in favor of devolution. The 40 percent rule was adopted because the people who proposed the bill in the House of Commons were constantly saying that an overwhelming majority of people in Scotland wanted devolution. As George Cunningham quite rightly said, we should find out, but the 40 percent rule is not a good way. One could satisfy the rule and still have 38 percent voting no; that would not be a satisfactory position. The rule may not achieve its purpose. It is not at all clear that it is a democratically acceptable practice to count abstainers in the same way that one counts voters on either side. This is exactly what happened.

TAM DALYELL: What would have happened if 20 percent of the electorate voted yes and 10 percent no? By Henry Drucker's criteria, that would have come to the same yes, but it would not have been evidence of overwhelming demand. It still would not have been passed unless people had accepted that there was overwhelming demand.

HENRY DRUCKER: If it had been 20 to 10, it would have come back to the House of Commons, and it would have been for the House of Commons to decide what was an acceptable result. A vote of 20 to 10 would be more acceptable than one of 40 to 38; it would be a much better indication that the Scottish people want devolution than 40 to 38, which is a very close vote. It would be unsatisfactory to proceed on 40 to 38.

PHILIP GOODHART: As someone who is fundamentally against separatism, I was fascinated by the story put forward by Professor Steiner. It seemed a success story rather than a story of failure. After all, what did one have? One had an endless argument and little balance, no action really of any sort. Perhaps at the end of the day everyone will get tired of it and go home and the status quo will prevail, which is on the whole what I want to happen. The argument can go on endlessly and that seems to be an advantage rather than a defect of this particular system. I agree with Thomas Foley and Enoch Powell that violence may well follow any referendum. Violence can always erupt out of these sorts of discussions. Violence is a little less likely to happen if those who are reaching for their guns are well aware that they are reaching for their guns against a clearly stated majority view against them. This is always a possibility. Violence is less likely if there is a referendum, rather than more likely.

I agree with Enoch Powell that there could be time to discuss all this in Parliament, and Parliament in its wisdom has decreed that there can be border polls at regular intervals. It seems almost certain that in the course of the next few years as a result of parliamentary debate and action there will be another border poll and, after that, another border poll in Northern Ireland. I agree with Henry Drucker that it might be better to find an alternative hurdle; yet this particular hurdle of the 40 percent rule has at least been enshrined in practice. There are precedents for it, and people tend to follow precedents. One could put in an additional hurdle requiring 10 percentage points difference between the yes and the no vote as well, but that would make it that much more difficult for the devolutionists to get their way. Thomas Foley talked about the placid majority. One of the advantages of requiring a certain proportion of turnout is that one knows before embarking on a major constitutional change that at least 40 percent of the people in any region are energetic enough to go to the polls and vote.

AUSTIN RANNEY: We turn now to Vernon Bogdanor's essay.

VERNON BOGDANOR: My essay approaches this question by looking at some of the plebiscites held at the end of the First World War. One conclusion emerges clearly: The referendum device can be an instrument of settlement of a territorial dispute where the parties on each side wish to settle. That was the case with Germany and Denmark over the province of Schleswig. Even with those who did not wish to settle, as in Upper Silesia, the referendum still can serve to defuse an issue.

There is reason to believe that referendum provides an element of legitimacy, and this may help to undermine terrorism. One reason for the strength of the Palestine Liberation Organization and its acceptance by some people in the West is precisely that it is associated not only with terrorism but also with some moral claim to the West Bank—just as Menachem Begin got support in the late 1940s not only because he had a gun but because it was thought that the Jews were entitled to a national home and their claims had been ignored. Even where there is not a will to settle, the referendum can do some good.

What sometimes happens when the will to settle is not there is that the parties disagree about the terms and conditions of the referendum, as Richard Scammon and Jürg Steiner have said. This shows the importance of settling the terms of the referendum in advance of any particular case. Where there is conflict, people will disagree over the significance of the result. One cannot settle all the issues in advance, but there must be some agreement on procedures in advance of particular referendums.

Modern ethnic nationalism, however, is a wholly different phenomenon from what we have been discussing. It poses fundamental problems for the future in Western Europe. Ethnic nationalists represent something wholly different from traditional nationalism, namely, the desire of many people in advanced and impersonal industrial societies to discover identities for themselves. It is difficult to believe that belonging to the United Kingdom means what it did fifty years ago, and the EEC inspires even less allegiance. The rise of ethnic nationalism is a response to the loss of identity felt by so many in industrial societies.

Notions of independence or separatism need to be qualified seriously when looking at the aims of modern nationalist parties. They are not seeking the same aims as nationalist movements in the nineteenth century because they understand that separation and independence are, strictly speaking, meaningless in the modern world. That world is an interdependent world. What does independence or separation mean in such a world? Nationalist parties on the whole have understood this fact of interdependence; the kind of powers that the Scottish Nationalist party and Plaid Cymru seek are compatible with a loose type of confederal arrangement.

How can anyone deny that the referendum in Wales was beneficial? If there had been no referendum and the Labour government had seen the issue as one of confidence affecting its retention of office, the Wales Act would have got through Parliament and an institution would have been set up which the vast majority of people in Wales did not want. The referendum prevented that, and so it was surely a good thing.

Analysis of the Scottish referendum poses much more complex problems. I used to agree with Enoch Powell that it was disgraceful for MPs opposed to devolution in Scotland to vote for the bill and then hope that it would be rejected by the voters in a referendum. It does not now seem so disgraceful, because it would have been perfectly tenable to say, "I'm very unhappy about devolution, but if I can be convinced that people in Scotland really want it and it's the price of keeping the union together, then I'm prepared to support it and therefore I am prepared to have a referendum to test that issue. If Scottish opinion is really overwhelmingly for devolution, I'm prepared to accept it."

Then one comes to the question of whether England should have been asked to vote as well, since devolution undoubtedly would have affected England as well as Scotland and Wales. England had a *right* to vote on the issue, but England's MPs, in the interests of good relations with Scotland, waived that right. They realized that if there had been an English majority against devolution, and a Scottish majority for devolution, it would not have helped to resolve the issue.

The 40 percent rule prevented devolution from being passed by a low majority on a low turnout. A small majority on a high turnout would be acceptable—for instance, 40 percent yes and 38 percent no. Similarly, devolution would have been accepted if there had been a large yes majority even if the turnout were low. What the 40 percent rule did was to stop devolution from being passed by a low majority on a low turnout.

My final point is one suggested by an article in the *Financial Times* by Malcolm Rutherford published after the Scottish referendum. He asked, What does it settle? We had the EEC referendum five years ago with a 2 to 1 majority in favor. The issue is being raised all over again and it is quite conceivable that Britain could withdraw. The referendum cannot settle anything irrevocably, and therefore it has only limited value. But then any political instrument has only limited value, and what better instrument is there for coping with the problems raised by modern separatism? I do not believe that there is one.

ROBIN DAY: The arguments of Mr. Bogdanor and Mr. Goodhart in favor of ground rules before a referendum are dangerous, wrongheaded, and un-British in the extreme. They are un-British because the essence of Britishness is never to decide anything in principle in abstract in advance. Wait until a problem arises, then decide it sensibly, and see what principles can be deduced from that decision: That is the tradition of the common law. We do not want any doctrinaire code of practice imposed on us. It is dangerous and wrongheaded to have a code of ground rules for the conduct of every conceivable referendum, because one is then in a straitjacket. If the circumstances are such as to make the 40 percent rule or some other requirement totally unsuitable to those unforeseeable circumstances, one is then in a position of having to change the rules in the middle of the game; that would look bad. Do not have any rules, and one will not have to change them.

This brings me to the six unwritten words of the constitution. This unwritten constitution of ours may create awful problems and risks, but it does have one great advantage and that is a glorious flexibility, a flexibility to be totally uninhibited by codes or by judges. It is responsive to unforeseeable events. It is swift to act in moments of crisis, such as the outbreak of war or the abdication of a monarch. It is slow to act as in the case of reforming the Second Chamber in 1967 or in the case of devolution, where Parliament dragged its feet beautifully. It is also competent to decide whenever it wishes to have a referendum—whether to have a referendum, when to have a referendum, and how to hold a referendum.

On the point about the unforeseeable circumstances, let us suppose a scenario in which the Common Market collapses under the weight of the common agricultural policy and Mrs. Thatcher is brought down by unrest, led by the general secretary of the Trades Union Congress of the time, perhaps David Lea. A general election is held, Labour wins, Peter Shore becomes prime minister, we come out of the Common Market, and then, to ensure our survival as a nation, the only opportunity open to us is to become the fifty-first state of the United States. Let us suppose that under President Kennedy, Jr., and Vice-President Foley, Prime Minister Shore's government decides to hold a referendum on joining the United States. It would be quite impossible, intolerable, to have the 40 percent rule, because the anti-American terrorists who would then presumably take action would have an inadequate warning of the scale and intensity of popular feeling unless there were an 80 percent hurdle. In such circumstances, therefore, a referendum could measure intensity because only a great intensity of feeling could result in an 80 percent turnout.

AUSTIN RANNEY: Let us remember that it was one of Robin Day's great countrymen, Thomas Hobbes, who said in the seventeenth century that life without rules would be nasty, simple, British, and short.

9
Summing Up:
Referendums for Britain?

Bryan Keith-Lucas

I will endeavor to pull together the main threads of these discussions. Everyone will realize that there are many threads running through this tangled skein. What we have learned in many cases is not what to do but what not to do. We in Britain can distill a certain amount of wisdom from the advice that we have gratefully received from the other side of the Atlantic and from Switzerland.

A question of the greatest concern to the British participants was, Is the concept of a referendum compatible with the British constitution? There are some doubts about whether there is a British constitution. There are some who said, "No, there's no such thing." There are others who said, "Yes, there is, and it is summed up in six words." There are still others who know it as an extremely complicated concept.

The old high Tory view is that the referendum is completely incompatible with the constitution, because we are a parliamentary monarchy, governed by Her Majesty with the advice and consent of the two houses of Parliament. That view had only limited support from the conference as a whole as an entirely satisfactory definition of the situation. There was a less dogmatic but somewhat similar approach supported on the whole by members of Parliament, who saw the referendum as a threat to the status, importance, and independence of the member of Parliament, who brings his judgment and wisdom to the grand assembly of the nation. This too was perhaps a slightly high-flown picture that omitted such things as political parties and whips. The idea was clear, however: Referendums pose some degree of threat to the status of members of Parliament.

The question then was raised as to whether the use of the referendum excludes true debate. It was suggested that the one place where true debate takes place is on the floor of the House of Commons. Would the use of the referendum device, perhaps, not exclude debate but widen the debate from the floor of the House to the nation at large? Here again, the consensus was not to accept the view that referendums kill debate.

Does the referendum undermine the party system? Perhaps it does. Some would ask, Does that matter? Again, we reached no clear decision.

An important point raised was that the referendum, though it can measure numbers, cannot measure intensity of feeling; that is one of its great limitations. On the whole, in looking at it in the light of the constitution, the sense of the meeting was to disagree with the Duke of Wellington's view that the British constitution is so perfect that in no circumstances should anyone ever meddle with it.

Functions of the Referendum

What functions could the referendum perform in Great Britain? Why should we have it? The strongest argument in favor of referendums is the contention that the people of Britain have an inherent right to express their views on public questions, a right that is being more and more vigorously urged in demands for participation of one sort and another. There is the other argument that it can give a degree of authority to a decision of Parliament that Parliament itself cannot give, particularly if that Parliament should happen to be one in which the ruling party does not represent a majority of the electors. The feeling that some higher authority can endorse and legitimize decisions of Parliament is comparatively new, and clearly inconsistent with the high Tory view of the constitution. Other, less praiseworthy, functions were mentioned, such as getting the government off an embarrassing hook, solving a problem on which the cabinet cannot reach an agreement within itself, or taking the wind out of the sails of the other side.

It may be that there are alternatives to the referendum that would serve the same purposes, though not in the same way—petitions perhaps, though there seems to be some disagreement on the significance of petitions. Civil war was suggested as an alternative, but commanded comparatively little support.

Suppose that it is agreed that there are circumstances in which Great Britain could copy the experience of other countries and continue with referendums. Should we have an act of Parliament to declare this? It was suggested from one quarter that this might be part of a new constitutional settlement, linked perhaps with a bill of rights and other fundamental changes in our constitution. This, however, was attacked from another quarter because of the legal complications that would result; it might be a gift to the constitutional lawyers, the casuists, and the sophists. Another point of view was put forward that we do not need an act to make the referendum a part of the British constitution. The British constitution, it was said, consists essentially of precedents, one upon another. We have the three recent referendums as precedents—the EEC, Scotland, and Wales—and one might also perhaps call in aid the precedent of the occasions when general elections have been held on one point, single-issue elections, particularly on the reform act in 1832 and the Parliament act in 1911. That may be debatable, however.

If we assume that referendums have become part of the constitution, whether we wanted it or no, then we have to ask, For what purposes would we use a referendum in this country? Little interest was shown around this table having referendums on moral questions—on abortion, divorce, or homosexuality. They have been used extensively in other countries on such questions, but there was no support around the table for doing so in Britain. Should the referendum be reserved for constitutional issues? These are difficult to define, but yet one understands what the phrase means. This would bring us more or less into line with France, Ireland, Denmark, and a number of other countries, and it seems to command general support here. Of all such constitutional questions, the first and most obvious is separation of a part of the nation's territory.

The surrender of part of the sovereignty of our Parliament obviously is one of the great constitutional issues. Here again, definitions are difficult. We have many different points of view about the impact of changes in the constitution and the practice of the Common Market. Did that constitute a change in our sovereignty, a surrender of part of our sovereignty?

What happens to the voting system? The question of proportional representation was aired on occasion. It was also suggested that one of the great constitutional issues is that of relations between government and the trade unions. Most of us accepted the view that wage settlements certainly should not be a constitutional issue to be settled by referendums, but the basic principles of the status of the trade unions might indeed be a constitutional issue. Would enlargement of the Common Market be a constitutional issue? It was suggested that one can go too far into constitutional niceties that the man in the street would not understand and would greet with ribald bewilderment.

The Referendum as Entrenchment

While we were being told about how the referendum works in California and elsewhere, the picture was one of a wild public demanding all sorts of strange things and being restrained either by the legislature or, more often, by the courts. When we came to look at it in this country, one began to see the referendum device in a different light, as a restraint rather than as an opportunity for initiating change, indeed, as a form of entrenchment of our constitution. We may be the one country that has no entrenchment. When we exported the Westminster model to the African territories, we always entrenched, usually fairly deeply, the essential parts of the constitution. We thereby precipitated a number of entirely unnecessary revolutions, but we ourselves have never had any entrenchment. This could become a burning issue if the Labour party or a part of the Labour party were able to put through proposals for the abolition of the House of Lords. The referendum then could be seen as a form of entrenchment that could, if the people saw fit, reject that change in the constitution. One sees the referendum in that peculiar light as a rather odd form of entrenchment, because we cannot have any other form of entrenchment without a constitution.

If we get to the stage of agreeing that there is a case for the referendum in certain constitutional circumstances that we have not exactly defined but explored, there remain many further questions needing some sort of an answer. How does one frame the questions? Who does it? Is the referendum binding or advisory? Is there to be a hurdle, a 40 percent rule? How does one regulate access to television? Are there limits on expenditures in the campaigns? Who may subscribe to the campaigns? Should there be government subsidies? Should one recognize umbrella organizations? Who may vote?

The experience of the other countries was extraordinarily valuable in showing us how complicated, how difficult these questions are. This prompted some of us to ask whether, having accepted the broad principle, we should not start to lay down some guidelines so that when the next referendum comes we shall have already thought out the answers to some of the questions. Some said that this simply does not make sense, that each referendum should be fitted to its own special problems, that one should not lay down such general guidelines in advance. Others said it would be folly not to try to lay down some guidelines in advance, that we should have some sort of a commission to look at this so that we are ready when the time comes. There was no consensus, but I would like to throw out a suggestion. We should have a look at this problem by a group of people who are interested but who are not official, not appointed by Her Majesty's government. Perhaps the Hansard Society might be willing to go on from this conference to try to pinpoint these problems and see what useful guidance can be given for the future.

Appendix

In October 1979, a conference on referendums was held at Ditchley Park, Oxfordshire, sponsored jointly by the Hansard Society and the American Enterprise Institute. One byproduct of this conference was a suggestion that it would be useful to draw up some guidelines for the conduct of a fair referendum under British conditions.

The Hansard Society therefore sponsored a further meeting, held at Nuffield College, Oxford, in June 1980, to discuss a draft report on the subject. Among those present were:

Kenneth Baker, M.P.	Paul McKee
Vernon Bogdanor	David Magleby
David Butler	David Marquand
George Cunningham, M.P.	Geoffrey Marshall
Tam Dalyell, M.P.	Austin Ranney
Thomas Fuglister	Michael Steed
Philip Goodhart, M.P.	Maxine Vlieland
Richard Holme	Gordon Wasserman
Bryan Keith-Lucas	

The report, prepared and revised by David Butler, is presented here. At all points, it has been shaped by the comments of those who were present at the meeting and of others who were consulted. No one has been asked to endorse every word of what follows, but it does broadly express a collective view.

It should be stressed that the purpose of this report is not to advocate or to oppose the holding of referendums. (That was an issue on which views differed widely among those involved in the discussion.) The aim is simply to explore the problems involved in holding a referendum in such a way as to allow a fair debate and to produce a verdict that, as far as possible, would be accepted as having been arrived at legitimately, with due opportunity for all views to be given a reasonable airing.

Background

Although occasionally discussed since the 1890s, referendums were not tried in Britain at the national or regional level until the 1970s, when four were held in the course of six years. The possibility of using them again is frequently ventilated. It is not a party matter. A Conservative government was responsible for the referendum in Northern Ireland on March 8, 1973; the Liberal party in 1969 had first called for such a referendum; and a Labour government sponsored the referendum on membership in the European Community on June 5, 1975. A back-bench cross-party coalition pushed the provisions in the devolution legislation leading to the Scottish and Welsh referendums on March 1, 1979.

Many statesmen, including a majority of British prime ministers in this century, have at some time endorsed referendums as a way of resolving particular dilemmas. In 1978, the present prime minister approved a party report advocating a wider use of referendums.

This study is concerned with referendums at the national or regional level. It should be noted, however, that local referendums have an extensive history in the United Kingdom. A number of acts give local authorities power to hold polls on issues. The Sunday opening of cinemas and public houses has frequently been voted upon; recently, there have been local polls on development plans and even on the siting of missiles at nearby bases.[1]

Parliament has been prepared to concede sovereignty on certain issues to the people; it acknowledges that there are questions better solved this way than by the normal confrontational democratic machinery. These may be grand constitutional matters "above" the ordinary play of politics or humble issues "below" partisan consideration.

Existing Purposes of Referendums. In world experience, a nationwide referendum is usually held to give legitimacy to a policy on which the government of the day has decided.[2] Its holding is a political act by the government, seeking to reinforce its own authority or to impress opinion abroad and improve its negotiating position. In the majority of cases, the verdict has been affirmative (though there have been some notable exceptions, as in France in 1969 and in Ireland in 1959 and 1968). Sometimes a referendum is held as a matter of constitutional necessity (as in Australia, where it is required for all constitutional amendments).

---

[1] For a survey of British experience in this area, see Philip Goodhart, *Referendum* (London: Tom Stacey, Ltd., 1971).

[2] In these generalizations, Switzerland is excepted. It is entirely a special case among nation states. It provides 300 of the 600 referendums that have ever occurred at nationwide level and these cover a wide range of policy issues. Referendums at the state level in the United States do so also, with a large proportion of referendum issues coming from popular initiatives. For a full list of all nationwide referendums held up to 1978, see David Butler and Austin Ranney, *Referendums* (Washington, D.C.: American Enterprise Institute, 1979).

Occasionally it is a device to enable a government to avoid responsibility for an awkward decision that divides parties. (In Sweden in 1979, all parties agreed to hold a referendum on nuclear development in order to separate the issue from the general election.) It may also be used to ease through the legislature a measure that is unpalatable to a sizable number of the government's supporters (as the Scottish and Welsh referendums of 1979 illustrate). It may be called, too, in the light of evidence from opinion polls or other sources of a strong public demand for a referendum.

Referendums have been invoked as a means of entrenchment. The referendum can be an instrument of veto as well as one of authorization. The legitimacy conferred on a decision by a referendum vote can be a check on political power as well as the source of such power. Each of the four United Kingdom referendums has resulted in a decision against change.

Mandatory or Advisory. Referendums cannot be mandatory or advisory except in the sense that they can be incorporated in legislation or they can merely provide information as a prelude to legislation. It is not possible for a British government or parliament to surrender power formally to the verdict of a referendum since Parliament cannot be disabled from exerting its legal sovereignty at any time.

In practice, referendums may give absolute political verdicts. Mr. Wilson committed his government before the 1975 (advisory) referendum on Europe by saying that a majority of even a single vote would be enough to reject the renegotiation. Parliament declared that the bringing into force of the Scotland and Wales acts of 1979 should in effect depend on whether 40 percent of the electorate voted yes (subject to the secretary of state's interpretation of what constituted 40 percent and Parliament's ultimate endorsement). In short, even if a referendum is not incorporated in legislation, both government and members of Parliament may treat its verdict as mandatory in the sense of being morally and politically binding.

Authority for Referendums. Referendums can be called through the action of the public, of the legislature, or of the government or as the result of some provision in a written constitution. At the moment, Switzerland is the only nation in which referendums have come from popular initiative (though Italy has provision for legislation to be vetoed by popular demand). Denmark is the only nation where a minority in the legislature can insist on a referendum. In several countries, constitutional or territorial amendments are not valid unless endorsed by referendum. In France, Australia, and one or two other countries, there is a provision for a political impasse to be automatically solved in referendum. Most written constitutions contain no reference to referendums, and most countries are in the same position as Britain, which has no written constitution: the calling of referendums is usually left to the government. Except in Switzerland, Italy, and Weimar Germany, almost every referendum taking place at the national level has done so on governmental initiative.

It is unlikely that any British government would open the floodgates to popular initiative, with every substantial pressure group having access to this court of appeal and this opportunity for propaganda. (Opinion poll findings on capital punishment and immigration are often adduced as a warning against referendums.) It is unlikely that any British government would allow a minority in the legislature to insist on a referendum, since this would give to the opposition a wonderful weapon for harassing those in power. Without a written constitution, constitutional amendment as a source of referendums does not formally arise in Britain. (If a written constitution were to be introduced, it might well include a provision for referendums. Even without a written constitution, a declaration or statute that a basic institution or policy should not be changed without a referendum might effectively bind future governments.)[3]

General Considerations

There can be no universal answers to all the problems involved in conducting referendums. What appears fair and reasonable in one situation may seem manifestly unfair in another. Some may therefore prefer to lay down the rules afresh every time there is a referendum. In 1975, legislation for a referendum was quickly prepared by the civil service, approved by the government, and enacted by Parliament; there may have been an element of luck. The device of umbrella organizations and their public subsidy could easily have gone awry. The Scottish referendum of 1979 provided an example of the awkwardness that may arise from the absence of preagreed procedure. Litigation over the ground rules distracted energies in the middle of the campaign.

Any referendum is likely to be on a matter that arouses strong

---

[3] It has been suggested, for example, that, if constitutional reformers were seeking to limit the power of a single-chamber legislature, it would be possible to give to, say, a third of the MPs the right to demand a referendum on a major issue. Equally, in a bicameral legislature, the veto power of the Second Chamber could be reduced to the right to insist on a referendum before legislation on a given issue or a right to make the holding of a referendum and a specified majority in it, a condition of the validity of such legislation.

emotions and that crosses party frontiers. In such circumstances, it may be helpful to establish guidelines well in advance, free from any suggestion of being prepared ad hoc to favour a particular answer to a particular question. If a referendum is conducted under general rules, it will at least be harder for the losers to repudiate the verdict as illegitimate (although other factors, like the weather on polling day or the conduct of the media, may provide an excuse). A sense that the rules of fair play have been observed is easier to maintain if the rules have been long agreed upon. Indeed, actual cheating or unfairness may be restrained.

Any legislation regulating the conduct of British referendums would have to be general at some points. Yet it is quite possible to draw up such legislation. Although there are specific defects in the Quebec law, partially revealed during its first test in May 1980, it does show how, in fifty-two clauses and thirteen pages, a framework for any referendum can be laid.

The existence of such an enabling law in Britain might, of course, encourage calls for referendums on specific issues. On the other hand, those who fear government-manipulated referendums might feel more optimistic about discouraging the holding of such referendums or at least of having a better chance of securing a no vote, if rules for their fair conduct were established. Any code or framework should be directed to questions of machinery and procedure that might be adopted (perhaps with modification) on the occasion of each referendum.

Suitable Issues. Any framework for referendums should not seek to specify or define the issues subject to it. A referendum may be desirable on a broad issue, as with the Northern Ireland referendum of 1973, or, in a different way, with the United Kingdom referendum of 1975. It may seek views about a specific piece of legislation (either being held in advance of it or being incorporated as one of the provisions of the legislation).

A referendum is most appropriate as a means of giving popular sanction to major constitutional or territorial change or as a means of securing an authoritative statement of public opinion on an issue that a general election could not settle. Some people would see it as a suitable way of deciding moral questions, issues like divorce, abortion, and criminal punishment that fall outside party politics.

Potential referendum subjects being so various and so controversial, it would be neither prudent nor practicable in a general enabling law to specify the categories of bills that either were open to referendum or had to be subject to referendum. The categories could not be defined in a simple way that would preclude argument; whatever categories were specified could always be disregarded by Parliament at any subsequent time.[4]

Suitable Electorate. It should be noted that the Scottish, Welsh, and Northern Ireland referendums were not, in the ordinary sense, nation-wide referendums. Referendums affecting the territorial integrity of the United Kingdom or the specific institutions of a specific part of it have so far only been voted on by those residents in the region especially concerned. The question has been raised whether citizens of the region residing elsewhere in the United Kingom (or abroad) or citizens of the United Kingdom as a whole should have a vote. It is hard to see in these cases how a wider franchise would have been politically or practically possible. It is most unlikely that any general enabling legislation on referendums should deal specifically with this sort of issue.

Qualified Majorities. What the verdict of a referendum is to mean can be established in advance. There is no reason why a simple majority of all those actually voting should be regarded as a definitive approval for some course of action. Support from a majority of states or cantons can be required (as in Australia and Switzerland). A two-thirds majority can be required (Sierra Leone) or 50 percent of the total electorate (Weimar Germany) or 40 percent yes (Denmark, for constitutional changes, and Scotland and Wales in 1979) or other figures (Denmark provides various examples). It is easy to understand the logic behind such arrangements: fundamental changes demand a clear-cut demonstration of support. Should abstention be regarded as a no vote? A majority on a low turnout carries little authority. The Cunningham amendment on which the Scottish and Welsh referendums were based was designed to impose a double test: a majority for change that was based on a substantial turnout. It is arguable that the turnout threshold increases interest and participation. It is also arguable that it allows people inclined to vote no to stay at home since that can be equivalent to voting no.

On the other hand, the idea that a majority is a majority and that the side with fewer votes should never come out of an election as the winner is deep-rooted. As the 40 percent rule in Scotland showed, ver-

---

[4] One particular and highly controversial area suggested for referendums concerns industrial relations. Opinions differ widely on what might have happened if a referendum rather than a general election had been resorted to in January 1974 or in subsequent disputes. Obviously, a referendum once under way may effectively suspend for some weeks action to settle a strike. On the one hand, it may demonstrate to one side or other that it had misjudged public sympathy; on the other hand, it may demonstrate the irrelevance of public opinion in enforcing settlements on embattled parties.

dicts based on percentages of the electorate can raise great technical difficulties. Since the United Kingdom electoral register is less than fully accurate, the percentage of "those actually entitled to vote" will always be a matter for dispute.[5] In the case of the referendums that are only advisory, it may be prudent not to lay down formal conditions on what is to constitute a yes verdict. It is obvious that a narrow majority on a low turnout would lack the authority of a decisive vote on a large turnout.

Administration

As the British referendums have shown, most of the basic rules for a fair referendum present no problem. Existing electoral law provides for the compilation of the register, the appointment of returning officers, the establishment and manning of polling stations, and the rules for the secrecy of the ballot. At this mechanical level, fair play in referendums is as easy to define and maintain as in ordinary elections. There is little need for special legislation, except possibly in areas of agency and equivalents to the "accredited representatives of the candidate" at the count. Some problems arise with referendums that are quite distinct from those occurring in ordinary elections. They provide the main subject matter of this report.

Identifying Two Sides. The central problem of defining fair play in a referendum is to identify the rival sides. In an election, the party system makes this relatively easy. The two or more main contestants are clearly identified. It is possible to lay down laws to regulate their conduct and to allocate facilities to them, whether it be free publicity, free postage, or access to broadcasting time. In a referendum, the composition of the rival sides is not clear. The yes advocates may not have a single position any more than the no advocates (and there may be a distinct and significant third set of groups urging abstention). Occasionally a referendum may divide the parties and the public on rigid party lines; if it does, an election may be a better way than a referendum to decide the matter. Normally a referendum is on an issue that in some measure crosses party lines: the public may in fact be consulted because the parties are divided.[6] Even if the main parties maintain monolithic posi-

---

[5] One suggested solution might be to define the qualifying percentage not in terms of the nominal electorate but of the numbers who actually voted in the last general election. Yet the number voting is a function of the age of the register. In a March referendum following a November general election, it would be easier to achieve the qualifying percentage than in a January referendum following a March election.
[6] There can, of course, be referendums that involve a multiple choice, not a yes/no, but these have been rare. There can also be referendums that are formal

tions, pro and anti, the essence of a referendum is that electors are being asked to exercise an independent judgment. It is unacceptable in a free society that the referendum battle should, by law, be made a monopoly of the established parties.

Umbrellas. The purpose of umbrella arrangements is to ensure fair play between the two sides in terms of money and of media access. If there is to be public subsidy of referendum campaigns, it is necessary to define who is entitled to receive it. If there is to be a limit on expenditure so that the richer side does not buy its way to victory, it is necessary to define who may spend money and be made accountable. If booklets presenting the yes and no cases are to be distributed by the authorities, it is necessary to define who is to prepare these statements. If the broadcast media are to offer balanced time, it is convenient to have some formal definition of who the representatives of the balanced arguments are.

The 1975 referendum was fought between two umbrella organizations, Britain in Europe and the National Referendum Campaign. These bodies were in existence as ad hoc self-appointed campaign coordinators before they were given legal status under the Referendum Act, which provided for them to receive money. Thereafter, they assumed an unchallenged status as the bodies to prepare a pamphlet for free distribution and to be entitled to broadcasting time. Both organizations had their troubles. The promarket organization was accused of being a stalking horse for a coalition; the prime minister was unhappy at the government being left out of the campaign. The antimarket organization had to keep in harmony such diverse people as Enoch Powell, Jack Jones, and Anthony Benn and to avoid being discredited by far more extreme elements on the no side, ranging from the National Front to the Trotskyists. The device of umbrella organizations worked quite well and did not lead to any serious recriminations. The media were particularly grateful at having the two sides formally defined.

Four years later, however, the Scottish referendum showed some of the difficulties inherent in umbrella organizations. Labour opponents of devolution were not, for tactical reasons, ready to team with the Conservatives. Labour supporters were equally unwilling to team with the Scottish National Party. It would have been intolerable if Mr. Dalyell had been silenced on the no side or Mr. Buchanan-Smith on the yes side because they could find a platform only with the consent of an

---

endorsements of a generally accepted *fait accompli* where an equal deployment of pro and anti cases would be inappropriate. For simplicity, this report confines itself to two-sided confrontations where there is clearly a strong case to be made in each direction.

umbrella organization dominated by a party opposed to their own. (This could have happened under a strict law limiting access to the air waves or expenditure of money to authorized umbrella organizations.)

In 1978, the Quebec legislature passed a general enabling act for the conduct of referendums that drew on the United Kingdom's 1975 experience. The Quebec Act provided for umbrella organizations controlled by those in the legislature who aligned themselves respectively with the yes and no sides. Only these organizations could spend any significant sums of money on the campaign or have access to broadcasting time. The goal was to prevent a referendum being distorted by lopsided intervention from wealthy interests. The consequence was to place the argument almost exclusively in the hands of the province's two main parties. People who wanted to urge a yes or no vote for reasons not approved by their side of the campaign seemed liable to be largely silenced.

When it was tested in 1980, the Quebec law worked more smoothly and proved less draconian than many had feared. There were no serious quarrels within the umbrella organizations—though it is arguable that the Liberals used their position to consolidate their complete preeminence over the other small parties as *the* opposition to the Parti Québécois. Other bodies managed to get a voice in the referendum by institutional advertising and by conferences, as well as by speeches in the federal parliament and other newsworthy activities. The press and its correspondence columns provided a forum for all sorts of views. It is not clear that the general law, providing for a duopoly by the umbrella organizations, served the public interest—or that, in other circumstances, it might not prove a serious restraint on free discussion.[7]

It would be possible to devise general rules for umbrella organizations less restrictive than those in Quebec, though the administration might prove complex and provoke litigation. Each party with at least 1 percent (or 3 percent or 5 percent) of the vote at the last election, for example, could be invited to declare a position. If it chose, it could decide yes or no on a divided vote, making plain its internal balance (on a conference vote or on the division of its members in Parliament). The controlling bodies of the umbrella organization would then have to contain representatives of the parties in proportion to their popular support and to allocate money and air time, as far as practicable, in

---

[7] One umbrella committee, for example, could have been based on thirty-eight members of the legislature who came from two bitterly opposed parties with different lines of objection to the proposal, one with twenty members and one with eighteen. In that event, the larger party could have gagged the smaller one; access to funds and, to some extent, to the media would have been reserved to those who controlled a majority on the committee—an intolerable restriction of free speech and fair play.

those proportions. Even if setting out such arrangements seems to argue against having umbrella organizations, the possibilities of their being appropriate in specific circumstances should not be neglected.

Government Activity. The government of the day will seldom be neutral about the outcome of a referendum. Any government has access to a vast publicity machine and is making news every day: Parliament, if it is in session, provides an exceptional platform. It is difficult, as the United Kingdom learned in 1975 and Quebec in 1980, for all government activities and opinions relevant to the referendum to be subsumed under one of the umbrella campaigns. Should the government be silent or should it be allowed a free voice so that, in effect, there are two campaigns on one side of the referendum argument against one on the other?

It is impossible to see how a government could be silenced, but it is well to allow for this dilemma in any drawing up of rules for umbrella organizations. This is perhaps part of a wider dilemma. Should *anyone* be silenced by rules defining the operation of umbrella associations? Should there be any attempt to confine discussion or propaganda to that emanating from the umbrella organizations?

Media Allocation. In the absence of mandatory and monopolistic umbrella organizations, it is still necessary to allocate resources to the yes and no forces. Since most people say that they get most of their information about politics from television, fair access to television outlets is essential to a fair referendum. It is possible to surrender all decisions on fair access to the broadcasting organizations as they exercise their normal editorial judgment (under the supervision of the British Broadcasting Corporation governors and the Independent Broadcasting Authority), and follow their duty to maintain political neutrality. The broadcasters seem confident of their ability to do a good job in these circumstances, particularly if the event is newsworthy enough for them to allocate a substantial amount of time to it. The more air time, the more possibility of ensuring that every significant interest and personality is allowed a voice, both in news bulletins and magazine programs and in large-scale "Great Debates."

The main problem with the media arises if there are to be referendum broadcasts (as in the United Kingdom in 1975) in which the protagonists are allotted time to present their own case in their own way. In default of two umbrella organizations, each taking an equal share, it is hard to see how such referendum broadcasts can be managed (and it is arguable that the two sides would get across their diverse cases more effectively within the framework of prolonged discussion programs, arranged by the broadcasting authorities, than in the ten-minute format of party political broadcasts). Another way of airing the rival arguments is to allow parties to use some of their routine political broadcasts during the referendum campaign. In Scotland in 1979, broadcasts were initially allocated to the parties, but this implied three yes broadcasts to one no. The Labour Vote No group was not prepared to participate in a Conservative broadcast. Tam Dalyell secured from the courts an injunction that prevented any of the broadcasts taking place.

There can never be a guarantee that party time will be available in equal proportion to the two sides nor, perhaps, is it desirable that control over the presentation of the referendum argument should be left in party hands. It might well be appropriate to place a formal ban on party political broadcasts during a referendum campaign. There is no danger that the parties and their main spokesmen will not be heard. There is a danger that party broadcasts will provoke litigation that, quite apart from the cost in money and in internal party disharmony, will distract attention from the main arguments of the campaign.

In a closely fought campaign, disputes are bound to arise about access to the air waves. The choice of spokesmen and the right of reply can have a powerful influence on the outcome; securing a quick right of reply or a hearing for a complaint must be central to "fairness." These questions could be left to the normal machinery of the broadcasters, reinforced by the new broadcasting complaints board. Alternatively, a referendum commissioner or referee could be established to regulate such matters quickly and costlessly, with a full statement of reasons.

One broad question that may trouble broadcasters is the extent to which they should accept as mandatory a fifty-fifty division in time allocated to the two sides. Certainly, broadcasters would resist any suggestion that exact balance should be sought within each program; the goal could not be more than approximate equality over the campaign as a whole. Even that might present difficulties in some situations where all the main parties were on the same side. The compilers of news bulletins might then have to depart a long way from ordinary news values if they were to produce equal coverage. In all normal circumstances, however, it is hard to see how anything other than a fifty-fifty division of time would be acceptable if the referendum were to be regarded as fair.

As far as the press is concerned, any attempt to regulate its editorial content or reporting to ensure a just balance would certainly be unacceptable. Referendum advertising (which would, under present rules, be banned on television) could only be limited in the press as part of some general limitation on expenses.

Finance. Few countries have attempted to regulate the amount of money spent in referendum campaigns. Subsidy to the rival sides (except in kind, through media time or the distribution of pamphlets) has been almost unknown. In the 1975 United Kingdom referendum and in the Quebec law, however, provision was made for public subsidies and for publicity about expenditure and, in Quebec, for a ceiling on costs.

Obviously, there are great difficulties about subsidies or expenditure ceilings. If there are people with things to say in a referendum campaign who are not prepared to submit to an umbrella organization, expenditure can hardly be limited without serious violation of the principles of free speech. The law of agency works in parliamentary elections; it is reasonable to make a candidate answerable for all that is spent on his behalf. An idea or a principle cannot be treated in this monopolistic way. Anyone can stand in an election, but there are only two sides to a yes/no question. It is possible to limit what any one organization may spend, but it is scarcely possible to limit the number of organizations that claim a right to speak for a cause. It seems that the only restraint must be publicity. It is possible to legislate effectively to ensure the declaration of any sums spent on promoting a yes or no vote and the revelation of where the money came from. Disclosure is, inevitably, retrospective. To affect the issue, it must be timely disclosure.

Ceilings on expenditure require full reporting (but full reporting does not require ceilings). Switzerland, California, and Australia—the three places with most experience of referendums—have not found it possible to place any ceiling. One comfort to those worried by this conclusion must be the evidence of the slight correlation between campaign expenditure and success (in referendums as well as in elections). Granted reasonable access to the media, the poorer side can make effective play with its opponent's lavishness. A fair referendum, however, does require that a minimum amount of money should be available to each side. Awareness of how meagre the resources of the anti-marketeers were in 1975, led to the government, with the full support of the well-financed, promarket group, asking Parliament to vote £ 125,000 to each side, on condition that they published their accounts.

In default of umbrella organizations, it is hard to see how this money could have been distributed. Nor is it clear how effective penalties could be imposed on those who failed to produce accounts—or produced inadequate ones. After an election, a candidate who fails to meet the accounting requirement can be punished (perhaps by loss of his seat). After a referendum, little would be served by punishing officials of an umbrella organization. As for the general question of subsidy, it may be argued that any major cause with a hope of getting 50 percent of the national vote can surely, by voluntary efforts, raise the few hundred thousand pounds needed to fight a referendum. Shortage of money was not a central problem in the Scottish or Welsh referendums. If, looking back at 1975, it is decided that state support is desirable, the best answer may lie in giving aid in kind, in making available broadcasting time, and in distributing pamphlets. Broadcasts and pamphlets published for one side can include different strands of opinion.

Yes and No Pamphlets. It is desirable that the electors should understand the issues at stake in the referendum. In places such as California and Australia, where referendums have been widely used, there has been provision either for protagonists or for neutrals to draw up a statement of the pro and anti cases and for these to be distributed to all electors. In 1975, the two umbrella organizations were each invited to prepare a 2,000-word pamphlet that the state printed and distributed free to every household (together with a similar government pamphlet, that meant there were two yes pamphlets and only one no). This whole operation cost nearly £4 million. It is certainly arguable that the government should not have used its resources to intervene on one side, either with its own separate pamphlet or with other publicity material. Yet, is a government ever going to surrender its voice to an umbrella organization that it does not control?

It is usually believed that such pamphlets are little noticed. But, on the eve of the 1975 referendum, a poll found that 75 percent of the electorate claimed to have seen the pamphlets from cover to cover and 27 percent to have read them from cover to cover. It can be argued, however, that the money (about £4 million) would have been more effectively spent on press or television advertisements. If there is no consensus on umbrella organizations, it is hard to see how such pamphlets could be produced fairly. If it is thought that the state should instruct the voters, the task of explaining the issues at stake should probably be left to a neutral body to prepare a fair summary of the various arguments on each side of the case. The existence of official information about a referendum may have a significant effect on turnout, which could be especially important in any referendum dependent upon a qualifying majority.

Simultaneous Referendums and Elections. Referendums are different when they take place by themselves, as a simplified version of a single-issue general election, from what they are when they come in batches, often in conjunction with an ordinary legislative election. Switzerland has referendums every three months, usually involving several quite separate questions. Australia in 1974, and on other occasions, has combined referendums with general elections. California has up to thirty propositions on the biennial November ballot, at the same time as federal and state contests.

When referendums come frequently, and come mixed up with other issues, the public attention given to them is likely to be much less. The turnout and the decision may be shaped by the other matters being voted. When there are continuous referendums, as in Switzerland, turnout may fall to a low level.

The legislation for the 1979 referendums in Scotland and Wales provided that they should not take place in the three months after a general election. If the referendums are to be reserved as a special device to give an authoritative mass verdict on a major issue, it would seem that, as in 1975, they should be allowed to stand alone, separate from the ordinary party struggle. There could be situations when considerations of cost and of turnout might argue for simultaneity, either with general or with local elections. It is not clear whether party loyalty would carry over into the referendum vote—or whether it would be a challenge to show independence of mind.[8]

The Count. In Westminster elections, votes are counted and recorded by complete constituencies. In the 1973 Northern Ireland referendum, the vote was announced for the whole province. In the United Kingdom in 1975, a government proposal for a national count (designed to conceal regional differences) was rejected by Parliament: votes were counted and announced at the county level (MPs were not to be embarrassed by constituency returns). In 1979, the region was the counting unit in Scotland and the county in Wales.

Britain is alone among the major democracies in not counting and recording votes at the ward, or even the polling district, level. There can be no need, on the grounds of the secrecy of the individual ballot, to count centrally. The only argument for counting centrally is that a referendum is designed to produce a firm central decision that should be seen as a collective verdict (and to prevent attempts, of the sort anticipated in Quebec, to show that one language group at least votes yes). The cost and delay of a national count make it inevitable that, at the least, the pattern of 1975 would be repeated. Once any figures below those for the whole electorate are released, there can be no reason in principle for not counting and publishing the figures for the most local of counting places. It is arguable that a community's knowing how it has voted is a stimulus to interest and to turnout.

The circumstances in which a referendum might be declared in-

---

[8] In Ireland in 1959, the electorate on the same day elected Eamonn de Valera as president and rejected in a referendum the change in the electoral system that he advocated. In England and Wales in 1979, when general and local elections were simultaneous for the first time, there was a surprisingly wide variation between Westminster and local council voting.

valid or a recount granted can hardly be specified in advance. The questions may best be left for resolution by the usual judicial processes. It might be unwise to rule out the possibility of judicial challenge since a narrow result on which doubt was, with some reason, cast would not command great parliamentary or public respect if left unresolved.

Campaign Duration. British election campaigns are, in contrast with some other countries, short. Their length is not defined, though by statute twenty days must elapse between the dissolution and the poll, and the parties are reluctant (for reasons of expense and for fear of public tedium) to extend the period of full-scale electioneering. The twenty-day period allows ten days for nomination and ten days for printing ballot papers and distributing and collecting postal votes. But with a referendum, once the question is defined, there is no reason for delay in printing ballot papers. It would probably be administratively practicable to organize a referendum with a bare two weeks' notice (though the abrupt dislocation of arrangements for local officials and politicians and for broadcasting schedules would be unpopular).

The length of time needed to develop the argument of the issues at stake is another matter. On some questions, the public is well informed and has decided views that would be unlikely to change; on other issues, the educational effect of the campaign might be decisive. To leave too much freedom over the duration of the campaign might give too much advantage to the government that called the referendum. It would at least be desirable to specify a minimum period (say, seventeen days) between the proclamation of a referendum and the vote, so that the media could give the arguments due coverage.

The beginning of the campaign may not be clear. It may effectively start with the mere publicizing of the proposal for a referendum, with the introduction of the legislation or with its passage or at some arbitrary date laid down in the legislation, with the day that the yes or no forces choose to deem it to begin, or with the day the media begin to give it full coverage. As a referendum comes into view, the decisive propaganda effort may take place months in advance, unregulated by any law. The thirty-five-hour televised debate in Quebec in March 1980 on the referendum wording was dominated two to one by the yes advocates, in line with the parliamentary majority.

Money comes into the question. If the amount to be spent is unrestricted, the richer side could take advantage of an elongated campaign by sustained advertising. If the amount to be spent is limited, the two sides, husbanding their resources for the finale, may not be able to make effective use of the early weeks.

It has to be recognized that the timing of a campaign may have a decisive effect on its outcome, which cannot be separated from the temporary popularity or unpopularity of a government.

Question Wording. The broad issue put to the public in a referendum is likely to be controversial, even before its exact formulation into a ballot question. Certainly, the debate over how the proposition is to be worded can be an important part of the whole campaign, educating the protagonists and the electorate about what is at stake. Those sponsoring a referendum naturally want the phraseology likely to elicit the most favourable result. The Quebec government was much criticized for putting forward an involved hundred-word question in its sovereignty-association referendum. General de Gaulle tangled two issues deceptively in his ill-judged 1969 referendum. In Britain in 1975, there was argument over the exact wording of the question, "Do you think that the United Kingdom should stay in the European Community (the Common Market)?" The words "(the Common Market)" were added as a concession to the antimarketeers. Indeed, in February 1975, a National Opinion Poll testing seven possible wordings found the majority varied from 0 percent to 16 percent.

In fact, though Quebeckers might deny this, worries over wording may be exaggerated. People do not read the ballot to make up their minds. They go to the polls in order to vote yes or no, and their decisions will be based on the broad issue and the way in which it has been presented during the campaign. If the question is a loaded one, that fact will have been an issue in the debate; a loaded question may well boomerang in the faces of its drafters.

Nonetheless, fair referendums do require the question to be as balanced and unambiguous as possible. One would hope for a British compromise based on mutual agreement between pros and antis. However, if the government and Parliament insist on a monopoly in calling referendums and if each referendum is to be sanctioned by Parliament, the government, if it controls a majority in Parliament, will inevitably have the last word.

Conclusion

Referendums are likely to be invoked again in the United Kingdom, on a nationwide scale or in one of the components of the country. While it would be possible to treat each referendum as a one-off affair, subject to its own rules in a specific act of Parliament, it might be better to set out the main machinery for the conduct of future United Kingdom referendums within the framework of a general law. The holding of a referendum is likely to be a controversial issue. It may lessen the tension to have rules of fair play established in advance, so that no one can charge that they have been specially devised to aid the victory of one side. In addition, if the rules are generally agreed, the preparation and holding of a referendum could be substantially accelerated. It would be possible for a referendum act to give ministers power to make provision for individual referendums by statutory instrument, subject to parliamentary approval. Specific matters, like the wording of the particular question, could then be subject to debate when the instrument came before Parliament. The presumption would be that the basic rules would not become a matter of controversy when a referendum is decided upon, any more than electoral law becomes an important issue when a general election is called.

A NOTE ON THE BOOK

The typeface used for the text of this book is
Times Roman, designed by Stanley Morison.
The type was set by
Maryland Linotype Composition Company, of Baltimore.
BookCrafters, Incorporated, of Chelsea, Michigan, printed
and bound the book, using Glatfelter paper.
The cover and format were designed by Pat Taylor.
The manuscript was edited by Ann Petty, and
by Donna Spitler of the AEI Publications staff.

Selected AEI Publications

AEI Associates Program